BOLLINGEN SERIES XX

THE COLLECTED WORKS

OF

C. G. JUNG

VOLUME 19

EDITORS

† SIR HERBERT READ

MICHAEL FORDHAM, F.R.C.PSYCH., HON. F.B.PS.S.

GERHARD ADLER, PH.D.

WILLIAM MC GUIRE, *executive editor*

GENERAL

BIBLIOGRAPHY

of C. G. Jung's Writings

COMPILED BY LISA RESS

WITH COLLABORATORS

BOLLINGEN SERIES XX

PRINCETON UNIVERSITY PRESS

THIS EDITION IS BEING PUBLISHED IN THE
UNITED STATES OF AMERICA FOR BOLLINGEN
FOUNDATION BY PRINCETON UNIVERSITY
PRESS AND IN ENGLAND BY ROUTLEDGE &
KEGAN PAUL, LTD. IN THE AMERICAN EDI-
TION, ALL THE VOLUMES COMPRISING THE
COLLECTED WORKS CONSTITUTE NUMBER XX
IN BOLLINGEN SERIES. THE PRESENT VOL-
UME IS NUMBER 19 OF THE COLLECTED
WORKS AND IS THE LAST TO BE PUBLISHED.

LIBRARY OF CONGRESS CATALOGUE CARD NUMBER: 75-156
ISBN 0-691-09893-X
MANUFACTURED IN THE U.S.A.

EDITORIAL NOTE

In the compilation of the following list of published writings, it has been the intention to record (through 1975) the initial publication of each original work of C. G. Jung, each translation, and subsequent substantial revisions and/or expansions thereof, with reciprocal cross-references. The items are ordered chronologically by years of publication, and within the year to the best of our knowledge (books first); items that cannot be dated closely enough appear at the end of the year's listings. Unless otherwise indicated (by an initial asterisk), each publication in German, English, and French has been examined by the compilers and described accordingly. This principle could not, practically, be observed for works in other languages, though these have been examined insofar as possible. Translations are related by cross-references to the work from which the translation was made, though it has not been possible to ascertain this in every case.

Unrevised reprintings of a text are not recorded unless brought out by a different publisher or altered in format, as in the case of a paperback edition. In such instances, the reissue is noted under the original entry. Separately reprinted brief extracts have generally been omitted as well. The proliferation of reprints, particularly in paperback, and of extract and anthologized use of Jung's writings both in brief and in extenso has made a policy of inclusiveness unrealistic.

In addition to all books and articles written by Jung solely or in collaboration with others, it has been the intention to record all forewords and the like written for other authors' works, letters included in other writers' publications, book reviews, newspaper articles both popular and scholarly, published texts of lectures appearing either in full or as summarized by their author ("Auto-referat"), and announcements issued in his capacity as editor.

In order to give as nearly complete a record as possible of Jung's publication, as well as to throw light on the sequence of development of his ideas, we have included, duly distinguished and with the permission of the responsible organizations, those items issued initially for private circulation. For the same reasons, we have included whatever information became available to us in regard to the delivery of a publication on some occasion in lecture form, and other useful secondary information. A separate list records chronologically the volumes of Seminar Notes, for the most part issued privately and under restriction. The numerous interviews with Jung—either published in periodicals and books or recorded for radio, television, or film, or by tape—have not been listed. Those of most interest and value are published in a volume, outside the *Collected Works*, entitled *C. G. Jung Speaking: Interviews and Encounters*.

The *Collected Works* (in English) and the *Gesammelte Werke* (in German) are separately listed, in volume sequence, with the necessary reciprocal cross-references. (Lists of contents of volumes 2 and 13 in the *Gesammelte Werke*, though still in press, were added in proof but could not be included in the indexes.)

While we have aimed at citing every substantial publication of Jung's writings, we are aware that in the case of items appearing in newspapers, books by other authors, etc., and particularly in the case of translations, omissions undoubtedly have occurred. We shall be grateful to be informed of these—and of any omissions and errors whatever—looking toward a revised edition of the General Bibliography.

*

This bibliography of Jung's writings was originally compiled, as a working tool for the English collection edition at the outset, by Michael Fordham, who based it on a list published by Jolande Jacobi in her *The Psychology of C. G. Jung*; he was indebted also, for advice, to Professor Jung's secretary at that time, Marie-Jeanne Schmid. This "draft bibliography," more or less in the form of the present publication, underwent revision and augmentation by the Editors and staff in a printed version that was privately distributed to workers in the field. The project of compiling a definitive General Bibliography was undertaken by A.S.B. Glover. After his death, in 1966, the work was carried on, under William McGuire's supervision, first by Jasna P. Heurtley and then by Lisa Ress, who is responsible for the present comprehensive state of the Bibliography.

The editors and publishers of the *Gesammelte Werke*, in Switzerland, have been of assistance throughout. Others to whom the compilers are especially indebted are Doris Albrecht, Roland Cahen, Aldo Carotenuto, G. Dreifuss, Aniela Jaffé, and Mihoko Okamura. The resources of two collections have been of particular value: the library of Professor C. G. Jung, at his house in Küsnacht/ Zürich, subsequently in the care of Mr. and Mrs. Franz Jung, and the Kristine Mann Library of the Analytical Psychology Club of New York.

*

ABBREVIATIONS AND SYMBOLS. The bibliographical abbreviations will, it is assumed, be obvious to users of the Bibliography. Abbreviations of titles of periodicals are explained in the index of periodicals. CW = *Collected Works*; GW = *Gesammelte Werke* (both listed by volumes in Part II). BS = Bollingen Series. An asterisk preceding an entry in the German, English, and French sections indicates that the publication could not be examined.

CONTENTS

EDITORIAL NOTE   V

I. THE PUBLISHED WRITINGS OF C. G. JUNG:
Original Works and Translations

German	3
English	61
Danish	107
Dutch	108
Finnish	113
French	114
Greek	126
Hebrew	127
Hungarian	128
Italian	129
Japanese	134
Norwegian	136
Portuguese	138
Russian	140
Serbo-Croatian	141
Slovenian	142
Spanish	143
Swedish	148
Turkish	150

II. THE COLLECTED WORKS OF C. G. JUNG / DIE
GESAMMELTEN WERKE VON C. G. JUNG   151

III. SEMINAR NOTES 209

INDEXES

    1. Titles (of all English and German items and of
original works in other languages)   219

    2. Personal Names   242

    3. Congresses, Organizations, Societies, etc.   249

    4. Periodicals   253

ADDENDA   259

I

THE PUBLISHED WRITINGS OF C. G. JUNG

Original Works and Translations

GERMAN

1902a *Zur Psychologie und Pathologie sogenannter occulter Phänomene. Eine psychiatrische Studie.* Leipzig: Oswald Mutze. pp. 121. Repub. as GW 1,1. Inaugural dissertation for the doctoral degree, presented to the Universität Zürich, Medizinische Fakultät. TR.—English: 1916a,2/CW 1,1//French: 1939a,2/1956a,4//Russian: 1939a.

1902b "Ein Fall von hysterischem Stupor bei einer Untersuchungsgefangenen." *J. Psychol. Neurol.*, I:3, 110–22. Repub. as GW 1,5. TR.—English: CW 1,5.

1903a "Über manische Verstimmung." *Allgemeine Zeitschrift für Psychiatrie und psychisch-gerichtliche Medizin*, LXI:1, 15–39. Repub. as GW 1,4. TR.—English: CW 1,4.

1903b "Über Simulation von Geistesstörung." *J. Psychol. Neurol.*, II:5, 181–201. Repub. as GW 1,6. TR.—English: CW 1,6.

1904a With F. Riklin: "Experimentelle Untersuchungen über Assoziationen Gesunder." (Diagnostische Assoziationsstudien, I. Beitrag.) *J. Psychol. Neurol.*, as follows: Pt. I—III:1/2, 55–83; Pt. II—III:4, 145–64; Pt. III—III:5, 193–215; Pt. IV—III:6, 283–308; Pt. V—IV:1/2, 24–67. Combined and pub. as G.1906a,1 with slight title change.

1904b "Über hysterisches Verlesen: eine Erwiderung an Herrn Hahn (pr. Arzt in Zürich)." *Archiv für die gesamte Psychologie*, III:4 (May), 347–50. Repub. as GW 1,2. TR.—English: CW 1,2.

1904c "Ärztliches Gutachten über einen Fall von Simulation geistiger Störung." *Schweiz. Z. Strafrecht*, XVII, 55–75. Repub. as GW 1,7. TR.—English: CW 1,7.

1905a "Kryptomnesie." *Die Zukunft*, Jhg. 13, L (25 Feb.), 325–34. Repub., slightly rev., as GW 1,3. TR.—English: CW 1,3.

1905b Review of Willy Hellpach: *Grundlinien einer Psychologie der Hysterie. Zbl. Nervenhk.*, XXVIII (n.s. XVI) (15 Apr.), 318–21. TR.—English: CW 18,19.

1905c "Experimentelle Beobachtungen über das Erinnerungsvermögen." *Zbl. Nervenhk.*, XXVIII (n.s. XVI):196 (1 Sept.), 653–66. Repub. as GW 2,4. TR.—English: CW 2,4.

1905d "Zur psychologischen Tatbestandsdiagnostik." *Zbl. Nervenhk.*, XXVIII (n.s. XVI):200 (1 Nov.), 813–15. Repub. as GW 1,9. TR.— English: CW 1,9.

1905e "Über spiritistische Erscheinungen." *Basl. Nach.*, Nos. 311–16 (12–17 Nov.). Extract pub. in *Volksrecht* (22 Nov.). Given as lecture at the Bernoullianum, Basel, 5 Feb. 1905. TR.—English: CW 18,4.

1905f "Die psychologische Diagnose des Tatbestandes." *Schweiz. Z. Strafrecht*, XVIII, 369–408. Repub. as G. 1906k with last (minor) sentence omitted.

1905g "Analyse der Assoziationen eines Epileptikers." (Diagnostische Assoziationsstudien, III. Beitrag.) *J. Psychol. Neurol.*, V:2, 73–90. Repub. as G. 1906a,2.

1905h "Über das Verhalten der Reaktionszeit beim Assoziationsexperimente." (Diagnostische Assoziationsstudien, IV. Beitrag.) *J. Psychol. Neurol.*, VI:1/2, 1–36. Also issued as pamphlet, Leipzig: Barth. pp. 38. Jung's "Habilitationsschrift," Universität Zürich, Medizinische Fakultät. Repub. as G. 1906a,3.

1906a *Diagnostische Assoziationsstudien: Beiträge zur experimentellen Psychopathologie.* Ed. by C. G. Jung. Vol. I. Leipzig: Barth. pp. 281. Subsequently issued bound as one with G. 1909a. Contains the following works wholly or partly by Jung:

    1. With F. Riklin: "Experimentelle Untersuchungen über Assoziationen Gesunder." (7–145) G. 1904a repub. with slight title change. Repub. as GW 2,1. TR.—English: 1918a,1/CW 2,1.

    2. "Analyse der Assoziationen eines Epileptikers." (175–92) G. 1905g repub. Repub. as GW 2,2. TR.—English: 1918a,2/CW 2,2.

    3. "Über das Verhalten der Reaktionszeit beim Assoziations-

experimente." (193–228) G. 1905h repub. Repub. as GW 2,3.
TR.—English: 1918a,3/CW 2,3.

4. "Psychoanalyse und Assoziationsexperiment." (258–81) G. 1906i
repub. Repub. as GW 2,5. TR.—English: 1918a,4/CW 2,5.
Contents also summarized in French by Jung. Cf. Fr. 1908a.

1906b "Die psychopathologische Bedeutung des Assoziationsexperimentes." *Archiv für Kriminalanthropologie und Kriminalistik,*
XXII:2–3 (15 Feb.), 145–62. Given as inaugural lecture upon Jung's
appointment as Lecturer in Psychiatry, Universität Zürich, 21 Oct.
1905. Repub. as GW 2,8. TR.—English: CW 2,8.

1906c "Statistisches von der Rekrutenaushebung." *CorrespBl. schweizer
Ärzte,* XXXVI:4 (15 Feb.), 129–30. Repub. as GW 2,15. TR.—English: CW 2,15.

1906d "Obergutachten über zwei sich widersprechende psychiatrische
Gutachten." *Monatsschrift für Kriminalpsychologie und Strafrechts-
reform,* II:11/12 (Feb.–Mar.), 691–98. Repub. as GW 1,8 with minor
title change. TR.—English: CW 1,8.

1906e Review of L. Bruns: *Die Hysterie im Kindesalter. CorrespBl.
schweizer Ärzte,* XXXVI:19 (1 Oct.), 634–35. TR.—English: CW
18,20.

1906f Review of E. Bleuler: *Affektivität, Suggestibilität, Paranoia.
CorrespBl. schweizer Ärzte,* XXXVI:21 (1 Nov.), 694–95. TR.—
English: CW 18,20.

1906g "Die Hysterielehre Freuds. Eine Erwiderung auf die Aschaffenburgsche Kritik." *Münchener medizinische Wochenschrift,* LIII:47
(20 Nov.), 2301–02. Repub. as GW 4,1. TR.—English: CW 4,1.

1906h Review of Carl Wernicke: *Grundriss der Psychiatrie in klinischen
Vorlesungen. CorrespBl. schweizer Ärzte,* XXXVI:23 (1 Dec.),
790–91. TR.—English: CW 18,20.

1906i "Psychoanalyse und Assoziationsexperiment." (Diagnostische Assoziationsstudien, VI. Beitrag.) *J. Psychol. Neurol.,* VII:1/2, 1–24.
Also pub. in *Schweiz. Z. Strafrecht,* XVIII, 396–403. Repub. as G.
1906a,4. TR.—English: 1918a,4.

1906j   "Assoziation, Traum und hysterisches Symptom." *J. Psychol. Neurol.*, VIII:1/2, 25–60. Repub. as G. 1909a,1.

1906k   "Die psychologische Diagnose des Tatbestandes." *Juristisch-psychiatrische Grenzfragen*, IV:2, 3–47. Also pub. as pamphlet (bound with article by another author). Halle: Carl Marhold. At head of title: "Aus der psychiatrischen Universitätsklinik in Zürich." G. 1905f repub. with omission of last (minor) sentence. Repub. as monograph: G. 1941d; and as GW 2,6. TR.—English: CW 2,6.

1907a   *Über die Psychologie der Dementia praecox: Ein Versuch.* Halle a. S.: Carl Marhold. pp. 179. 1972: (Frühe Schriften II; "Studienausgabe.") Olten: Walter. pp. 180.

         Vorwort. (Dated July 1906.)

       I. Kritische Darstellung theoretischer Ansichten über die Psychologie der Dementia praecox.

       II. Der gefühlsbetonte Komplex und seine allgemeinen Wirkungen auf die Psyche.

       III. Der Einfluss des gefühlsbetonten Komplexes auf die Association.

       IV. Dementia praecox und Hysterie. Eine Parallele.

       V. Analyse eines Falles von paranoïder Demenz, als Paradigma. Schlusswort.

     Repub. as GW 3,1. TR.—English: 1909a/CW 3,1//Russian: 1939a.

1907b   Review of Albert Moll: *Der Hypnotismus, mit Einschluss der Hauptpunkte der Psychotherapie und des Occultismus. CorrespBl. schweizer Ärzte*, XXXVII:11 (1 June), 354–55. TR.—English: CW 18,20.

1907c   Review of Albert Knapp: *Die polyneuritischen Psychosen. CorrespBl. schweizer Ärzte*, XXXVII:11 (1 June), 355. TR.—English: CW 18,20.

1907d   Review of M. Reichhardt: *Leitfaden zur psychiatrischen Klinik. CorrespBl. schweizer Ärzte*, XXXVII:23 (1 Dec.), 742–43. TR.—English: CW 18,20.

1907e   "Über die Reproduktionsstörungen beim Assoziationsexperiment." (Diagnostische Assoziationsstudien, IX. Beitrag.) *J. Psychol. Neurol.*, IX:4, 188–97. Repub. as G. 1909a,2.

1907f Contribution to discussion of paper by Frank and Bezzola: "Über die Analyse psychosomatischer Symptome," p. 185, in "II. Vereinsbericht. 37. Versammlung südwestdeutscher Irrenärzte in Tübingen am 3. und 4. November 1906." *Zbl. Nervenhk.*, n.s. XVIII:5, 176–91.

1908a *Der Inhalt der Psychose.* (Schriften zur angewandten Seelenkunde, 3.) Leipzig and Vienna: Franz Deuticke. pp. 26. Repub. with supplement as G. 1914a. Academic lecture, given at the Rathaus, Zurich, 16 Jan. 1908. TR.—Russian: 1909a.

1908b With E. Bleuler: "Komplexe und Krankheitsursachen bei Dementia praecox." *Zbl. Nervenhk.*, XXXI (n.s. XIX), (Mar.), 220–27.

1908c 7 abstracts. *Folia neuro-biol.*, 1:3 (Mar.) , 493–94, 497–99. Listed but not trans. at the end of CW 18,26. Articles abstracted by Jung:

1. 388) Jung, C. G. "Associations d'idées familiales."
2. 389) Métral, M. "Expériences scolaires sur la mémoire de l'orthographe."
3. 394) Lombard, Emile. "Essai d'une classification des phénomènes de glossolalie."
4. 395) Claparède, Ed. "Quelques mots sur la définition de l'hystérie."
5. 396) Flournoy, Th. "Automatisme téléologique antisuicide. . . ."
6. 397) Leroy, E.-Bernard. "Escroquerie et hypnose. . . ."
7. 398) Lemaître, Aug. "Un nouveau cycle somnambulique de Mlle. Smith. Les peintures religieuses."

All of the above articles reviewed appeared originally in the *Archives de psychologie 1907*, VII:25&26. Cf. CW 18,26,ii.

1908d "Über die Bedeutung der Lehre Freuds für Neurologie und Psychiatrie" (Autoreferat). *CorrespBl. schweizer Ärzte*, XXXVIII:7 (1 Apr.), 218. Summary of lecture given to the Gesellschaft der Ärzte des Kantons Zürich, autumn meeting, 26 Nov. 1907. TR.— English: CW 18,21.

1908e Review of Franz C. R. Eschle: *Grundzüge der Psychiatrie. CorrespBl. schweizer Ärzte*, XXXVIII:8 (15 Apr.), 264–65. TR.— English: CW 18,20.

7

1908f Review of P. Dubois: *Die Einbildung als Krankheitsursache.* *CorrespBl. schweizer Ärzte*, XXXVIII:12 (15 June), 399. TR.—English: CW 18,20.

1908g Review of Georg Lomer: *Liebe und Psychose. CorrespBl. schweizer Ärzte*, XXXVIII:12 (15 June), 399–400. TR.—English: CW 18,20.

1908h Review of E. Meyer: *Die Ursachen der Geisteskrankheiten.* *CorrespBl. schweizer Ärzte*, XXXVIII, 706. TR.—English: CW 18,20.

1908i 9 abstracts. *Folia neuro-biol.*, II:1 (Oct.), 124–25, 132–35. Listed but not trans. at the end of CW 18,26. Articles abstracted by Jung:

1. 122) Piéron, H. "La théorie des émotions et les données actuelles de la physiologie."

2. 123) Revault d'Allones, [G.] "L'explication physiologique de l'émotion."

3. 124) Hartenberg, P. "Principe d'une physiognomie scientifique."

4. 130) Dumas, G. "Qu'est-ce que la psychologie pathologique?"

5. 131) Dromard, [G.] "De la dissociation de la mimique chez les aliénés."

6. 132) Marie, A. "Sur quelques troubles fonctionnels de l'audition chez certains débiles mentaux."

7. 133) Janet, P. "Le renversement de l'orientation ou l'allochirie des représentations."

8. 134) Pascal, [Constanza]. "Les maladies mentales de Robert Schumann."

9. 135) Vigouroux, [A.] et Juquelier, [P.] "Contribution clinique à l'étude des délires du rêve."

All the articles reviewed appeared originally in the *Journal de psychologie normal et pathologique*, IV (Sept.–Oct. 1907), V (Mar.–Apr. 1908). Cf. CW 18,26,ii.

1908j Review of Wilhelm Stekel: *Nervöse Angstzustände und ihre Behandlung. Medizinische Klinik*, IV:45 (8 Nov.), 1735–36. TR.—English: CW 18,22.

1908k Review of Sigmund Freud: *Zur Psychopathologie des Alltagslebens.* *CorrespBl. schweizer Ärzte*, XXXVIII:23 (1 Dec.), 775–76. TR.—English: CW 18,20.

1908l 5 abstracts. *Folia neuro-biol.*, II:3 (Dec.), 366–68. Listed but not trans. at the end of CW 18,26. Articles abstracted by Jung:
1. 348) Varendonck, J. "Les idéals des enfants."
2. 349) Claparède, Ed. "Classification et plan des méthodes psychologiques."
3. 350) Katzaroff, Dimitre. "Expériences sur le rôle de la récitation comme facteur de la mémorisation."
4. 351) Maeder, Alphonse. "Nouvelles contributions à la psychopathologie de la vie quotidienne."
5. 352) Rouma, Georges. "Un cas de Mythomanie. . . . ."
All of the above articles reviewed appeared originally in the *Archives de psychologie 1908*, VII:27&28. Cf. CW 18,26,ii.

1908m "Die Freudsche Hysterietheorie." *Monatsschrift für Psychiatrie und Neurologie*, XXIII:4, 310–22. Repub. as GW 4,2. Lecture given to the First International Congress of Psychiatry and Neurology, Amsterdam, Sept. 1907. TR.—English: CW 4,2//Dutch: 1908a.

1908n "Zur Tatbestandsdiagnostik." *Z. angew. Psychol.*, I:1/2, 163.

1908o Contribution entitled "Deutsche Schweiz" to "Der gegenwärtige Stand der angewandten Psychologie in den einzelnen Kulturländern." *Z. angew. Psychol.*, I, 469–70. TR.—English: CW 18,9.

1909a *Diagnostische Assoziationsstudien: Beiträge zur experimentellen Psychopathologie*. Ed. by C. G. Jung. Vol. II. Leipzig: Barth. Subsequently issued bound as one with G. 1906a. Contains the following works by Jung:
1. "Assoziation, Traum und hysterisches Symptom." (31–66) G. 1906j repub. Repub. as GW 2,7. TR.—English: 1918a,5/CW 2,7.
2. "Über die Reproduktionsstörungen beim Assoziationsexperiment." (67–76) G. 1907e repub. Repub. as GW 2,9. TR.—English: 1918a,6/CW 2,9.

1909b "Vorbemerkung der Redaktion." *Jb. psychoanal. psychopath. Forsch.*, I:1. 1 p. Dated Jan. 1909. TR.—English: CW 18,23.

1909c "Die Bedeutung des Vaters für das Schicksal des Einzelnen." *Jb. psychoanal. psychopath. Forsch.*, I:1, 155–73. Also pub. as pamphlet, Leipzig and Vienna: Franz Deuticke. pp. 19. "Zweite, unveränderte, mit einer Vorrede versehene Auflage." Pub., rev. and exp., as G. 1949a. TR.—English: 1916a,4/ (Pts. only) CW 4,14// French: 1935a,3.

1909d Review of Karl Kleist: *Untersuchungen zur Kenntnis der psycho-motorischen Bewegungsstörungen bei Geisteskranken. CorrespBl. schweizer Ärzte*, XXXIX:1 (1 Jan.), 176. TR.—English: CW 18,20.

1909e Review of L. Loewenfeld: *Homosexualität und Strafgesetz. CorrespBl. schweizer Ärzte*, XXXIX:1 (1 Jan.), 176. TR.—English: CW 18,20.

1909f Review of Oswald Bumke: *Landläufige Irrtümer in der Beurteilung von Geisteskranken. CorrespBl. schweizer Ärzte*, XXXIX:6 (15 Mar.), 205. TR.—English: CW 18,20.

1909g Review of Christian von Ehrenfels: *Grundbegriffe der Ethik. CorrespBl. schweizer Ärzte*, XXXIX:6 (15 Mar.), 205. TR.—English: CW 18,20.

1909h Review of Isidor Sadger: *Konrad Ferdinand Meyer. Eine patho-graphisch-psychologische Studie. Basl. Nach.* (Nov.), 1 p. TR.—English: CW 18,11.

1909i Review of Louis Waldstein: *Das unbewusste Ich und sein Verhältnis zur Gesundheit und Erziehung. Basl. Nach.* (9 Dec.), 1 p. TR.—English: CW 18,12.

1910a Review of Christian v. Ehrenfels: *Sexualethik. CorrespBl. schweizer Ärzte*, XL:6 (20 Feb.), 173. TR.—English: CW 18,20.

1910b Review of Alexander Pilcz: *Lehrbuch der speziellen Psychiatrie für Studierende und Aerzte. CorrespBl. schweizer Ärzte*, XL:6 (20 Feb.), 174. TR.—English: CW 18,20.

1910c Review of Max Dost: *Kurzer Abriss der Psychologie, Psychiatrie und gerichtlichen Psychiatrie . . . CorrespBl. schweizer Ärzte*, XL:6 (20 Feb.), 174. TR.—English: CW 18,20.

1910d Review of W. v. Bechterew: *Psyche und Leben. CorrespBl. schweizer Ärzte*, XL:7 (1 Mar.), 206. TR.—English: CW 18,20.

1910e Review of M. Urstein: *Die Dementia praecox und ihre Stellung zum manisch-depressiven Irresein. CorrespBl. schweizer Ärzte*, XL:7 (1 Mar.), 206. TR.—English: CW 18,20.

1910f Review of Albert Reibmayer: *Die Entwicklungsgeschichte des Talentes und Genies. I. Band. CorrespBl. schweizer Ärzte*, XL:8 (10 Mar.), 237. TR.—English: CW 18,20.

1910g Review of P. Näcke: *Ueber Familienmord durch Geisteskranke. CorrespBl. schweizer Ärzte*, XL:8 (10 Mar.), 237–38. TR.—English: CW 18,20.

1910h Review of Th. Becker: *Einführung in die Psychiatrie. CorrespBl. schweizer Ärzte*, XL:29, 942. TR.—English: CW 18,20.

1910i Review of A. Cramer: *Gerichtliche Psychiatrie. CorrespBl. schweizer Ärzte*, XL:29, 942. TR.—English: CW 18,20.

1910j Review of August Forel: *Ethische und rechtliche Konflikte im Sexualleben in- und ausserhalb der Ehe. CorrespBl. schweizer Ärzte*, XL:29, 942–43. TR.—English: CW 18,20.

1910k "Über Konflikte der kindlichen Seele." *Jb. psychoanal. psychopath. Forsch.*, II:1, 33–58. Also pub. as monograph: Leipzig and Vienna: Franz Deuticke. pp. 26. Repub., with addn. of new foreword, as G. 1916b. Cf. E. 1910a,3 for English version. Lecture delivered to the Depts. of Psychology and Pedagogy, Clark University, Worcester, Mass., Sept. 1909. TR.—Russian: 1939a.

1910l "Randbemerkungen zu dem Buch von [Fritz] Wittels: *Die sexuelle Not.*" *Jb. psychoanal. psychopath. Forsch.*, II:1, 312–15. TR.—English: 1973d,2.

1910m "Referate über psychologische Arbeiten schweizerischer Autoren (bis Ende 1909)." *Jb. psychoanal. psychopath. Forsch.*, II:1, 356–88. TR.—English: CW 18,26.

1910n "Bericht über Amerika." In "Bericht über die II. private psychoanalytische Vereinigung in Nürnberg am 30. und 31. März." *Jb. psychoanal. psychopath. Forsch.*, II:2, 737. Abstract, recorded by

Otto Rank, of Jung's paper. Briefer abstract, also by Rank, pub. in *Zbl. Psychoanal.*, I:3 (Dec.), 130. TR.—English: CW 18,64.

1910o "Zur Kritik über Psychoanalyse." *Jb. psychoanal. psychopath. Forsch.*, II:2, 743–46. Repub. as GW 4,7. TR.—English: CW 4,7.

1910p "Buchanzeige." Review of Erich Wulffen: *Der Sexualverbrecher. Jb. psychoanal. psychopath. Forsch.*, II:2, 747. TR.—English: CW 18,25.

1910q "Ein Beitrag zur Psychologie des Gerüchtes." *Zbl. Psychoanal.*, I:1/2, 81–90. Repub. as GW 4,4. TR.—English: 1916a,5/CW 4,4//French: 1935a,2.

1910r "Die an der psychiatrischen Klinik in Zürich gebräuchlichen psychologischen Untersuchungsmethoden." *Z. angew. Psychol.*, III, 390. Contribution to a survey of clinical methods. Repub. as GW 2,17. TR.—English: CW 2,17.

1910s "Über Dementia praecox." *Zbl. Psychoanal.*, I:3 (Dec.), 128. Summary of lecture given at the I. private Psychoanalytische Vereinigung, Salzburg, 27 Apr. 1908. TR.—English: CW 18,10.

1911a "Wandlungen und Symbole der Libido. Beiträge zur Entwicklungsgeschichte des Denkens." [Pt. I.] *Jb. psychoanal. psychopath. Forsch.*, III:1, 120–227. Contents:
  1. Einleitung.
  2. Über die zwei Arten des Denkens.
  3. Vorbereitende Materialen zur Analyse der Millerschen Phantasien.
  4. Der Schöpferhymnus.
  5. Das Lied von der Motte.
Repub., with G. 1912c, as G. 1912a. The 1st of 2 pts.

1911b "Morton Prince, M.D.: *The Mechanism and Interpretation of Dreams.* Eine kritische Besprechung." *Jb. psychoanal. psychopath. Forsch.*, III:1, 309–28. Repub. as GW 4,6. TR.—English: CW 4,6.

1911c "Kritik über E. Bleuler: 'Zur Theorie des schizophrenen Negativismus.'" *Jb. psychoanal. psychopath. Forsch.*, III:1, 469–74. Repub. as GW 3,3. TR.—English: 1916a,7/CW 3,4.

1911d "Buchanzeige." Review of Eduard Hitschmann: *Freuds Neurosen-lehre. Jb. psychoanal. psychopath. Forsch.*, III:1, 480. TR.—English: CW 18,27.

1911e "Ein Beitrag zur Kenntnis des Zahlentraumes." *Zbl. Psychoanal.*, I:12, 567–72. Repub. as GW 4,5. TR.—English: 1916a,6/CW 4,5// French: 1956a,3.

1911f "Beiträge zur Symbolik." *Zbl. Psychoanal.*, II:2 (Nov.), 103–04. Summary by Otto Rank of lecture given at the 3d Congress of the Internationale Psychoanalytische Vereinigung, Weimar, 22 Sept. 1911. (Ms. of lecture never discovered.) TR.—English: CW 18,34.

1911g "Bericht über das Vereinsjahr 1910–11." *Korrespondenzblatt der Internationalen Psychoanalytischen Vereinigung*, pp. 16–17, in *Zbl. Psychoanal.*, II:3 (Dec.), 233–34. Annual report by the president, delivered to the 3d Congress of the Internationale Psychoanalytische Vereinigung, Weimar, 21–22 Sept. 1911. TR.—English: CW 18,28.

1911h Contribution on ambivalence to the discussion following a paper by E. Bleuler. *Psychiatrisch-neurologische Wochenschrift*, XII:43 (21 Jan.), 406. (Also pub. in *Zbl. Psychoanal.*, I:5 (Feb.–Mar.), 267–68, and in *CorrespBl. schweizer Ärzte*, XLI:6 (20 Feb.).) Brief remarks to papers by Von Speyr and Riklin follow. Recorded at a Winter Meeting of the Verein schweizer Irrenärzte, Bern, 27 Nov. 1910. TR.—English: CW 18,33.

1912a *Wandlungen und Symbole der Libido. Beiträge zur Entwicklungsgeschichte des Denkens.* Leipzig and Vienna: Franz Deuticke. pp. 422. With 8 text illus. G. 1911a and 1912c repub., combined as one. Repub., with addn. of new foreword, as G. 1925a. TR.—English: 1916b.

1912b *"Über Psychoanalyse beim Kinde." Ier congrès international de Pédagogie, Brussels, August, 1911. [Published Papers.] Vol. II, pp. 332–43. Brussels: Librairie Misch et Thron. Subsequently incorporated into G. 1913a.

1912c "Wandlungen und Symbole der Libido. Beiträge zur Entwicklungsgeschichte des Denkens." [Pt. II.] *Jb. psychoanal. psychopath. Forsch.*, IV:1, 162–464. Contents:
   1. Einleitung.

2. Über den Begriff und die genetische Theorie der Libido.

3. Die Verlagerung der Libido als mögliche Quelle der primitiven menschlichen Erfindungen.

4. Die unbewusste Entstehung des Heros.

5. Symbole der Mutter und der Wiedergeburt.

6. Der Kampf um die Befreiung von der Mutter.

7. Das Opfer.

Repub., with G. 1911a, as G. 1912a. The 2d of 2 pts.

1912d "Neue Bahnen der Psychologie." *Raschers Jahrbuch für schweizer Art und Kunst* (Zurich), III, 236–72. Repub. as GW 7,3. Pub., rev. and exp., with title change, as G. 1917a. TR.—English: 1916a,15/ CW 7,3 (2d edn.).

1912e "Psychoanalyse." *Neue Zür. Z.*, CXXXIII:38 (10 Jan.). Jung's response to article by J[ohann] M[ichelsen], "Psychoanalyse," which appeared earlier in the same paper, 2 Jan. 1912. Cf. G. 1912f and 1912g. TR.—English: CW 18,29.

1912f "Zur Psychoanalyse." *Neue Zür. Z.*, CXXXIII:72 (17 Jan.). Jung's reply to a response to his G. 1912e. Cf. G. 1912e and 1912g. TR.—English: CW 18,29.

1912g "Zur Psychoanalyse." *Wissen und Leben,*† IX:10 (15 Feb.), 711–14. Jung's reply to the editor's request for a concluding word on the controversy carried in the *Neue Zür. Z.* (cf. G. 1912e and 1912f) in the form of a letter to the editor, dated 28 Jan. 1912. Repub. as GW 4,8. TR.—English: CW 4,8.

† *Neue Schweizer Rundschau* published as *Wissen und Leben*, 1907–1918.

1912h "Über die psychoanalytische Behandlung nervöser Leiden." (Autoreferat.) *CorrespBl. schweizer Ärzte*, XLII:28 (1 Oct.), 1079–84. Abstract of a report given at a meeting of the Medizinisch-pharmazeutischer Bezirksverein, Bern, 4 June 1912. TR.—English: CW 18,30.

1913a "Versuch einer Darstellung der psychoanalytischen Theorie. Neun Vorlesungen, gehalten in New-York im September 1912." *Jb. psychoanal. psychopath. Forsch.*, V:1, 307–441. The text of 9 lectures written in German but given in an English trans. as an Extension Course at Fordham University, Sept. 1912. Cf. E. 1913b. Repub. as monograph: Leipzig and Vienna: Franz Deuticke. pp. 135. Pub.

with addns. as G. 1955b. Incorporates G. 1912b. TR.—English: 1913b/ 1914a/1915b/CW 4,9//French: 1932a//Spanish: 1935b.

1913b "Erklärung der Redaktion." *Jb. psychoanal. psychopath. Forsch.*, V:2, 757. Repub. in G. 1974a following 357J. TR.—English: 1974b.

1913c "Zur Psychologie des Negers." *Korrespondenzblatt der Internationalen Psychoanalytischen Vereinigung*, p. 8, in *Internationale Zeitschrift für ärztliche Psychoanalyse*, I:1, 115. Abstract of lecture given to the Zurich Branch Society of the Internationale Psychoanalytische Vereinigung, Zurich, 22 Nov. 1912. TR.—English: CW 18,65.

1913d "Eine Bemerkung zur Tauskschen Kritik der Nelkenschen Arbeit." *Internationale Zeitschrift für ärztliche Psychoanalyse*, I:3, 285–88. TR.—English: 1973d,3/CW 18,31.

1914a *Der Inhalt der Psychose.* (Schriften zur angewandten Seelenkunde, 3.) Leipzig and Vienna: Franz Deuticke. pp. 44. G. 1908a exp. by the addn. of the rev. German version of E. 1915c as Suppl. Repub. as GW 3,2. TR.—English: 1916a,14/CW 3,2&3//Russian: 1939a.

1914b *Psychotherapeutische Zeitfragen. Ein Briefwechsel mit Dr. C. G. Jung.* Ed. by Dr. R. Loÿ. Leipzig and Vienna: Franz Deuticke. pp. 51. Repub. as GW 4,12. TR.—English: 1916a,10/CW 4,12//French: 1953a,7.

1914c Editorial note to *Psychologische Abhandlungen*, 1, ed. by C. G. Jung. Leipzig and Vienna: Franz Deuticke. 1 p. TR.—English: CW 18,134.

1916a *VII Sermones ad Mortuos. Die sieben Belehrungen der Toten.* Geschrieben von Basilides in Alexandria, der Stadt, wo der Osten den Westen berührt. Übersetzt aus dem griechischen Urtext in die deutsche Sprache. Printed for private circulation by the author. pp. XXVIII. Repub. as G. 1962a,15,x. TR.—English: 1925a/1966a,19 //?Portuguese: 1969a//Spanish: 1966b. Presentation copy examined, inscribed: "To R.F.C. Hull. A souvenir from C. G. Jung. June, 1959."

1916b *Über Konflikte der kindlichen Seele.* Leipzig and Vienna: Franz Deuticke. pp. 35. G. 1910k repub. with the addn. of the "Vorwort zur zweiten Auflage," dated Dec. 1915. Pub. with further addns. as G. 1939a. TR.—French: 1935a,1//Russian: 1939a.

1917a *Die Psychologie der unbewussten Prozesse. Ein Überblick über die moderne Theorie und Methode der analytischen Psychologie.* (Schweizer Schriften für allgemeines Wissen, 1.) Zurich: Rascher. pp. 135. G. 1912d, rev. and exp., with title change and the addn. of a preface dated Dec. 1916. Repub., slightly rev. and with new preface, as G. 1918a. TR.—English: 1917a,15.

1918a *Die Psychologie der unbewussten Prozesse. Ein Überblick über die moderne Theorie und Methode der analytischen Psychologie.* Zurich: Rascher. pp. 149. G. 1917a, slightly rev., pub. with the addn. of a preface to the second edition, dated Oct. 1918. Pub., further rev. and exp., with title change, as G. 1926a.

1918b "Über das Unbewusste." *Schweizerland*, IV:9, 464–72; IV:11–12, 548–58. In 2 pts. Repub. as GW 10,1. TR.—English: CW 10,1.

1921a *Psychologische Typen.* Zurich: Rascher. pp. 704. Repr. with varying pp. Index added 1930. Contents:
Einleitung. (7–13)
    I. Das Typenproblem in der antiken und mittelalterlichen Geistesgeschichte. (17–94)
    II. Über Schillers Ideen zum Typenproblem. (97–189)
    III. Das Apollinische und das Dionysische. (193–207)
    IV. Das Typenproblem in der Menschenkenntnis. (211–36)
    V. Das Typenproblem in der Dichtkunst. (239–380)
    VI. Das Typenproblem in der Psychiatrie. (383–404)
    VII. Das Problem der typischen Einstellungen in der Ästhetik. (407–21)
    VIII. Das Typenproblem in der modernen Philosophie. (425–55)
    IX. Das Typenproblem in der Biographik. (459–70)
    X. Allgemeine Beschreibung der Typen. (473–583)
    XI. Definitionen. (587–691)
Schlusswort. (693–704)
Repub. as GW 6,1&3. TR.—Dutch: 1949b // English: 1923a/CW 6,1,2,&4 // French: 1950a // Greek: 1935a/1954a // Italian: 1948d // Japanese: (Pts. only) 1957a // Portuguese: 1967b // Russian: (Pts. only) 1924a/1929a//Spanish: 1934a//Swedish: 1941a.

1922a "Über die Beziehungen der analytischen Psychologie zum dichterischen Kunstwerk." *Wissen und Leben*, XV:19 (1 Sept.), 914–25;

XV:20 (15 Sept.), 964–75. (Parts I and II respectively.) Repub. as G. 1931a,3. Given as lecture to the Gesellschaft für deutsche Sprache und Literatur, Zurich, May 1922, and to the Psychologischer Club Zurich, same year. TR.—English: 1923b/CW 15,6//French: 1931a,4.

1925a *Wandlungen und Symbole der Libido. Beiträge zur Entwicklungsgeschichte des Denkens.* Leipzig and Vienna: Franz Deuticke. pp. 428. G. 1912a repub., with addn. of the "Vorrede zur zweiten Auflage," dated Nov. 1924, which appears on the recto and verso of the unnumbered page between the title page and the table of contents. Pub., greatly rev. and exp., with title change, as G. 1952d. TR.— French: 1931b//Spanish: 1953b.

1925b "Die Ehe als psychologische Beziehung." *Das Ehebuch.* pp. 294–307. Ed. by Hermann Keyserling. Celle: Kampmann. Repub. as G. 1931a,11. TR.—English: 1926a/1928a,6//French: 1931a,5.

1925c "Psychologische Typen." *Zeitschrift für Menschenkunde; Blätter für Charakterologie.* . . , I:1 (May), 45–65. Repub. as GW 6,5. Lecture given at the Congrès international de Pédagogie, Territet/ Montreux, 1923. TR.—English: 1925b/CW 6,6.

1926a *Das Unbewusste im normalen und kranken Seelenleben.* . . *Ein Überblick über die moderne Theorie und Methode der analytischen Psychologie.* "III. vermehrte und verbesserte Auflage." Zurich: Rascher. pp. 166. Contents:
> Vorworten. (5–10)
>   I. Die Anfänge der Psychoanalyse. (11–28)
>   II. Die Sexualtheorie. (29–45)
> III. Der andere Gesichtspunkt. Der Wille zur Macht. (46–59)
> IV. Die zwei psychologischen Typen. (60–92)
>   V. Das persönliche und das überpersönliche oder kollektive Unbewusste. (93–115)
> VI. Die synthetische oder konstruktive Methode. (116–29)
> VII. Die Dominanten des kollektiven Unbewussten. (130–58)
> VIII. Zur Auffassung des Unbewussten. Allgemeines zur Therapie. (159–64)
> Schlusswort. (165–66)

G. 1918a rev. and exp. with title change. Again rev. and exp., with title change, as G. 1943a. TR.—English: 1928b,1/CW 7,1//French: 1928a//Spanish: 1938a//Swedish: 1934a.

1926b   *Analytische Psychologie und Erziehung. 3 Vorlesungen gehalten in London im Mai 1924.* Heidelberg: N. Kampmann. pp. 95. Repr. 1936: Zurich: Rascher. pp. 95. First written and given as lectures in English (cf. E. 1928a,13, Lectures II–IV, London, May 1924). First pub., however, in this German version. Pub., rev. and exp., as G. 1946b,1. TR.—Dutch: 1928a.

1926c   "Geist und Leben." *Form und Sinn*, II:2 (Nov.), 33–44. Repub. as G. 1931a,13. Lecture given to the Literarische Gesellschaft Augsburg, 29 Oct. 1926, contributed to the series "Natur und Geist." TR.—English: 1928a,2.

1927a   "Die Erdbedingtheit der Psyche." *Mensch und Erde.* pp. 83–137. Ed. by Hermann Keyserling. (Der Leuchter; Weltanschauung und Lebensgestaltung, 8.) Darmstadt: Otto Reichl. Subsequently divided and largely rewritten as G. 1931a,8 and G. 1928d. Originally given as lecture to the Conference of the Gesellschaft für freie Philosophie, Darmstadt, 1927. TR.—French: 1931a,3.

1927b   "Die Frau in Europa." *Europ. Rev.*, III:7 (Oct.), 481–99. Repub. as G. 1929a. TR.—English: 1928a,5.

1928a   *Die Beziehungen zwischen dem Ich und dem Unbewussten.* Darmstadt: Reichl. pp. 208. Repr. 1933: Zurich: Rascher. Half title: *Das Ich und das Unbewusste.* Contents:
    I. Die Wirkungen des Unbewussten auf das Bewusstsein.
      1. Das persönliche und das kollektive Unbewusste. (11–30)
      2. Die Folgeerscheinungen der Assimilation des Unbewussten. (31–60)
      3. Die Persona als ein Ausschnitt aus der Kollektivpsyche. (61–73)
      4. Die Versuche zur Befreiung der Individualität aus der Kollektivpsyche. (74–88)
    II. Die Individuation.
      1. Die Funktion des Unbewussten. (91–116)
      2. Anima und Animus. (117–58)
      3. Die Technik der Unterscheidung zwischen dem Ich und den Figuren des Unbewussten. (159–83)
      4. Die Mana-Persönlichkeit. (184–208)
Orig. given as lecture, in German, and pub. in trans. as Fr. 1916a.

Subsequently much rev. and exp. from the German ms., and pub. as above. Pub. with the addn. of a new foreword as G. 1935a. TR.— Dutch: 1935a // English: 1928b,2.

1928b *Über die Energetik der Seele.* (Psychologische Abhandlungen, 2.) Zurich: Rascher. pp. 224. Contents:
　　1. Vorwort. Repub. as G. 1948b,1.
　　2. "Über die Energetik der Seele." (9–111) Repub. as G. 1948b,2. TR.—English: 1928a,1.
　　3. "Allgemeine Gesichtspunkte zur Psychologie des Traumes." (112–84) First pub. in an English trans. (cf. E. 1916a,13). Orig. German text considerably rev. and exp., and pub. here. Subsequently pub., rev. and exp., as G. 1948b,4. TR.—French: 1944a,6.
　　4. "Instinkt und Unbewusstes." (185–99) First pub. in an English trans. (cf. E. 1919b). Pub., rev. and with the addn. of brief concluding note, as G. 1948b,6. Contribution to symposium, "Instinct and the Unconscious," presented at a joint meeting of the Aristotelian Society, The Mind Association, and the British Psychological Association, London, July 1919. TR.— English: 1919b.
　　5. "Die psychologischen Grundlagen des Geisterglaubens." (200– 24) Pub., rev., as G. 1948b,7. Paper read in an English trans. before the Society for Psychical Research, London, 4 July 1919. TR.—English: 1920b // French: 1939a,4.
Whole book pub., exp., with addns. and title change, as G. 1948b.

1928c "Heilbare Geisteskranke? Organisches oder funktionelles Leiden?" *Berliner Tageblatt,* 189 (21 Apr.), 1. Beiblatt. The orig. ms. bears the title "Geisteskrankheit und Seele" and was presumably given as a lecture before a meeting of the III. Allgemeiner Ärztlicher Kongress für Psychotherapie, Baden-Baden, 20–22 Apr. 1928. Repub. under the orig. title as GW 3,6. TR.—English: CW 3,7.

1928d "Die Struktur der Seele." *Europ. Rev.,* IV:1 (Apr.), 27–37; and IV:2 (May), 125–35. (In two parts.) Derived from G. 1927a. Pub., rev. and exp., as G. 1931a,7.

1928e "Die Bedeutung der schweizerischen Linie im Spektrum Europas." *Neue Schw. R.,* XXXIV:6 (June), 1–11, 469–79. A retort to Keyserling's *Das Spektrum Europas.* Repub. as GW 10,19. TR.—English: 1959k / CW 10,19 // French: 1948a,3.

1928f "Das Seelenproblem des modernen Menschen." *Europ. Rev.*, IV:9 (Dec.), 700–15. Brief, much simplified version pub. as G. 1929e. Pub., rev. and exp., as G. 1931a,14. Read before the Tagung des Verbandes für intellektuelle Zusammenarbeit, Prague, Oct. 1928. TR.—English: 1931c // French: 1931a,2.

1928g "Psychoanalyse und Seelsorge." *Ethik (Sexual- und Gesellschafts-Ethik)* (Halle), V:1, 7–12. Repub. as GW 11,8. TR.—English: CW 11,8.

1929a *Die Frau in Europa.* Zurich: Verlag der Neuen Schweizer Revue. pp. 46. Reset, 1932: "Zweite Auflage." Zurich: Rascher. pp. 39. Reset, 1965: "Rascher Paperback," pp. 25. G. 1927b repub. as monograph. Repub. as G. 1971a,2. TR.—Dutch: 1949c // English: CW 10,6 // French: 1931a,6 // Italian: 1963a,4 // Japanese: 1956b,3 // Spanish: 1940a.

1929b With Richard Wilhelm: *Das Geheimnis der goldenen Blüte. Ein chinesisches Lebensbuch.* Munich: Dorn. pp. 161. A 1929 Berlin edn. with 150 pp. has been reported but not seen. Contains the following work by Jung:
   I. "Einführung." (7–[88])
     1. Einleitung. (9–27)
     2. Die Grundbegriffe. (28–40)
     3. Die Erscheinungen des Weges. (41–57)
     4. Die Loslösung des Bewusstseins vom Objekt. (58–64)
     5. Die Vollendung. (65–73)
     6. Schlusswort. (74–75)
     7. Beispiele europäischer Mandalas. ([77–88]) Includes 10 black and white plates.
G. 1929h pub., rev. and exp. Pub., rev. and with addns., as G. 1938a. TR.—English: 1931a,1&2 // Italian: 1936a.

1929c *"Ziele der Psychotherapie." *Bericht über den IV. allgemeinen ärztlichen Kongress für Psychotherapie* in Bad Neuheim [April]. pp. 1–14. Given as lecture to the Congress, 12 Apr. 1929. Repub. as G. 1931a,5.

1929d "Die Probleme der modernen Psychotherapie." *Schweizerisches medizinisches Jahrbuch.* pp. 74–86. Repub. as G. 1931a,2. Lecture given to the Ärztlicher Verein and to the Psychotherapeutische Gesellschaft, Munich, 21 March 1929. TR.—English: 1931d.

1929e "Das Seelenproblem des modernen Menschen." *Allgemeine Neueste Nachrichten* (23 Jan.). A much abbreviated, simplified version of G. 1928f.

1929f "Der Gegensatz Freud und Jung." *Kölnische Zeitung*, Saturday, 4 May and Tuesday, 7 May. (In two parts.) Repub. as G. 1931a,4.

1929g "Paracelsus. Ein Vortrag gehalten beim Geburtshaus an der Teufelsbrücke bei Einsiedeln am 22. Juni 1929." *Lesezirkel*, XVI:10 (Sept.), 117–25. Repub. as G. 1934b,5. Lecture given at Paracelsus' birthplace to the Literarische Club Zurich, 22 June 1929.

1929h With Richard Wilhelm: "Tschang Scheng Schu. Die Kunst das menschliche Leben zu verlängern." *Europ. Rev.*, V:8 (Nov.), 530–56. Contains the following work by Jung:
    1. "Einleitung." (530–42)
Pub., rev. and exp., as G. 1929b.

1929i "Die Bedeutung von Konstitution und Vererbung für die Psychologie." *Die Medizinische Welt*, III:47 (Nov.), 1677–79. Repub. as GW 8,4. TR.—English: CW 8,4.

1930a "Psychologie und Dichtung." *Philosophie der Literaturwissenschaft.* pp. 315–30. Ed. by Emil Ermatinger. Berlin: Junker und Dünnhaupt. Pub., rev. and exp., as G. 1950a,2. TR.—English: 1930c / 1933a,8.

1930b "Einführung." W. M. Kranefeldt: *Die Psychoanalyse.* pp. 5–16. (Sammlung Göschen, 1034.) Berlin and Leipzig: Walter de Gruyter. Reset, 1950: new title: *Therapeutische Psychologie.* Jung's introduction, pp. 5–17. Repub. as GW 4,15. TR.—English: 1932a / CW 4,15.

1930c "Nachruf für Richard Wilhelm." *Neue Zür. Z.*, CLI:422 (6 Mar.), 1. Repub. as G. 1931b. Delivered as contribution to a memorial service for Wilhelm, Munich, 10 May 1930. Cf. G. 1931b and 1938a,2. TR.—English: 1931a,3.

1930d "Die seelischen Probleme der menschlichen Altersstufen." *Neue Zür. Z.* (14 and 16 Mar.). (In 2 pts.) Pub., largely rewritten, as G. 1931a,10, with title change. TR.—French: 1931a,1.

1930e "Der Aufgang einer neuen Welt." A review of Hermann Keyserling: *Amerika; der Aufgang einer neuen Welt. Neue Zür. Z.,* no. 2378, iv (7 Dec.), Bücherbeilage, p. 6. Repub. as GW 10,20. TR.—English: CW 10,20.

1931a *Seelenprobleme der Gegenwart.* (Psychologische Abhandlungen, 3.) Zurich: Rascher. pp. 435. 1950: rev. edn. pp. 392. Reset, 1969: "Rascher Paperback." pp. 323. Repr., 1973: ("Studienausgabe.") Olten: Walter. pp. 323. Contents:

    1. Vorwort(e). (v–vii) Dated Dec. 1930 and July 1932. TR—English: CW 18,67 with addn. // Japanese: 1955a // Swedish: 1936a,1.

    2. "Die Probleme der modernen Psychotherapie." (1–39) G. 1929d repub. Repub. as GW 16,6. TR.—English: CW 16,6 // French: 1953a,3 // Japanese: 1955a // Swedish: 1936a,2.

    3. "Über die Beziehungen der analytischen Psychologie zum dichterischen Kunstwerk." (40–73) G. 1922a repub. Repub. as GW 15,6. TR.—Danish: 1964a // English: CW 15,6 // Japanese: 1955a // Serbo-Croat: 1969a,8 // Swedish: 1936a,3.

    4. "Der Gegensatz Freud und Jung." (74–86) G. 1929f repub. Repub. as GW 4,16. TR.—English: 1933a,6 / CW 4,16 // French: 1953a,8 // Swedish: 1936a,4.

    5. "Ziele der Psychotherapie." (87–114) G. 1929c repub. Repub. as GW 16,5. TR.—English: 1933a,3 / CW 16,5 // French: 1953a,6.

    6. "Psychologische Typologie." (115–43) A lecture to a meeting of the Schweizer Irrenärzte, Zurich, 1928. Repub. as GW 6,6. TR.—English: 1933a,4 / CW 6,7 // French: 1961b,7 // Swedish: 1936a,5.

    7. "Die Struktur der Seele." (144–75) G. 1928d rev. and exp. Repub. as GW 8,7. TR.—English: CW 8,7 // French: 1961b,1 // Japanese: 1955a // Swedish: 1936a,6.

    8. "Seele und Erde." (176–210) Derived from G. 1927a; title changed. Repub. as GW 10,2. TR.—English: 1928a,3 / CW 10,2 // Japanese: 1955a.

    9. "Der archaische Mensch." (211–47) G. 1931f, somewhat rev.

Repub. as GW 10,3. TR.—Dutch: 1940a,5 // English: 1933a,7 /
CW 10,3 // French: 1961b,5 // Japanese: 1955a // Swedish:
1936a,7.

10. "Die Lebenswende." (248–74) G. 1930d, much rev., with title
change. Repub. as GW 8,16. TR.—Dutch: 1940a,3 // English:
1933a,5 / CW 8,16 // French: 1961b,8 // Swedish: 1936a,8.

11. "Die Ehe als psychologische Beziehung." (275–95) G. 1925b
repub. Repub. as GW 17,8. TR.—Dutch: 1940a,2 // English:
CW 17,8 // Japanese: 1955a // Swedish: 1936a,9.

12. "Analytische Psychologie und Weltanschauung." (296–335) A
rev. and exp. version of the orig. unpub. ms, 1st pub. in trans.
as E. 1928a,4. Repub. as GW 8,14. Lecture given in Karlsruhe,
1927, and to the Philosophische Gesellschaft, Zurich, 4 March
1930. TR.—Dutch: 1940a,7 // English: CW 8,14 // French:
1961b,4 // Swedish: 1936a,10.

13. "Geist und Leben." (369–400) G. 1926c repub. Repub. as
GW 8,12. TR.—English: CW 8,12 // French: 1961b,3 // Japanese: 1955a.

14. "Das Seelenproblem des modernen Menschen." (401–35) G.
1928f, rev. and exp. Repub. as GW 10,4. TR.—Dutch: 1940a,1
// English: 1933a,10 / CW 10,4 // ?Greek: 1949a // Japanese:
1955a // Spanish: 1932a // Swedish: 1936a,11.

TR. of entire work: Dutch: 1956a // ?Greek: 1962c // Italian: 1942a.

1931b * "Richard Wilhelm." *Chinesisch-Deutscher Almanach für das Jahr
1931. pp. 7–14. Frankfurt a. M.: China-Institut. G. 1930c repub.?
Repub. as G. 1938a,2 with title change.

1931c * "Die praktische Verwendbarkeit der Traumanalyse." *Bericht über
den VI. allgemeinen ärztlichen Kongress für Psychotherapie*. Dresden. Delivered as a lecture to the 6th Congress of the Allgemeine
ärztliche Gesellschaft für Psychotherapie, Dresden, 31 Apr. 1931.
Cf. G. 1934b,4. TR.—English: 1933a,1.

1931d "Vorwort." H. Schmid-Guisan: *Tag und Nacht*. pp. vi–x. Zurich and
Munich: Rhein. TR.—English: CW 18,108.

1931e "Einführung." Francis [error for Frances] G. Wickes: *Analyse der
Kindesseele. Untersuchung und Behandlung nach den Grundlagen
der Jungschen Theorie*. pp. 13–20. Stuttgart: Julius Hoffmann. The

first 3½ paragraphs only of the above were previously pub. in trans. as E. 1927a. Repub. as GW 17,2. TR.—Dutch: 1957b // English: (Pt. only) 1927a / 1966c / CW 17,2 // Italian: 1948e.

1931f "Der archaische Mensch." *Europ. Rev.*, VII:3 (Mar.), 182–203. Pub., rev. somewhat, as G. 1931a,9. Lecture delivered to the Hottinger Lesezirkel, Zurich, 22 Oct. 1930, and pub. abridged as the above. TR.—Spanish: 1931a.

1931g "Die Entschleierung der Seele." *Europ. Rev.*, VII:7 (July), 504–22. Pub. with minor alterations and title change as G. 1934b,2. Lecture given to the Kulturbund, Vienna, 1931. TR.—English: 1933a,9.

1932a *Die Beziehung der Psychotherapie zur Seelsorge.* Zurich: Rascher. pp. 30. Reset, 1948; pp. 39. Repub. as GW 11,7 with title change. Text of lecture to the Elsässische Pastoralkonferenz, Strassburg, May 1932, and to the Psychologischer Club Zurich, 1932. TR.—Dutch: 1935b // English: 1933a,11 / CW 11,7 // French: 1953a,13.

1932b "Vorwort zum Märchen vom Fischotter." O. A. Schmitz: *Märchen aus dem Unbewussten.* pp. 7–12. Munich: Hanser. TR.—English: CW 18,110.

1932c * Answers to questions on Goethe. *Kölnische Zeitung,* (22 Mar.) Letter to the editor, Max Rychner (28 Feb. 1932). Letter pub. in G. 1972a, and trans. in E. 1973b.

1932d "Dr. Hans Schmid-Guisan." *Basl. Nach.,* (25 Apr.). Obituary article. TR.—English: CW 18,109.

1932e "Ulysses." *Europ. Rev.*, VIII:2/9 (Sept.), 547–68. Pub. with the addn. of "forenote" as G. 1934b,7. TR.—Spanish: 1933a.

1932f "Sigmund Freud als kulturhistorische Erscheinung." *Charakter*, I:2 (Sept.), 65–70. Repub. as G. 1934b,6. Excerpts pub. as "Entlarvung der viktorianischen Epoche. Freud kulturhistorisch gesehen." *Vossische Zeitung* (4 Aug.). Simultaneously issued in trans. in the U.S. edn. of this journal as E. 1932b. TR.—English: 1932b // Spanish: 1935c.

1932g "Picasso." *Neue Zür. Z.*, CLIII:2 (Sun., 13 Nov.), 1. Repub. as G. 1934b,8. TR.—Spanish: 1933b / 1934b.

1932h "Wirklichkeit und Überwirklichkeit." *Querschnitt*, XII:12 (Dec.), 844–45. Repub. as GW 8,15. TR.—English: CW 8,15.

1932i "Die Hypothese des kollektiven Unbewussten." (Autoreferat.) *Vierteljahresschrift der Naturforschenden Gesellschaft in Zürich*, LXXVII:2, "Sitzungsberichte," IV–V. Abstract of lecture read before a meeting of the Naturforschende Gesellschaft held at the Eidgenössische Technische Hochschule, Zurich, 1 Feb. 1932. Lecture ms not discovered. TR.—English: CW 18,51.

1933a "Blick in die Verbrecherseele. Das Doppelleben des Kriminellen. Ungewöhnliche Fälle von Übertragung verbrecherischer Absichten auf Andere. . . . Aus einem Gespräch." *Neues Wiener Journal*, (15 Jan.). 1 p. For English versions, see E. 1932c.

1933b "Über Psychologie." *Neue Schw. R.*, n.s. I:1 (May), 21–28 and 1:2 (June), 98–106. (In 2 pts.) Rev. and expanded into G. 1934b,3 with change of title. An expanded version of a lecture originally delivered in Dresden, 1931, then at a conference, Town Hall, Zurich, 18 Dec. 1932, and in Cologne and Essen, Feb. 1933. TR.—French: (Pts. only) 1933a.

1933c "Bruder Klaus." *Neue Schw. R.*, n.s. I:4 (Aug.), 223–29. Repub. as GW 11,6. TR.—English: 1946c / CW 11,6.

1933d Review of Gustav Richard Heyer: *Der Organismus der Seele. Europ. Rev.*, IX:10 (Oct.), 639. TR.—English: CW 18,124.

1933e "Geleitwort des Herausgebers." *Zbl. Psychotherap.*, VI:3 (Dec.), 139–40. Repub. as GW 10,25. TR.—English: CW 10,25.

1933f Contribution on hallucination to the "Discussion-Aussprache" following papers on "Das Problem der Sinnestäuschungen" in "Bericht über die Wissenschaftlichen Sitzungen der 84. Versammlung der Schweizerischen Gesellschaft für Psychiatrie in Prangins près Nyon, 7–8 Octobre 1933." *Schweizer Archiv für Neurologie und Psychiatrie. . . ,* XXXII:2, 382. TR.—English: CW 18,38.

1934a *Allgemeines zur Komplextheorie.* (Kultur- und staatswissenschaftliche Schriften der Eidgenössischen Technischen Hochschule, 12.)

Aarau: Sauerländer. pp. 20. Pub., slightly rev. and with minor title change, as G. 1948b,3. Text of lecture originally entitled "Über Komplextheorie," given as "Antrittsvorlesung," at the Eidgenössische Technische Hochschule, 5 May 1934, and at the 7. [Allgemeiner ärztlicher] Kongress für Psychotherapie, Bad Nauheim, 10–13 May 1934. Summary of lecture pub. in *Zbl. Psychotherap.*, VII: 3, 139–42. TR. of whole—French: 1944a,5.

1934b   *Wirklichkeit der Seele. Anwendungen und Fortschritte der neueren Psychologie.* With contributions by Hugo Rosenthal, Emma Jung and W. M. Kranefeldt. (Psychologische Abhandlungen, 4.) Zurich: Rascher. pp. 409. Reset, 1969: Olten: Walter. pp. 265. Contains the following works by Jung:

    1. Vorwort. Dated Sept. 1933. TR.—English: CW 18,113 // Japanese: 1955b.

    2. "Das Grundproblem der gegenwärtigen Psychologie." (1–31) G. 1931g, slightly rev. and with title change. Repub. as GW 8,13. TR.—English: CW 8,13 // French: 1944a,1 // Japanese: 1955b // Spanish: 1935a.

    3. "Die Bedeutung der Psychologie für die Gegenwart." (32–67) G. 1933b, rev. and exp. with title change. Repub. as GW 10,7. TR.—English: CW 10,7 // French: 1944a,2 // Japanese: 1955b.

    4. "Die praktische Verwendbarkeit der Traumanalyse." (68–103) Cf. G. 1931c. Repub. as GW 16,12. TR.—English: 1933a,1 / CW 16,12 // French: 1944a,7 // Japanese: 1955b.

    5. "Paracelsus." (104–18) G. 1929g repub. Repub. as G. 1952c. TR.—English: CW 15,1 // French: 1961b,14.

    6. "Sigmund Freud als kulturhistorische Erscheinung." (119–31) G. 1932f repub. Repub. as GW 15,3. TR.—English: CW 15,3 // French: 1961b,15 // Japanese: 1955b.

    7. "Ulysses." (132–69) G. 1932e pub. with the addn. of a forenote. Repub. as GW 15,8. TR.—English: 1949c / CW 15,8 // French: 1961b,16 // Japanese: 1955b // Spanish: 1933a / ?1944a.

    8. "Picasso." (170–79) G. 1932g repub. Repub. as GW 15,9. TR.—English: 1940a / 1953i / CW 15,9 // French: 1961b,17 // Italian: 1946a // Japanese: 1955b // Spanish: 1933b / 1934b.

    9. "Vom Werden der Persönlichkeit." (180–211) Lecture delivered to the Kulturbund, Vienna, Nov. 1932, titled "Die Stimme des Innern." Repub. as GW 17,7. TR.—Dutch: 1940a,4. // English: 1939a,6 / CW 17,7 // French: 1955b // Japanese: 1955b.

10. "Seele und Tod." (212–30) G. 1934h repub. Pub., abridged and with title change, as G. 1935i. Repub. as whole as GW 8,17. TR.—Dutch: 1940b,6 // English: 1945a / 1959c / CW 8,17 // French: 1939a,3 / 1956a,5 // Japanese 1955b. TR. of entire work—Dutch: 1957a // Italian: 1949b // Spanish: 1935a / (Pts. only?) 1940a.

1934c "Zur Empirie des Individuationsprozesses." *Eran. Jb. 1933.* pp. 201–14. Includes 5 black and white plates. (The *Eranos Jahrbuch* articles were originally given as lectures at the Eranos Tagung, Ascona, in August of the year indicated.) Pub., completely rewritten and exp., as G. 1950a,4. TR.—English: 1939a,2.

1934d "Geleitwort." Gerhard Adler: *Entdeckung der Seele. Von Sigmund Freud und Alfred Adler zu C. G. Jung.* pp. vii–viii. Zurich: Rascher. Dated Dec. 1933. TR.—English: CW 18,52.

1934e "Geleitwort." Carl Ludwig Schleich: *Die Wunder der Seele.* pp. 3–11. Berlin: S. Fischer. Reset, 1953: Frankfurt: G. B. Fischer. pp. 5–11. TR.—English: CW 18,39.

1934f Rejoinder to Dr. Bally's article "Deutschstämmige Psychotherapie," headlined "Zeitgenössisches." *Neue Zür. Z.,* CLV:437,1 (13 Mar.) and CLV:443,1 (14 Mar.). (In 2 pts.) Cf. G. 1934g. Repub., with G. 1934g, as GW 10,26. TR.—English: CW 10,26 (with trans. of G. 1934g).

1934g "Ein Nachtrag." *Neue Zür. Z.,* CLV:457 (15 Mar.). Second and third paragraphs *only* by Jung. Cf. G. 1934f. Repub., with G. 1934f, as GW 10,26. TR.—English: CW 10,26 (p. 544, last 3 parags., ftnote 5) with trans. of G. 1934f.

1934h "Seele und Tod." *Europ. Rev.,* X:4 (Apr.), 229–38. Extract pub. in *Berliner Tageblatt,* (17 Apr.). Entire article repub. as G. 1934b,10.

1934i "Ein neues Buch von Keyserling." Review of Hermann Keyserling: *La Révolution mondiale. Basl. Nach.,* Sonntagsblatt, XXVIII: 19 (13 May), 78–79. Repub. as GW 10,21. TR.—English: CW 10,21.

1934j Circular letter: "Sehr geehrte Kollegen! . . . Zürich-Küsnacht 1.12.34." *Zbl. Psychotherap.,* VII:6 (Dec.), 1p. (separatum). Repub. as GW 10,27. TR.—English: 1946d,1 / CW 10,27.

1934k "Zur gegenwärtigen Lage der Psychotherapie." *Zbl. Psychotherap.*, VII:1, 1–16. Repub. as GW 10,8. TR.—English: CW 10,8 // French: 1953a,9.

1934l With M. H. Göring: "Geheimrat Sommer zum 70. Geburtstag." *Zbl. Psychotherap.*, VII, 313–14.

1935a *Die Beziehungen zwischen dem Ich und dem Unbewussten.* Zurich: Rascher. pp. 208. 1966: 7th rev. edn. ("Rascher Paperback.") pp. 151. 1971: ("Studienausgabe.") Olten: Walter. pp. 160. G. 1928a pub. with addn. of the "Vorrede zur zweiten Auflage," dated Oct. 1934, on 4 unnumbered pp. between the title page and the table of contents. (An insignificant, prefatory parag. was added to the 1938 repr.) Repub. as GW 7,2, with slight title change. TR.—Danish: 1962a // English: CW 7,2 // French: 1938a / 1964a // ?Greek: 1962a,2 // Hebrew: 1973a // Italian: 1948a // Norwegian: 1966a // Spanish: 1936a // Swedish: 1967a.

1935b "Über die Archetypen des kollektiven Unbewussten." *Eran. Jb. 1934.* pp. 179–229. (See G. 1934c.) Pub., rev., as G. 1954b,2. TR.— English: 1939a,3.

1935c "Einleitung." M. Esther Harding: *Der Weg der Frau.* pp. 9–13. Zurich: Rhein. The original German version, of which an English trans. was previously pub. as E. 1933b. TR.—English: 1933b / CW 18,130.

1935d "Geleitwort." Olga von Koenig-Fachsenfeld: *Wandlungen des Traumproblems von der Romantik bis zur Gegenwart.* pp. iii–vi. Stuttgart: F. Enke. TR.—English: CW 18,115.

1935e "Vorwort." Rose Mehlich: *J. H. Fichtes Seelenlehre und ihre Beziehung zur Gegenwart.* pp. 7–11. Zurich: Rascher. TR.—English: (Pts. only) 1950e / CW 18,114.

1935f "Einführung." *Das tibetanische Totenbuch.* pp. 15–35. Ed. by W. Y. Evans-Wentz. Zurich: Rascher. Jung's "Einführung" consists of:
    1. "Geleitwort." (15–16)
    2. "Psychologischer Commentar zum Bardo Thödol." (17–35)
Repub. as GW 11,11. TR.—English: 1957f.

1935g "Was ist Psychotherapie?" *Schweizerische Ärztezeitung für Standesfragen,* XVI:26 (28 June), 335–39. Repub. as GW 16,3. Contribution to a symposium of the Allgemeine ärztliche Gesellschaft für Psychotherapie, "Psychotherapie in der Schweiz," May 1935. Cf. G. 1935h. TR.—English: CW 16,3 // French: 1953a,1.

1935h "Votum C. G. Jung." *Schweizerische Ärztezeitung für Standesfragen,* XVI:26 (28 June), 345–46. Repub. as GW 10,31, with sl. title change. Contribution to discussion at symposium, "Psychotherapie in der Schweiz," May 1935. Cf. G. 1935g. TR.—English: CW 10,31.

1935i "Von der Psychologie des Sterbens." *Münchener Neueste Nachrichten,* 269 (2 Oct.), 3. G. 1934b,10 abridged and with title change.

1935j "Geleitwort." *Zbl. Psychotherap.,* VIII:1, 1–5. Repub. as GW 10,28. TR.—English: CW 10,28.

1935k "Vorbemerkung des Herausgebers." *Zbl. Psychotherap.,* VIII:2, 65. Repub. as GW 10,29. TR.—English: CW 10,29.

1935l "Grundsätzliches zur praktischen Psychotherapie." *Zbl. Psychotherap.,* VIII:2, 66–82. Repub. as GW 16,2. Given as lecture to the Medizinische Gesellschaft, Zurich, 1935. TR.—English: CW 16,2 // French: 1953a,5.

1936a "Traumsymbole des Individuationsprozesses . . ." *Eran. Jb. 1935.* pp. 13–133. (See G. 1934c.) Pub., rev. and exp., as G. 1944a,3. TR.—English: 1939a,4 / 1959d.

1936b "Psychologische Typologie." *Süddeutsche Monatshefte,* XXXIII:5 (Feb.), 264–72. Repub. as GW 6,7. TR.—English: CW 6,8.

1936c "Wotan." *Neue Schw. R.,* n.s. III:11 (Mar.), 657–69. Repub. as G. 1946a,2. TR.—English: (abridged) 1937c / 1947a,3 / CW 10,10.

1936d Review of Gustav Richard Heyer: *Praktische Seelenheilkunde.* *Zbl. Psychotherap.,* IX:3, 184–86. TR.—English: CW 18,125.

1936e "Über den Archetypus, mit besonderer Berücksichtigung des Animabegriffes." *Zbl. Psychotherap.,* IX:5, 259–74. Pub., rev., as G. 1954b,3.

1937a "Die Erlösungsvorstellungen in der Alchemie." *Eran. Jb. 1936.* pp. 13–111. (See G. 1934c.) Pub., rev. and exp., as G. 1944a,4. TR.— English: 1939a,5.

1937b "Zur psychologischen Tatbestandsdiagnostik. Das Tatbestands- experiment im Schwurgerichtsprozess Näf." *Archiv für Kriminologie,* C (Jan.–Feb.), 123–30. Repub. as GW 2,19. TR.—English: CW 2,19.

1938a With Richard Wilhelm: *Das Geheimnis der goldenen Blüte. Ein chinesisches Lebensbuch.* "II. Auflage." Zurich: Rascher. pp. 150. Contains the following works by Jung:
    1. "Vorrede zur II. Auflage." (v–viii) TR.—English: 1962b,1.
    2. "Zum Gedächtnis Richard Wilhelms." (ix–xviii) G. 1930c repub. with title change. TR.—English: 1962b,3.
    3. Europäischer Kommentar. (1–66) (Untitled here) G. 1928b,I, 1–6 rev. and exp. TR.—English: 1962b,2.
    4. "Beispiele europäischer Mandalas." (67–68 + 10 plates) Plates (excepting #2) incorporated into G. 1950a,5. TR.—English: 1962b,2.
G. 1929b pub. rev. and with addns. Pub. reset and with further addns. as G. 1957b. TR.—Dutch: 1953a // English: 1962b // Spanish: 1955a.

1938b "Ueber das Rosarium Philosophorum." *Aus d. Jhrsb. 1937/38.* pp. 25–29. Printed for private circulation. Summary of 2 lectures to the Psychologischer Club Zürich, given presumably late in 1937 or early in 1938. TR.—English: CW 18,126.

1938c "Einige Bemerkungen zu den Visionen des Zosimos." *Eran. Jb. 1937.* pp. 15–54 (See G. 1934c.) Pub., rev. and considerably exp., with title change, as G. 1954b,5.

1938d "Begleitwort." Gertrud Gilli: *Der dunkle Bruder.* 2 pp. Zurich/Elgg: Volksverlag. TR.—English: CW 18,116.

1939a *Über Konflikte der kindlichen Seele.* "Dritte Auflage." Zurich: Rascher. pp. 36. G. 1916b pub. as a pamphlet with a new foreword and supplement. Pub., slightly rev. and exp., as G. 1946b,2. TR.— Spanish: 1945a.

1939b "Die psychologischen Aspekte des Mutterarchetypus." *Eran. Jb. 1938.* pp. 403–43. (See G. 1934c.) Pub., rev., as G. 1954b,4. TR.— English: 1943a.

1939c "Geleitwort." D. T. Suzuki: *Die grosse Befreiung. Einführung in den Zen-Buddhismus.* pp. 7–37. Leipzig: Curt Weller. Repub. as GW 11,13. TR.—English: 1949d / CW 11,13 // ?Spanish: 1964c.

1939d "† Sigmund Freud." *Basl. Nach.*, Sonntagsblatt, XXXIII:40 (1 Oct.), 157–59. Obituary article. Repub. as GW 15,4. TR.—English: CW 15,4 // Norwegian: 1956a.

1939e "Bewusstsein, Unbewusstes und Individuation." *Zbl. Psychotherap.*, XI:5, 257–70. Orig. written in English and pub. as E. 1939a,1. Subsequently rev. considerably and pub. in this German version. Repub. as GW 9,i,10. TR.—English: CW 9,i,10 // French: 1953a,12.

1940a *Psychologie und Religion. Die Terry Lectures 1937 gehalten an der Yale University.* Zurich: Rascher. pp. 192. 1962: 4th edn., rev. and reset. ("Rascher Paperback.") pp. 125. Orig. written in English and trans. from E. 1938a by Felicia Froboese and Toni Wolff. Subsequently rev. and exp. and pub. in this version. Contents:
  Vorrede. (Oct. 1939.)
  1. Die Autonomie des Unbewussten. (9–61)
  2. Dogma und natürliche Symbole. (63–116)
  3. Geschichte und Psychologie eines natürlichen Symbols. (117–90)
Repub. as GW 11,1. TR.—Danish: 1968a // Dutch: 1951a // English: CW 11,1 // French: 1958b // Greek: 1962b // Italian: 1948c // Japanese: 1956b,1 // Norwegian: 1965a // Portuguese: 1956a // Spanish: 1949b // Turkish: 1965a (from English).

1940b "Die verschiedenen Aspekte der Wiedergeburt." *Eran. Jb. 1939.* pp. 399–447. (See G. 1934c.) Pub., rev. and exp., with title change, as G. 1950a,3. TR.—English: 1944a.

1940c "Geleitwort." Jolande Jacobi: *Die Psychologie von C. G. Jung.* pp. 17–18. Zurich: Rascher. Dated Aug. 1939. Paging varies in successive edns. TR.—Danish: 1963a / English: 1942c / 1962c / CW 18,40 // Italian: 1949c // Spanish: 1947a.

1941a With K. Kerényi: *Das göttliche Kind in mythologischer und psychologischer Beleuchtung.* (Albae Vigiliae, 6/7.) Amsterdam: Pantheon Akademische Verlagsanstalt. pp. 124. Contains the following work by Jung:
"Zur Psychologie des Kind-Archetypus." (85–124)
Pub. rev., together with G. 1941b, as G. 1941c.

1941b With K. Kerényi: *Das göttliche Mädchen. Die Hauptgestalt der Mysterien von Eleusis in mythologischer und psychologischer Beleuchtung.* (Albae Vigiliae, 8/9.) Amsterdam: Pantheon Akademische Verlagsanstalt. pp. 109. Contains the following work by Jung:
"Zum psychologischen Aspekt der Korefigur." (85–109)
Pub. rev., together with G. 1941a, as G. 1941c.

1941c With K. Kerényi: *Einführung in das Wesen der Mythologie.* Amsterdam: Pantheon Akademische Verlagsanstalt; Zurich: Rascher. pp. 251. Contains the following works by Jung:
1. "Zur Psychologie des Kind-Archetypus." (105–44)
2. "Zum psychologischen Aspekt der Korefigur." (217–41)
G. 1941a and 1941b rev. and pub. as one vol. Repub. as G. 1951b.
TR.—English: 1949a // Italian: 1948b.

1941d *Die psychologische Diagnose des Tatbestandes.* Zurich: Rascher. pp. 47. G. 1906k repub. Repub. as GW 2,6. TR.—English: CW 2,6.

1941e "Rückkehr zum einfachen Leben." *Du,* Jhg. I:3 (May), 6–7, 56. Summation of answers to a questionnaire on the effect of wartime conditions in Switzerland. TR.—English: (Pts. only) 1945b / CW 18,71.

1941f "Paracelsus als Arzt." *Schweizerische medizinische Wochenschrift,* LXXI:40 (Oct.), 1153–70. Repub. as G. 1942a,1. Simplified version pub. in *Basler Nachrichten* (21 Sept.). Lecture given at the annual meeting of the Naturforschende Gesellschaft Basel, of the Schweizerische Gesellschaft zur Geschichte der Medizin und der Naturwissenschaften, Basel, 7 Sept. 1941 and to the Psychologischer Club Zürich, 21 Feb. 1942.

1942a *Paracelsica. Zwei Vorlesungen über den Arzt und Philosophen Theophrastus.* Zurich: Rascher. pp. 188. With 3 plates and 5 text illus.

Contents:

 Vorwort. (7–8)

 1. "Paracelsus als Arzt." (9–41) G. 1941f repub. Repub. as GW
  15,2. TR.—English: CW 15,2.

 2. "Paracelsus als geistige Erscheinung." (43–178) Lecture contributed to the Schweizerische Paracelsus Gesellschaft Celebration, Einsiedeln, 5 Oct. 1941. Repub. as GW 13,3. TR.—English:
  CW 13,3.

Two lectures delivered on the occasion of the 400th anniversary of
Paracelsus' death, Autumn 1941.

1942b "Zur Psychologie der Trinitätsidee." *Eran. Jb. 1940/41.* pp. 31–64.
  (See G. 1934c.) Pub., rev. and exp. with title change, as G. 1948a,4.
  Lecture given also to the Psychologischer Club Zurich, 5 Oct. 1940.

1942c "Das Wandlungssymbol in der Messe." *Eran. Jb. 1940/41.* pp. 67–
  155. (See G. 1934c.) Pub., rev. and exp., as G. 1954b,6. Lecture given
  also to the Psychologischer Club Zurich, 17 May 1941. TR.—English:
  1955b / 1955l (Pt. only).

1943a *Über die Psychologie des Unbewussten.* Zurich: Rascher. pp. 213.
  1960: reset, "7. vermehrte und verbesserte Auflage." pp. 135. 1966:
  reset. ("Rascher Paperback.") pp. 148. Contents:
  Vorworte. (7–15)
  1. Die Psychoanalyse. (17–34)
  2. Die Erostheorie. (35–53)
  3. Der andere Gesichtspunkt: Der Wille zur Macht. (54–73)
  4. Das Problem des Einstellungstypus. (74–115)
  5. Das persönliche und das überpersönliche oder kollektive Unbewusste. (116–44)
  6. Die synthetische oder konstruktive Methode. (145–60)
  7. Die Archetypen des kollektiven Unbewussten. (161–202)
  8. Zur Auffassung des Unbewussten: Allgemeines zur Therapie.
   (203–11)
  Schlusswort. (212–13)
  G. 1926a rev. and exp. with title change. Repub. as GW 7,1. TR.—
  Danish: 1961a // Dutch: 1950b // English: CW 7,1 // Finnish:
  1966a // French: 1952a // ?Greek: 1956a / 1962a,1 // Hebrew: 1973b
  // Hungarian: 1948a // Italian: 1947b / 1968a // Norwegian: 1963a
  // Portuguese: 1967a // Swedish: 1965a.

1943b "Der Geist Mercurius." *Eran. Jb. 1942.* pp. 179–236. (See G. 1934c.) Pub., rev. and exp., as G. 1948a,3.

1943c "Zur Psychologie östlicher Meditation." *Mitteilungen der Schweizerischen Gesellschaft der Freunde ostasiatischer Kultur,* V, 33–53. Repub. as G. 1948a,5. Lecture given to the Psychologischer Club Zurich, 8 May 1943, and to the Schweizerische Gesellschaft der Freunde ostasiatischer Kultur, Zurich/Basel/Bern, Mar.–May 1943. TR.—English: 1947b.

1943d * "Votum. Zum Thema: Schule und Begabung." *Schweizer Erziehungs-Rundschau,* XVI:1 (Apr.), 3–8. Lecture presented as contribution to a meeting of the Basler staatliche Schulsynode, 4 Dec. 1942. Repub. with title change as G. 1946b,3.

1943e "Psychotherapie und Weltanschauung." *Schweizerische Zeitschrift für Psychologie und ihre Anwendungen,* I:3, 157–64. Repub. as G. 1946a,4. Contribution to the Tagung für Psychologie, Zurich, 26 Sept. 1942.

1943f "Ein Gespräch mit C. G. Jung. Über Tiefenpsychologie und Selbsterkenntnis." *Du,* III:9 (Sept.), 15–18. Written in answer to questions from Jolande Jacobi. Repub. as G. 1947c with title change. TR.—English: 1943b.

1944a *Psychologie und Alchemie.* (Psychologische Abhandlungen, 5.) Zurich: Rascher. pp. 696. Contents:
 1. Vorwort. (7–8)
 2. Einleitung in die religionspsychologische Problematik der Alchemie. (13–62) Repub. as G. 1957a,2.
 3. Traumsymbole des Individuationsprozesses. (69–305) G. 1936a rev. and exp.
 4. Die Erlösungsvorstellungen in der Alchemie. (313–631) G. 1937a rev. and exp.
 5. Epilog. (635–46)
Pub., rev. and with addn. of new foreword, as G. 1952d. TR.—English: CW 12 (1st edn.) // Italian: 1949a.

1944b "Vorwort" and essay: "Über den indischen Heiligen." Heinrich Zimmer: *Der Weg zum Selbst.* pp. 5–6, and pp. 11–24. Ed. by C. G. Jung. Zurich: Rascher. Essay repub. as GW 11,15. TR.—Dutch: 1948b // English: (essay only) CW 11,15.

1945a *Psychologische Betrachtungen.* A selection from the writings of C. G. Jung, comp. and ed. by Jolande Jacobi. Zurich: Rascher. pp. 455. A collection of short passages from a wide range of writings; contains no new material. Pub., rev. and exp. with title change, as G. 1971b. TR.—Dutch: 1949a // English: 1953a // French: 1965a.

1945b "Das Rätsel von Bologna." *Festschrift Albert Oeri.* pp. 265–79. Basel: Basler Nachrichten. Cf. G. 1955a,II,3. TR.—English: 1946f.

1945c "Nach der Katastrophe." *Neue Schw. R.,* n.s. XIII:2 (June), 67–88. Repub. as G. 1946a,5. TR.—English: 1946a.

1945d "Vom Wesen der Träume." *Ciba Zeitschrift* (Basel), IX:99 (July), 3546–57. Repub. as G. 1952i. Pub., rev. and exp., as G. 1948b,5. TR.—Dutch: 1947b // English: 1948a // French: 1945a / 1953a,4 // Portuguese: 1947a / 1948a // Spanish: 1946a.

1945e "Medizin und Psychotherapie." *Bulletin der schweizerischen Akademie der medizinischen Wissenschaften,* I:5, 315–28. Repub. as GW 16,8. Lecture delivered to a scientific meeting of the Senate of the Academy, Zurich, 12 May 1945. TR.—English: CW 16,8 // French: 1953a,2.

1945f "Die Psychotherapie in der Gegenwart." *Schweizerische Zeitschrift für Psychologie und ihre Anwendungen,* IV:1, 3–18. First pub. in an English trans., E. 1942b. Repub. as G. 1946a,3. Given as the opening address to the Kommission für Psychotherapie, Schweizerische Gesellschaft für Psychiatrie, Zurich, 4th annual meeting, 19 July 1941. TR.—English: 1942b / 1947a,4 / CW 16,9.

1945g "Der philosophische Baum." *Verhandlungen der Naturforschenden Gesellschaft Basel,* LVI:2, 411–23. Pub., greatly rev. and exp., as G. 1954b,7. Written as contribution to a Festschrift for Gustav Senn, professor of botany, which was never published.

1946a *Aufsätze zur Zeitgeschichte.* Zurich: Rascher. pp. 147. Contents:
　　　　1. Vorwort. (vii–ix) Repub. as GW 10,9. TR.—English: 1947a,1 / CW 10,9.
　　　　2. "Wotan." (3–23) Repub. as GW 10,10. G. 1936c repub. TR.—English: (abridged) 1937c / 1947a,3 / CW 10,10 // French: 1948a,2.

3. "Die Psychotherapie in der Gegenwart." (25–55) G. 1945f repub. with slight title change. Repub. as GW 16,9. TR.—English: 1947a,4 / CW 16,9 // French: 1953a,10.

4. "Psychotherapie und Weltanschauung." (57–72) G. 1943e repub. Repub. as G. 1954c,3 and GW 16,7. TR.—English: 1947a, 5 / CW 16,7 // French: 1953a,14.

5. "Nach der Katastrophe." (73–116) G. 1945c repub. Repub. as GW 10,11. TR.—English: 1947a,6 / CW 10,11 // French: 1948a,4.

6. "Nachwort." (117–47) Repub. as GW 10,13. TR.—English: 1947a,7 / CW 10,13 // ?French: 1948a,5.

TR. of entire work—Dutch: 1947a // Spanish: 1968a.

1946b *Psychologie und Erziehung.* Zurich: Rascher. pp. 204. 1963: ("Rascher Paperback.") pp. 135. Contents:

1. "Analytische Psychologie und Erziehung: Drei Vorlesungen." (3–124) G. 1926b rev. and exp., with addn. of new foreword dated June 1945. Repub. as GW 17,4. TR.—English: CW 17,4 // French: 1963a,1 // Japanese: 1956a,1.

2. "Über Konflikte der kindlichen Seele." (125–81) G. 1939a slightly exp. Repub. as GW 17,1. TR.—English: CW 17,1 // French: 1963a,2 // Japanese: 1956a,2.

3. "Der Begabte." (183–203) G. 1943d repub. with title change. Repub. as GW 17,5. TR.—English: CW 17,5 // French: 1963a,5 // Japanese: 1956a,3.

TR. of entire work—Dutch: 1948a // Hebrew: 1958a // Italian: 1947a // Norwegian: 1967a // Spanish: 1949a.

1946c *Die Psychologie der Übertragung. Erläutert anhand einer alchemistischen Bilderserie. Für Ärzte und praktische Psychologen.* Zurich: Rascher. pp. 283. Contents:

Vorrede. (vii–xii) Dated Fall 1945.

I. Einleitende Überlegungen zum Problem der Übertragung. (1–63)

II. Die Bilderserie des Rosarium Philosophorum als Grundlage für die Darstellung der Übertragungsphänomene. (65–253)

    1. Der Mercurbrunnen.

    2. König und Königin.

    3. Die nackte Wahrheit.

    4. Das Eintauchen im Bade.

5. Die Conjunction.
6. Der Tod.
7. Der Aufstieg der Seele.
8. Die Reinigung.
9. Die Wiederkehr der Seele.
10. Die neue Geburt.
Schlusswort. (255–60)
Repub. as GW 16,13. TR.—English: CW 16,13 // Italian: 1962a //
Spanish: 1954a.

1946d "Gérard de Nerval." (Autoreferat.) *Aus d. Jhrsb. 1945/46.* p. 18.
Printed for private circulation. Summary of lecture to the Psychologischer Club Zurich, 9 June 1945. TR.—English: CW 18,117.

1946e "Zur Psychologie des Geistes." *Eran. Jb. 1945.* pp. 385–448. (See G. 1934c.) Pub., rev. and exp., with title change, as G. 1948a,2. TR.—English: 1948d.

1946f Foreword to K. A. Ziegler: "Alchemie II," List no. 17 (May). pp. 1–2. Printed in Bern. Foreword, in both German and English, to a bookseller's catalog. For English version, see E. 1946b.

1946g "Zur Umerziehung des deutschen Volkes." *Basl. Nach.*, No. 486, "Sondernummer . . ." (Centennial edn.) (ca. 16 Nov.), 85. The last 9 paragraphs of an essay, "Randglossen zur Zeitgeschichte," dated 1945, never pub. as a whole in German, although trans. and pub. in its entirety in English as CW 18,73. TR.—English: (full text) CW 18,73.

1946h Excerpts of letter (published to anon.) to James Kirsch (26 May 1934), pp. 225–27. Ernest Harms: "Carl Gustav Jung—Defender of Freud and the Jews." *Psychiatric Quarterly*, 20:2 (Apr.), 199–233. Entire letter pub. in G. 1972a and trans. in E. 1973b. TR.—English: 1946d,2.

1947a "Der Geist der Psychologie." *Eran. Jb. 1946.* pp. 385–490. (See G. 1934c.) Pub., rev. and with title change, as G. 1954b,8. TR.—English: 1954b,2 / (sl. abbrev.) 1957e.

1947b "Vorwort." Linda Fierz-David: *Der Liebestraum des Poliphilo; ein Beitrag zur Psychologie der Renaissance und der Moderne.* pp. 5–7. Zurich: Rhein. Dated Feb. 1946. TR.—English: 1950c.

1947c "Über Tiefenpsychologie und Selbsterkenntnis. Ein Gespräch zwischen Prof. C. G. Jung und Dr. Jolan Jacobi." *Hamburger Akademische Rundschau*, II:1 / 2, 11–19. G. 1943f repub. with title change.

1948a *Symbolik des Geistes. Studien über psychische Phänomenologie.* . . . With a contribution by Riwkah Schärf. (Psychologische Abhandlungen, 6.) Zurich: Rascher. pp. 500. 1965: ("Rascher Paperback.") pp. 206. Contains the following works by Jung:

1. Vorwort. (vii–viii) Dated June 1947. TR.—English: CW 18,90.
2. "Zur Phänomenologie des Geistes im Märchen." (3–67) G. 1946e, rev. and exp., with title change. Repub. as G. 1957a,3 and GW 9,i,8. TR.—English: 1954b,1 / CW 9,i,8 // Japanese: 1956a,4.
3. "Der Geist Mercurius." (69–149) G. 1943b rev. and exp. Repub. as GW 13,4. TR.—English: 1953b / CW 13,4.
4. "Versuch zu einer psychologischen Deutung des Trinitätsdogmas." (321–446) G. 1942b, greatly rev. and exp., with title change. Repub. as GW 11,2, with slight title change. TR.—English: CW 11,2 // French: (1 ch., "Das Problem des Vierten," sl. abridged, in 2 pts.) 1957b and 1958c.
5. "Zur Psychologie östlicher Meditation." (447–72) G. 1943c repub. Repub. as G. 1957a,4 and GW 11,14. TR.—English: CW 11,14 // Japanese: 1956b,2.

TR. of entire work—Dutch: 1955a // Italian: 1959a // Spanish: 1962a.

1948b *Über psychische Energetik und das Wesen der Träume.* (Psychologische Abhandlungen, 2.) "2., vermehrte und verbesserte Auflage." Zurich: Rascher. pp. 311. 1965: 3d edn., rev. and reset. ("Rascher Paperback.") pp. 206. Contents:

1. Vorwort(en). (1–3) G. 1928b,1 repub. with new foreword (dated May 1947) added for this edn. TR.—English: CW 18,37.
2. "Über die Energetik der Seele." (5–117) G. 1928b,2 repub. Repub. as GW 8,1. TR.—English: CW 8,1 // French: 1956a,1.
3. "Allgemeines zur Komplextheorie." (119–43) G. 1934a, sl. rev. and with minor title change. Repub. as GW 8,3, with reversion to title of G. 1934a. TR.—English: CW 8,3 // French: 1962a,5.
4. "Allgemeine Gesichtspunkte zur Psychologie des Traumes."

(145–225) G. 1928b,3, rev. and exp. Repub. as GW 8,9. TR.—English: 1956b / CW 8,9 // French: 1962a,6.

5. "Vom Wesen der Träume." (227–57) G. 1945d, rev. and exp. Repub. as G. 1954c,1 and GW 8,10. TR.—English: CW 8,10.

6. "Instinkt und Unbewusstes." (259–76) G. 1928b,4, rev. and with addn. of brief concluding note. Repub. as GW 8,6. TR.—English: CW 8,6 // French: 1956a,2.

7. "Die psychologischen Grundlagen des Geisterglaubens." (277–311) G. 1928b,5 rev. Repub. as GW 8,11. TR.—English: CW 8,11 // French: 1956a,6.

G. 1928b exp., with title change. New foreword and items 2. and 4. added. TR. of entire work—Danish: 1969a // Norwegian: 1968a // Spanish: 1954b.

1948c "De Sulphure." *Nova Acta Paracelsica, V.* pp. 27–40. Pub., exp., as part of G. 1955a,III,3. TR.—English: ?1947c.

1948d "Vorwort." Esther Harding: *Das Geheimnis der Seele.* pp. 9–10. Zurich: Rhein. Written in German as introduction for the original English pub. and first pub. in trans. TR.—English: 1947e.

1948e "Vorwort." Stuart Edward White: *Uneingeschränktes Weltall.* pp. 7–14. Zurich: Origo. Written in German to accompany the German trans. of White's *The Unobstructed Universe* (New York, 1940). Dated July 1948. Also pub. as "Psychologie und Spiritismus." *Neue Schw. R.,* n.s. XVI:7 (Nov.), 430–35. TR.—English: CW 18,6.

1948f "Schatten, Animus und Anima." *Wiener Zeitschrift für Nervenheilkunde* . . . , I:4 (June), 295–307. Incorporated as part of G. 1951a,II & III. Lecture given to the Schweizerische Gesellschaft für praktische Psychologie, Zurich, 1948. TR.—English: 1950a.

1949a *Die Bedeutung des Vaters für das Schicksal des Einzelnen.* "Dritte, umgearbeitete Auflage." Zurich: Rascher. pp. 38. G. 1909c rev. and exp., with addn. of new foreword. Repub. as GW 4,14. TR.—English: CW 4,14 (with addns. from G. 1909c) // French: 1963a,4.

1949b "Über das Selbst." *Eran. Jb. 1948.* pp. 285–315. Incorporated into G. 1951a,IV. Lecture given also to the Psychologischer Club Zurich, 22 May 1948. TR.—English: 1951a.

1949c "Vorwort." Robert Crottet: *Mondwald. Lappengeschichten.* pp. 7–9. Zurich: Fretz und Wasmuth. Dated March 1949. TR.—English: CW 18,119.

1949d "Geleitwort." Esther Harding: *Frauen-Mysterien, einst und jetzt.* pp. viii–xii. Zurich: Rascher. Dated Aug. 1948. TR.—Dutch: 1938a // English: 1955e / CW 18,53 // French: 1953d.

1949e "Geleitwort zu den 'Studien aus dem C. G. Jung-Institut Zürich'." C. A. Meier: *Antike Inkubation und moderne Psychotherapie.* (Studien aus dem C. G. Jung-Institut Zürich, 1.) Zurich: Rascher. 2 unno.'d pp. after title page. Introduction to the series, of which Jung was the editor. Dated Sept. 1948. TR.—English: (Pts. only) 1950e / 1967d / CW 18,45.

1949f "Vorwort." Erich Neumann: *Ursprungsgeschichte des Bewusstseins.* pp. 1–2. Zurich: Rascher. Dated 1 March 1949. TR.—English: 1954f.

1949g Letter to the editors on the effect of technology on the psyche. *Zürcher Student,* Jhg. 27:5 (Nov.), 129–30. Written in reply to the eds.' question and dated 14 Sept. 1949. TR.—English: CW 18,76.

1949h * "Dämonie." (Definition.) *Schweizer Lexikon,* Vol. I. Zurich: Encyclios. Written July 1945 at the request of the publishers. Only the 1st sentence and the references appear here as the definition, which is published without attribution. TR.—Full text of Jung's definition pub. in trans. as CW 18,89.

1950a *Gestaltungen des Unbewussten.* With a contribution by Aniela Jaffé. (Psychologische Abhandlungen, 7.) Zurich: Rascher. pp. 616. Contains the following works by Jung:
   1. Vorwort. (1–2) Dated Jan. 1949. TR.—English: CW 18,56.
   2. "Psychologie und Dichtung." (5–36) G. 1930a, rev. and exp. Repub. as G. 1954c,2 and GW 15,7. Excerpt pub. 1955 as "Der Dichter." *Internationale Bodensee-Zeitschrift für Literatur* . . . , IV:6 (July), 88–91. TR.—English: (with addn.) CW 15,7 // French: 1955a.
   3. "Über Wiedergeburt." (37–91) G. 1940b, rev. and exp. with title change. Repub. as GW 9,i,5. TR.—English: CW 9,i,5.

4. "Zur Empirie des Individuationsprozesses." (93–186) G. 1934c, rev. and exp. Repub. as GW 9,i,11. TR.—English: CW 9,i,11.

5. "Über Mandalasymbolik." (187–235) Contains 9 of the plates pub. in G. 1938a,4. Repub. as GW 9,i,12. TR.—English: CW 9,i,12.

1950b "Faust und die Alchemie." (Autoreferat.) *Aus d. Jhrsb. 1949/50.* pp. 29–32. Printed for private circulation. Summary of lecture to the Psychologischer Club Zurich, 8 Oct. 1949. TR.—English: CW 18,105.

1950d "Geleitwort." Lily Abegg: *Ostasien denkt anders.* pp. 3–4. Zurich: Atlantis. Dated Mar. 1949. Omitted from pub. of the English trans., *The Mind of East Asia* (London and New York, 1952). TR.—English: 1953f.

1950e "Vorrede" and "Fall von Prof. C. G. Jung." Fanny Moser: *Spuk. Irrglaube oder Wahrglaube.* pp. 9–12 and pp. 253–61. Baden bei Zurich: Gyr. "Vorrede" dated Apr. 1950. "Vorrede" pub. as G. 1956b, with the omission of the first few sentences and the addn. of a title. TR. of both—English: CW 18,7.

1950f "Wo leben die Teufel? Zur Psychologie der Ehe." *Welt,* (26 July). 1 p.

1950g Contribution to "Rundfrage über ein Referat auf der 66. Wanderversammlung der südwestdeutschen Psychiater und Neurologen in Badenweiler." pp. 464–65. *Psyche,* Jhg. 4:8 (Nov.), 448–80. Answer to questionnaire concerning a report given by Dr. Medard Boss at the above congress and sent out by the editors to Boss's colleagues. TR.—English: CW 18,14.

1951a *Aion. Untersuchungen zur Symbolgeschichte.* With a contribution by Marie-Louise von Franz. (Psychologische Abhandlungen, 8.) Zurich: Rascher. pp. 561. Contains the following work by Jung: "Beiträge zur Symbolik des Selbst."
    I.   Das Ich. (15–21)
    II.   Der Schatten. (22–26) Incorporates G. 1948f.
    III. Die Syzygie: Anima und Animus. (27–43) Incorporates G. 1948f.

IV.   Das Selbst. (44–62) Incorporates G. 1949b.

V.   Christus, ein Symbol des Selbst. (63–110)

VI.   Das Zeichen der Fische. (111–41)

VII.   Die Prophezeiung des Nostradamus. (142–51)

VIII.   Über die geschichtliche Bedeutung des Fisches. (152–71)

IX.   Die Ambivalenz des Fischsymbols. (172–83)

X.   Der Fisch in der Alchemie. (184–224)

XI.   Die alchemistische Deutung des Fisches. (225–50)

XII.   Allgemeines zur Psychologie der christlich-alchemistischen Symbolik. (251–66)

XIII. Gnostische Symbole des Selbst. (267–320)

XIV. Die Struktur und Dynamik des Selbst. (321–78)

XV. Schlusswort. (379–84)

I–IV repub. as G. 1954c,4. Jung's work repub. with rearranged title as GW 9,ii.

On the advice of Dr. von Franz, it is construed that the title *Aion* belongs to Prof. Jung's part of the book rather than to hers. The present entry, however, records the title-page data of the Swiss edn. The CW trans. bears the title *Aion* as well. TR.—English: CW 9,ii.

1951b With K. Kerényi: *Einführung in das Wesen der Mythologie. Das göttliche Kind; Das göttliche Mädchen.* "4. revidierte Auflage." Zurich: Rhein. pp. 260. Contains the following works by Jung:

    1. "Zur Psychologie des Kind-Archetypus." (105-47) Repub. as GW 9,i,6. TR.—English: CW 9,i,6.

    2. "Zum psychologischen Aspekt der Korefigur." (223–50) Repub. as GW 9,i,7. TR.—English: CW 9,i,7.

G. 1941c repub. with the addn. of new foreword by Kerényi. TR.—French: 1953b // Italian: 1972a.

1951c "Tiefenpsychologie." (Definition.) *Lexikon der Pädagogik.* Vol. II, pp. 768–73. Bern: A. Francke. Written in 1948. TR.—English: CW 18,44.

1951d "Grundfragen der Psychotherapie." *Dialectica*, V:1 (15 Mar.), 8–24. Repub. as GW 16,10. TR.—English: CW 16,10 // French: 1953a,11.

1951e "Das Fastenwunder des Bruder Klaus." *Neue Wissenschaft*, Jhg. 1950/51:7 (Apr.), 14. Rev. from letter written 10 Nov. 1948 in response to Fritz Blanke's "Bruder Klaus von der Flüe." *Neue Wissenschaft*, Jhg. 1950/51:4. Orig. text of letter pub. in G. 1972b and trans. in E. 1973b. TR.—English: CW 18,94.

1952a   *Antwort auf Hiob*. Zurich: Rascher. pp. 169. Pub. with addn. as G. 1961a. TR.—English: 1954a/CW 11,9 // French: 1964b // Italian: 1965d // Norwegian: 1969b // Spanish: 1964a // Swedish: 1954a. Note: A paragraph written by Jung describing the book was printed as a blurb on the dust jacket of this edn. Repub. as GW 11,23, and trans. into English as CW 18,95.

1952b   With W. Pauli: *Naturerklärung und Psyche*. (Studien aus dem C. G. Jung-Institut Zürich, 4.) Zurich: Rascher. pp. 194. Contains the following work by Jung:

"Synchronizität als ein Prinzip akausaler Zusammenhänge." (1–107) Ch. 2 of Jung's article pub. rev. as G. 1958f. Whole article repub. as GW 8,18. TR.—Dutch: 1954a.
A rev. version with addns. by the author was trans. and pub. as E. 1955a. TR. of entire work—Spanish: 1964b.

1952c   * *Paracelsus*. (Der Bogen, 25.) St. Gallen: Tschudy. pp. 24. G. 1934b.5 repub. Repub. as GW 15,1. TR.—English: CW 15,1.

1952d   *Psychologie und Alchemie*. 2d rev. edn. Zurich: Rascher. pp. 708. G. 1944a pub. rev. and with the addn. of "Vorwort zur 2. Auflage." Repub. as GW 12. TR.—English: CW 12 // French: 1970a // Spanish: 1953a.

1952e   *Symbole der Wandlung. Analyse des Vorspiels zu einer Schizophrenie.* With 300 illus., selected and comp. by Jolande Jacobi. "Vierte, umgearbeitete Auflage . . ." Zurich: Rascher. pp. 821. 1971: "Sonderausgabe." Olten: Walter. (Same edn., in boards.) Contents:

Vorreden (vii–xviii)
Part I:
    I.   Einleitung. (3–8) TR.—English: 1954d.
    II.   Über die zwei Arten des Denkens. (9–51)
    III.   Vorgeschichte. (52–58)
    IV.   Der Schöpferhymnus. (59–129)
    V.   Das Lied von der Motte. (130–96)

Part II:

I.   Einleitung. (199–217)

II.   Über den Begriff der Libido. (218–33)

III.   Die Wandlung der Libido. (234–83)

IV.   Die Entstehung des Heros. (284–345)

V.   Symbole der Mutter und der Wiedergeburt. (346–468)

VI.   Der Kampf um die Befreiung von der Mutter. (469–528)

VII.   Das Opfer. (529–763)

VIII.   Schlusswort. (764–69)

G. 1925a, greatly rev. and exp. with title change. Repub. as GW 5. TR.—English: CW 5 // French: 1953c // Italian: 1965b / 1970a // Spanish: 1962b.

1952f "Über Synchronizität." *Eran. Jb. 1951.* pp. 271–84. (See G. 1934c.) Repub. as GW 8,19. Lecture given in 2 pts. also to the Psychologischer Club Zurich, 20 Jan. and 3 Feb. 1951. TR.—English: 1953c / 1957b / CW 8,19.

1952g "Vorwort." Gerhard Adler: *Zur analytischen Psychologie.* pp. 7–9. Zurich: Rascher. Dated May 1949. Not in orig. edn.: London and New York: Norton, 1948. TR.—English: 1966e / CW 18,55 // French: 1957a.

1952h "Zu unserer Umfrage 'Leben die Bücher noch?'" [Contribution] *Jungkaufmann; schweizer Monatsschrift für die kaufmännische Jugend,* XXVII:3 (Mar.), 51–52. Jung's reply to Hölderlin's famous question, written as a letter to the editor, A. Galliker (29 Jan. 1952). Text of letter pub. in G. 1972b and trans. in E. 1976a.

1952i * "Vom Wesen der Träume." *Ciba-Zeitschrift* (Wehr-Baden), V:55 (May), 1830–37. G. 1945d repub. Pub., rev. and exp., as G. 1948b,5.

1952j "Religion und Psychologie." *Merkur,* VI:5 (May), 467–73. Repub. with title change as GW 11,17. A reply to Prof. Buber. TR.—English: 1957d / 1973e.

1953a Contribution to *Trunken von Gedichten. Eine Anthologie geliebter deutscher Verse.* p. 63. Ed. by Georg Gerster. Zurich: Verlag der Arche. Partial trans. in E. 1976a, p. 193.

1953b "Vorwort." Frances G. Wickes: *Von der inneren Welt des Menschen.* pp. vii–viii. Zurich: Rascher. Dated Sept. 1953. Not included in original English publication: *The Inner World of Man* (New York: Farrar and Rinehart, 1938). TR.—English: 1954g / CW 18,57.

1954a With Paul Radin and Karl Kerényi: *Der göttliche Schelm. Ein indianischer Mythen-Zyklus.* Zurich: Rhein. pp. 219. Contains the following work by Jung:
"Zur Psychologie der Schelmenfigur." (185–207) Repub. as GW 9,i,9. TR.—English: 1955d / 1956a.
TR. of entire work—English: 1956a // French: 1958a // Italian: 1965a.

1954b *Von den Wurzeln des Bewusstseins. Studien über den Archetypus.* (Psychologische Abhandlungen, 9.) Zurich: Rascher. pp. 681. Contents:

1. Vorrede. (ix–x) Dated May 1953. TR.—Dutch: 1962a,1 // English: CW 18,58.

2. "Über die Archetypen des kollektiven Unbewussten." (1–56) G. 1935b rev. Repub. as G. 1957a,1 and GW 9,i,1. TR.—Dutch: 1962a,2 // English: CW 9,i,1 // Spanish: 1970a,1.

3. "Über den Archetypus mit besonderer Berücksichtigung des Animabegriffes." (57–85) G. 1936e rev. Repub. as GW 9,i,3. TR.—Dutch: 1962a,3 // English: CW 9,i,3 // Spanish: 1970a,2.

4. "Die psychologischen Aspekte des Mutterarchetypus." (87–135) G. 1939b rev. Repub. as GW 9,i,4. TR.—Dutch: 1962a,4 // English: (with pts. of E. 1943a) CW 9,i,4 // Spanish: 1970a,3.

5. "Die Visionen des Zosimos." (135–216) G. 1938c, rev. and considerably exp., with title change. Repub. as GW 13,2. TR.—English: CW 13,2.

6. "Das Wandlungssymbol in der Messe." (217–350) G. 1942c, rev. and exp. Repub. as GW 11,3. TR.—English: CW 11,3.

7. "Der philosophische Baum." (351–496) G. 1945g, greatly rev. and exp. Repub. as GW 13,5. TR.—English: CW 13,5.

8. "Theoretische Überlegungen zum Wesen des Psychischen." (497–608) G. 1947a, sl. rev. & with title change. Repub. as GW 8,8. Excerpts repub. as G. 1954c,5. TR.—Dutch: 1962a,5 // English: 1954b,2 / CW 8,8 // Spanish: 1970a,4.
TR. of entire work—French: 1971b.

1954c *Welt der Psyche. Eine Auswahl zur Einführung.* Ed. by A. Jaffé and G. P. Zacharias. Zurich: Rascher. pp. 165. 1965: reset. ("Geist und Psyche.") Munich: Kindler. pp. 149. Contains the following works by Jung:

    1. "Vom Wesen der Träume." (9–32) G. 1948b,5 repub. Repub. as GW 8,10.

    2. "Psychologie und Dichtung." (33–61) G. 1950a,2 repub. Repub. as GW 15,7.

    3. "Psychotherapie und Weltanschauung." (63–73) G. 1946a,4 repub. Repub. as GW 16,7.

    4. "Beiträge zur Symbolik des Selbst." (75–120) G. 1951a, Chs. I-IV, repub. Repub. as GW 9,ii, chs. I–IV.

    5. "Theoretische Überlegungen zum Wesen des Psychischen." (121–59) G. 1954b,8, Section 7 and "Nachwort," repub. Cf. GW 8,8.

    TR. of entire work—Dutch: 1955b // Norwegian: 1969a.

1954d Preface to John Custance: *Weisheit und Wahn.* pp. vii–xi. Zurich: Rascher. Written in German in 1951, according to ms. in Jung Library, Küsnacht. First pub., however, in an English trans. TR.— English: 1952a / CW 18,15.

1954e Two letters to the author. Georg Gerster: "C. G. Jung zu den fliegenden Untertassen." *Weltwoche,* Jhg. 22: 1078 (9 July). Interview request not granted. These letters used in article instead. TR.— English: 1954h / (Pts. only) 1955i / 1959i,3 / CW 18,80.

1954f "Mach immer alles ganz und richtig." *Weltwoche,* Jhg. 22:1100 (10 Dec.), 31. Answer to question on the rules of life. TR.—English: CW 18,79.

1955a *Mysterium coniunctionis. Untersuchung über die Trennung und Zusammensetzung der seelischen Gegensätze in der Alchemie.* With the collaboration of M.-L. von Franz. Pt. I. (Psychologische Abhandlungen, 10.) Zurich: Rascher. pp. 284. Contents:
    Die Symbolik der Polarität und Einheit.
        Vorwort.
        I. Die Komponenten der Coniunctio.
            1. Die Gegensätze. (1–4)
            2. Der Quaternio. (5–15)
            3. Die Waise und die Witwe. (16–37)

    4. Alchemie und Manichäismus. (38–42)
II. Die Paradoxa.
    1. Die Arkansubstanz und der Punkt. (43–50)
    2. Die Scintilla. (50–55)
    3. Das Enigma Bolognese. (56–95) Cf. G. 1945b.
III. Die Personifikationen der Gegensätze.
    1. Einleitung. (96–99)
    2. Sol. (100–20)
    3. Sulphur. (121–40) Includes an exp. G. 1948c.
    4. Luna. (141–200)
    5. Sal. (200–84)
Repub. as GW 14, vol. I. The 1st of 2 pts. Cf. G. 1956a for Pt. II.
TR.—English: CW 14.

1955b   *Versuch einer Darstellung der psychoanalytischen Theorie.* Zurich: Rascher. pp. 195. G. 1913a pub. with the addn. of a foreword. Repub. as GW 4,9. TR.—English: CW 4,9.

1955c   "Geleitwort." Gustav Schmaltz: *Komplexe Psychologie und körperliches Symptom.* pp. 7–8. Stuttgart: Hippokrates. TR.—English: CW 18,17.

1955d   "Psychologischer Kommentar." *Das tibetische Buch der grossen Befreiung.* pp. 13–54. Ed. by W. Y. Evans-Wentz. Munich: Barth. "Kommentar" trans. from E. 1954e by M. Niehus-Jung; written in English in 1939. Repub. as GW 11,10.

1955e   "Mandalas." *Du,* Jhg. 15:4 (Apr.), 16, 21. Repub. as GW 9,i,13. TR.—English: 1955g / CW 9,i,13.

1955f   Letter to Hans A. Illing (10 Feb. 1955). Hans A. Illing: "Jung und die moderne Tendenz in der Gruppentherapie." *Heilkunst,* no. 7 (July), 233. Full text of letter pub. in G. 1972b and trans. in E. 1976a. Excerpt pub. as G. 1956d,1. TR.—English: (excerpts) 1957i.

1956a   *Mysterium coniunctionis. . . .* Pt. II. (Psychologische Abhandlungen, 11.) Zurich: Rascher. pp. 418. Contents:
Die Symbolik der Polarität und Einheit. (cont.)
    IV. Rex und Regina.
        1. Einleitung. (1–5)
        2. Gold und Geist. (5–9)

3. Die königliche Wandlung. (9–19)

4. Die Heilung des Königs. (19–81)

5. Die dunkle Seite des Königs. (82–96)

6. Der König als Anthropos. (96–109)

7. Die Beziehung des Königssymbols zum Bewusstsein. (109–21)

8. Die religiöse Problematik der Königserneuerung. (121–33)

9. Regina. (134–39)

V. Adam und Eva.

1. Adam als Arkansubstanz. (140–49)

2. Die Statue. (150–57)

3. Adam als erster Adept. (157–67)

4. Die Gegensätzlichkeit Adams. (168–76)

5. Der "alte Adam." (176–78)

6. Adam als Ganzheit. (179–85)

7. Die Wandlung. (186–99)

8. Das Runde, Kopf und Gehirn. (199–223)

VI. Die Konjunktion.

1. Die alchemistische Anschauung der Gegensatzvereinigung. (224–38)

2. Stufen der Konjunktion. (238–47)

3. Die Herstellung der Quintessenz. (247–53)

4. Der Sinn der alchymischen Prozedur. (253–59)

5. Die psychologische Deutung der Prozedur. (259–69)

6. Die Selbsterkenntnis. (270–80)

7. Der Monoculus. (280–96)

8. Inhalt und Sinn der zwei ersten Konjunktionsstufen. (296–311)

9. Die dritte Stufe der Konjunktion: der unus mundus. (312–23)

10. Das Selbst und die erkenntnistheoretische Beschränkung. (324–34)

Nachwort. (335–337)

Repub. as GW 14, vol. II. The 2d of 2 pts. Cf. G. 1955a for Pt. I. (A third part was written by M.-L. von Franz. Cf. note under GW 14.) TR.—English: CW 14.

1956b "Die Parapsychologie hat uns mit unerhörten Möglichkeiten bekanntgemacht." *Gibt es Geister? Rundfrage—beantwortet von Psy-*

chologen, Schriftstellern, Philosophen . . . pp. 17–22. Bern: Viktoria. G. 1950e ("Vorrede" only) pub. with omission of the 1st few sentences, and addn. of title.

1956c Statement in publisher's brochure (with other statements) announcing publication of Karl Eugen Neumann's translation of *Die Reden Gotamo Buddhos*. 2 pp. Zurich and Stuttgart: Artemis; Vienna: Paul Zsolnay. Undated, but probably written in Jan. 1956. Repub. as GW 11,26. TR.—English: CW 18,101.

1956d Excerpts of letters to Hans A. Illing. Georg R. Bach and Hans A. Illing: "Historische Perspektive zur Gruppenpsychotherapie." *Zeitschrift für psychosomatische Medizin*, Jhg. 2 (Jan.), 141–42. Contains excerpts from the following letters by Jung:

    1. 10 Feb. 1955 (141) Excerpted from G. 1955f.

    2. 26 Jan. 1955 (141–42)

Full text of letters pub. in G. 1972b and trans. in E. 1976a. TR.—English: 1957i.

1956e "Wotan und der Rattenfänger. Bemerkungen eines Tiefenpsychologen." *Der Monat*, IX:97 (Oct.), 75–76. Letter to the editor, Melvin J. Lasky (Sept. 1956). Text of letter pub. in G. 1973a and trans. in E. 1976a.

1956f Contribution to symposium, "Das geistige Europa und die ungarische Revolution." *Die Kultur*, V:73 (1 Dec.), 8. Ca. 50 words long. TR.—English: CW 18,84,i.

1957a *Bewusstes und Unbewusstes. Beiträge zur Psychologie*. Ed. by Aniela Jaffé. ("Bücher des Wissens.") Frankfurt am Main and Hamburg: Fischer. pp. 184. Contents:

    1. "Über die Archetypen des kollektiven Unbewussten." (11–53) G. 1954b,2 repub. Repub. as GW 9,i,1.

    2. "Einleitung in die religionspsychologische Problematik der Alchemie." (54–91) G. 1944a,2 repub. Repub. as GW 12,3,I.

    3. "Zur Phänomenologie des Geistes im Märchen." (92–143) G. 1948a,2 repub. Repub. as GW 9,i,8.

    4. "Zur Psychologie östlicher Meditation." (144–63) G. 1948a, 5 repub. Repub. as GW 11,14.

1957b * With Richard Wilhelm: *Das Geheimnis der goldenen Blüte. Ein chinesisches Lebensbuch.* "Fünfte Auflage." Zurich: Rascher. pp. 161. Contains the following works by Jung:

1. "Vorrede zur II. Auflage. (vii–x) Repub. as part of GW 13,1. TR.—English: CW 13,1.

2. "Zum Gedächtnis Richard Wilhelms." (xiii–xxvi) Repub. as GW 15,5. TR.—English: CW 15,5.

3. "Europäischer Kommentar." (1–68 + 10 plates) Repub. as part of GW 13,1. TR.—English: CW 13,1.

G. 1938a reset, with new foreword by Salomé Wilhelm (xi–xii) and the addn. of the text of the *Hui Ming Ging.* (148–67). TR. of entire work—English: 1962b.

1957c * Contribution to symposium: *Aufstand der Freiheit. Dokumente zur Erhebung des ungarischen Volkes.* p. 104. Zurich: Artemis. Ca. 175 words long. TR.—English: CW 18,84,ii.

1957d "Vorwort." Eleanor Bertine: *Menschliche Beziehungen; eine psychologische Studie.* pp. 5–7. Zurich: Rhein. Dated Aug. 1956. TR.— English: 1958e / CW 18,61 // Italian: 1961a.

1957e * "Vorrede." Felicia Froboese-Thiele: *Träume—eine Quelle religiöser Erfahrung?* pp. 18–19. Göttingen: Vandenhoeck and Ruprecht. TR.—English: CW 18,102.

1957f "Vorwort." René J. van Helsdingen: *Beelden uit het onbewuste. Een geval van Jung.* pp. 7–8. Arnhem: Van Loghum Slaterus. Written for this pub. and dated May 1954. Foreword is in German, while the rest of the book is in Dutch. TR.—English: CW 18,59.

1957g "Vorwort." Jolande Jacobi: *Komplex, Archetypus, Symbol in der Psychologie C. G. Jungs.* pp. ix–xi. Zurich: Rascher. Dated Feb. 1956. TR.—English: 1959e // French: 1961c.

1957h "Vorwort." Victor White: *Gott und das Unbewusste.* pp. xi–xxvi. Zurich: Rascher. Repub. as GW 11,4. Originally written in German in 1952, but 1st pub. in an English trans. "Anhang" by Gebhard Frei contains extracts of letters written by Jung to Frei, reprinted from *Annalen der Philosophischen Gesellschaften Innerschweiz und Ostschweiz.* TR.—English: 1952c / CW 11,4.

1957i   * "Gegenwart und Zukunft." *Schweizer Monatshefte,* Supplement, XXXVI:12 (Mar.), 5–55. Also pub. as paperback: Zurich: Rascher. pp. 55. 1964: reset. ("Rascher Paperback.") pp. 68. Repub. as GW 10,14. TR.—Danish: 1959a // Dutch: 1958a // English: 1958b / CW 10,14 // Finnish: 1960a // French: 1962b // Italian: 1963a,10 // Norwegian: 1966c // Spanish: 1957a.

1957j   * Contribution to *Flinker Almanac 1958.* pp. 52–53. Paris: Librairie Française et Etrangère. Ca. 500 words long. Letter to the editor, Martin Flinker (17 Oct. 1957). Text of letter pub. in G. 1973a and trans. in E. 1976a.

1958a   *Ein moderner Mythus. Von Dingen, die am Himmel gesehen werden.* Zurich: Rascher. pp. 122. 1964: reset. ("Rascher Paperback.") pp. 143. Repub., with addns., as GW 10,15. Contents:
Vorrede. (7–9)
  1. Das Ufo als Gerücht. (11–25)
  2. Das Ufo im Traum. (26–75)
  3. Das Ufo in der Malerei. (76–93)
  4. Zur Geschichte des Ufophänomens. (94–98)
  5. Zusammenfassung. (99–104)
  6. Das Ufophänomen in nicht-psychologischer Beleuchtung.
    (105–09)
Epilog. (110–22)
Dedicated to Walter Niehus. TR.—English: (with addns.) 1959b // French: 1961a // Italian: 1960a // Portuguese: ?1962b // Spanish: 1961a.

1958b   "Die transzendente Funktion." *Geist und Werk. Aus der Werkstatt unserer Autoren. Zum 75. Geburtstag von Dr. Daniel Brody.* pp. 3–33. Zurich: Rhein. A rev. version of the original 1916 ms. first pub. in an English trans. as E. 1957a. Repub. as GW 8,2. TR.—English: CW 8,2.

1958c   "Das Gewissen in psychologischer Sicht." *Das Gewissen.* pp. 185–207. (Studien aus dem C. G. Jung-Institut, Zurich, 7.) Zurich: Rascher. Repub. as GW 10,16. Also pub. in *Universitas* (June). Lecture contributed to the series "Das Gewissen," C. G. Jung Institute, Zurich, Winter Semester 1957/58. TR.—English: CW 10,16 // French: 1971a,4.

1958e "Vorwort." Aniela Jaffé: *Geistererscheinungen und Vorzeichen. Eine psychologische Deutung.* pp. 9–12. Zurich: Rascher. Dated August 1957. TR.—English: 1963b / CW 18,8.

1958f "Ein astrologisches Experiment." *Zeitschrift für Parapsychologie und Grenzgebiete der Psychologie,* I:2/3 (May), 81–92. G. 1952b, ch. 2 extensively rev. and condensed. Prefatory note includes letter to the editor, Hans Bender (12 Feb. 1958), repub. in G. 1973a and trans. in E. 1976a. TR.—English: CW 18,48 (with addns.).

1958g "Drei Fragen an Prof. C. G. Jung." *Zürcher Student,* Jhg. 36:4 (July), 151. Dated 27 June 1958. Answers to questions on psycho-diagnostic methods. TR.—English: CW 18,85.

1958h "Zeichen am Himmel. C. G. Jung und die physische Realität der UFOs." *Badener Tagblatt* (29 Aug.). Ca. 220 words long. Press release to United Press International, probably also pub. in other newspapers. TR.—English: 1958h / 1958j / 1959i,1 / CW 18,81.

1958i "Die Schizophrenie." *Schweizer Archiv für Neurologie und Psychiatrie,* LXXXI:1/2, 163–77. Repub. as GW 3,9. Paper presented to the II. Internationaler Kongress für Psychiatrie, Zurich, 1957. Brief summary (in German, English, French, Spanish, and Italian) pub. as "Schizophrenia." *Synopses, Lectures to the Full Assemblies and Lectures to the Symposia. [Proceedings] Zurich, II. International Congress for Psychiatry, 1957.* pp. 49–52. [Zurich, ?1958.] TR.—English: CW 3,10.

1958j " 'Nationalcharakter' und Verkehrsverhalten." *Zentralblatt für Verkehrs-Medizin, Verkehrs-Psychologie und angrenzende Gebiete,* IV:3, 131–33. A letter written at the request of the editor, F. v. Tischendorf (19 Apr. 1958). Text of letter pub. in G. 1973a and trans. in E. 1976a. TR.—English: 1959j.

1959a "Über Psychotherapie und Wunderheilungen. Aus einem Brief von C. G. Jung." *Magie und Wunder in der Heilkunde. Ein Tagungsbericht.* pp. 8–9. Ed. by Wilhelm Bitter. (7. Kongressbericht der Stuttgarter Gemeinschaft "Arzt und Seelsorger.") Stuttgart: Klett. Letter (17 Apr. 1959), written at the request of the editor, Wilhelm Bitter, pub. with minor omissions. Entire letter pub. in G. 1973a and trans. in E. 1976a.

1959b "Gut und Böse in der analytischen Psychologie." *Gut und Böse in der Psychotherapie. Ein Tagungsbericht.* pp. 29–42. Ed. by Wilhelm Bitter. (8. Kongressbericht der Stuttgarter Gemeinschaft "Arzt und Seelsorger.") Stuttgart: "Arzt und Seelsorger." Extemporaneous address to the Gemeinschaft, Zurich, Fall 1958. Transcript prepared for pub. by Gebhard Frei, and approved, with corrections, by Jung. Repub. as GW 10,17 and GW 11,19. TR.—English: 1960e / CW 10,17. Also contains on pp. 56–57 the first 2 parags. of a letter to the editor (12 July 1958), the full text of which appears in G. 1973a and is trans. in E. 1976a.

1959c * Foreword to Frieda Fordham: *Eine Einführung in die Psychologie C. G. Jungs.* pp. 7–8. Zurich: Rascher. Trans. from E. 1953d by J. Meier.

1959d *"Geleitwort" and answers to questions. Otto Kankeleit: *Das Unbewusste als Keimstätte des Schöpferischen. Selbstzeugnisse von Gelehrten, Dichtern, und Künstlern.* pp. 9 and 68–69. Munich and Basel: Ernst Reinhardt. TR.—English: CW 18,121.

1959e "Vorrede." Toni Wolff: *Studien zu C. G. Jungs Psychologie.* pp. 7–14. Ed. by C. A. Meier. Zurich: Rhein. Dated Aug. 1958. Repub. as GW 10,18. TR.—English: 1960d / CW 10,18.

1959f "Neuere Betrachtungen zur Schizophrenie." *Universitas,* XIV:1 (Jan.), 31–38. Trans. from the original English text (cf. E. 1957h) by H. Degen. Repub. as GW 3,8. Text of contribution to the "Voice of America" symposium, "The Frontiers of Knowledge and Humanity's Hopes for the Future," broadcast 16 Dec. 1956; written up at the request of the Bollingen Foundation.

1959g Contribution to "Eine Tat-Umfrage: Das Interview mit dem anonymen Stimmbürger. Psychologen legen das unbewusste Nein des Bürgers bloss." *Tat* (23 Jan.). 1 p. Ca. 350 words long.

1959h Commentary on Walter Pöldinger: "Zur Bedeutung bildnerischen Gestaltens in der psychiatrischen Diagnostik." *Die Therapie des Monats,* IX:2, 67. TR.—English: CW 18,128.

1961a *Antwort auf Hiob.* 3d rev. edn. Zurich: Rascher. pp. 122. 1967: reset. ("Rascher Paperback.") pp. 143. 1973: ("Studienausgabe.")

Olten: Walter. pp. 143. G. 1952a repub. with the addn. of a "Nach-wort" trans. from E. 1956c by Marianne Niehus-Jung. Repub. as GW 11,9. TR.—Finnish: 1974a.

1961b "Nachwort." Arthur Koestler: *Von Heiligen und Automaten.* pp. 363–68. Zurich: Büchergilde Gutenberg. Bern, Stuttgart, Vienna: Scherz. 1965: Zurich: Buchclub Ex Libris. Trans. from E. 1961c by Hans Flesch-Brunningen. Written in English as a letter to Melvin J. Lasky, editor of *Encounter* (19 Oct. 1960), in response to excerpts of Koestler's book pub. therein, and itself pub. in a subsequent issue. Text of letter trans. into German in G. 1973a.

1961c "Ein Brief zur Frage der Synchronizität." *Zeitschrift für Parapsychologie und Grenzgebiete der Psychologie,* V:1 (Mar.), 1–8. Trans. from the English ms. by H. Bender, with corrections and additions by Jung. Originally written in English as letter to A.D. Cornell (9 Feb. 1960). TR.—English: 1961a.

1962a *Erinnerungen, Träume, Gedanken.* Recorded and ed. by Aniela Jaffé. Zurich: Rascher. pp. 422. 1968: Zurich: Buchclub Ex Libris. pp. 423. ?1971: Olten: Walter. pp. 423. Contents:
   1. Prolog. (10–12)
   2. Kindheit. (13–30)
   3. Schuljahre. (31–88)
   4. Studienjahre. (89–120)
   5. Psychiatrische Tätigkeit. (121–50)
   6. Sigmund Freud. (151–73)
   7. Die Auseinandersetzung mit dem Unbewussten. (174–203)
   8. Zur Entstehung des Werkes. (204–26)
   9. Der Turm. (227–41)
   10. Reisen. (242–92)
   11. Visionen. (293–301)
   12. Über das Leben nach dem Tode. (302–29)
   13. Späte Gedanken. (330–56)
   14. Rückblick. (357–61)
   15. Appendix.
       i. Aus den Briefen Jungs an seine Frau aus den USA. 1909. (363–70)
       ii. Aus Briefen von Freud an Jung. 1909–11. (370–73) Cf. G. 1974a.

  iii. Brief an seine Frau aus Sousse, Tunis. 1920. (373–75)
  iv. Aus einem Brief an einen jungen Gelehrten. 1952. (375–76)
      To Zwi Werblowsky (17 June 1952). Entire letter pub. in
      G. 1972b and trans. in E. 1975a.
   v. Aus einem Brief an einen Kollegen. 1959. (376–78) To
      Erich Neumann (10 Mar. 1959). Entire letter pub. as G.
      1967a and trans. in E. 1975a.
  vi. "Théodore Flournoy." (378–79)
 vii. "Richard Wilhelm." (380–84) Cf. G. 1930c and G. 1931b.
viii. "Heinrich Zimmer." (385–86)
  ix. Nachtrag zum "Roten Buch." (387)
   x. "VII Sermones ad Mortuos." (389–98) G. 1916a repub.
Also contains excerpts of letter to Gustav Steiner (30 Dec. 1957),
pp. 3–4. Cf. G. 1964b. TR. (Appendix content varies) —Dutch: 1963a
// English: 1962a / 1966a // French: 1966a // ?Japanese: 1972a and
1973a // Norwegian: 1966b // Portuguese: 1969a // Spanish: 1966b
// Swedish: 1964a. See E. 1962a for Danish and Italian trans.'s.
Uncertain whether Japanese trans. from German or English.

1963a "Vorwort." Cornelia Brunner: *Die Anima als Schicksalsproblem des
      Mannes.* pp. 9–14. (Studien aus dem C. G. Jung-Institut, Zürich,
      14.) Zurich: Rascher. Dated April 1959. TR.—English: CW 18,63.

1963b "Geleitbrief." *Der Mensch als Persönlichkeit und Problem.* Gedenk-
      schrift for Ildefons Betschart on his 60th birthday. pp. 14–15. Ed.
      by Elisabeth Herbrich. Munich: Anton Pustet. Letter to the editor
      (30 May 1960). Entire text of letter pub. in G. 1973a and trans. in
      E. 1976a.

1964a "Brief von Prof. C. G. Jung an den Verfasser." Josef Rudin: *Psycho-
      therapie und Religion.* pp. 11–13. 2d edn. Olten: Walter. Letter to
      the author written 30 Apr. 1960 in response to Jung's reading of the
      1st edn. of the above, and subsequently included in the 2d. Text
      of letter pub. in G. 1973a and trans. in E. 1976a. TR.—English:
      1968c.

1964b Letter to Gustav Steiner (30 Dec. 1957), pp. 125–28. Gustav Steiner:
      "Erinnerungen an Carl Gustav Jung. Zur Entstehung der Auto-
      biographie." *Basler Stadtbuch 1965.* Basel: Helbing und Lichten-
      hahn. A facsimile of the 1st part of the ms. appears on p. 127. Pub.

with omissions in G. 1962a, pp. 3–4. Repub. in G. 1973a. TR.—English: (Pt. only) 1962a / 1976a.

1967a Letter to Erich Neumann (10 March 1959). Aniela Jaffé: *Der Mythus vom Sinn im Werk von C. G. Jung.* pp. 182–84. Paperback. Zurich: Rascher. Repub. in G. 1973a. Pub. in abbrev. form as G. 1962a,15,V. TR.—English: 1976a.

1967b * Excerpt of letter to Ernst Hanhart (18 Feb. 1957). *Katalog der Autographen-Auktion* (Marburg), no. 425 (23–24 May). Also pub. in the *Tagesanzeiger für Stadt und Kanton Zürich* (27 May). TR.— English: 1976a.

1967c Letters to Richard Evans. Richard I. Evans: *Gespräche mit C. G. Jung und Äusserungen von Ernest Jones.* Zurich: Rhein. pp. 168. Trans. from E. 1964b by Lucy Heyer-Grote. Contains 2 letters dated April 1957 and one dated 30 May 1957. Also contains a lengthy interview.

1968a "Zugang zum Unbewussten." *Der Mensch und seine Symbole.* pp. 20–103. [Ed. by Carl G. Jung and after his death by M.-L. von Franz; coordinating editor, John Freeman.] Olten: Walter. pp. 320. Trans. from E. 1964a by Klaus Thiele-Dohrmann.

1968b Letters to August Forel. August Forel: *Briefe. Correspondance 1864–1927.* Ed. by Hans W. Walser. Bern: Hans Huber. Contains the following letters from Jung:
    1. 1 Apr. 1906. (381–82)
    2. 12 Oct. 1909. (403) Repub. in G. 1972a.
TR.—English: 1973b.

1969a *Über Grundlagen der analytischen Psychologie. Die Tavistock Lectures.* Zurich: Rascher. pp. 218. Trans. from E. 1968a by Hilde Binswanger. 1975: ("Studienausgabe.") Olten: Walter. TR.—Norwegian: 1972a.

1971a *Der Einzelne in der Gesellschaft.* ("Studienausgabe.") Olten: Walter. pp. 117. Contents:
    1. "Die Bedeutung des Vaters für das Schicksal des Einzelnen." (7–31) GW 4,14 repub.

2. "Die Frau in Europa." (33–55) G. 1929a repub. Repub. as GW 10,6.

3. "Das Liebesproblem des Studenten." (57–77) First pub. in English trans. Repub. as GW 10,5. Lecture to the student body, Universität Zürich, prob. in Dec. 1922. TR.—English: 1928a,7 / CW 10,5.

4. "Die Bedeutung der analytischen Psychologie für die Erziehung." (79–96) GW 17,3 prepub. Orig. German here pub. for the first time. Cf. E. 1928a,13, Lecture I, for English version. Lecture given at the Congrés international de Pédagogie, Territet / Montreux, 1923.

5. "Die Bedeutung des Unbewussten für die individuelle Erziehung." (97–115) GW 17,6 prepub. Orig. German here pub. for the 1st time. Lecture given at the International Congress of Education, Heidelberg, 1925. TR.—English: 1928a,14 / CW 17,6.

1971b *Mensch und Seele. Aus dem Gesamtwerk 1905 bis 1961.* Selected and ed. by Jolande Jacobi. Olten: Walter. pp. 391. "Dritte, erweiterte Auflage von *Psychologische Betrachtungen.*" G. 1945a, rev. and exp. Cf. E. 1970b for details. TR. (in effect)—English: 1970b.

1971c *Psychiatrie und Okkultismus.* (Frühe Schriften I; "Studienausgabe.") Olten: Walter. pp. 155. Contents:

1. "Zur Psychologie und Pathologie sogenannter okkulter Phänomene." (7–102) GW 1,1 repub.

2. "Über hysterisches Verlesen." (103–06) GW 1,2 repub.

3. "Kryptomnesie." (107–19) GW 1,3 repub.

4. "Über manische Verstimmung." (121–49) GW 1,4 repub.

1971d *Psychologie und Religion.* ("Studienausgabe.") Olten: Walter. pp. 280. Contents:

1. "Psychologie und Religion." (7–127) GW 11,1 repub.

2. "Über die Beziehung der Psychotherapie zur Seelsorge." (129–52) GW 11,7 repub.

3. "Psychoanalyse und Seelsorge." (153–61) GW 11,8 repub.

4. "Das Wandlungssymbol in der Messe." (163–267) GW 11,3 repub.

1972a *Briefe. Erster Band, 1906–1945.* Ed. by Aniela Jaffé in collaboration with Gerhard Adler. Olten: Walter. pp. 530. English and French letters trans. by Aniela Jaffé. The 1st of 3 vols. Cf. G. 1972b and G. 1973a. Letters arranged chronologically. Contains 381 letters. "With a very few exceptions . . . the selection of letters in the Swiss and American editions is identical." Cf. E. 1973b. TR.—English: 1973b and 1976a // French: 1975a.

1972b *Briefe. Zweiter Band, 1946–1955.* pp. 560. Bibliographical information the same as for G. 1972a. The 2d of 3 vols. Cf. G. 1972a and G. 1973a. Contains 333 letters. TR.—English: 1973b and 1976a // French: 1975a.

1972c *Probleme der Psychotherapie.* ("Studienausgabe.") Olten: Walter. pp. 107. Contents:
1. "Grundfragen der Psychotherapie." (7–22) GW 16,10 repub.
2. "Grundsätzliches zur praktischen Psychotherapie." (23–42) GW 16,2 repub.
3. "Was ist Psychotherapie?" (43–51) GW 16,3 repub.
4. "Einige Aspekte der modernen Psychotherapie." (52–59) GW 16,4 repub.
5. "Der therapeutische Wert des Abreagierens." (60–70) GW 16,11 repub.
6. "Psychotherapie und Weltanschauung." (71–78) GW 16,7 repub.
7. "Medizin und Psychotherapie." (79–88) GW 16,8 repub.
8. "Die Psychotherapie in der Gegenwart." (89–106) GW 16,9 repub.

1972d *Typologie.* ("Studienausgabe.") Olten: Walter. pp. 208. Contents:
1. "Zur Frage der psychologischen Typen." (7–17) GW 6,4 repub.
2. "Allgemeine Beschreibung der Typen." (18–104) GW 6,3,10 repub.
3. "Definitionen." (105–89) GW 6,3,11 repub.
4. "Psychologische Typen." (190–205) GW 6,5 repub.

1972e *Zur Psychoanalyse.* (Frühe Schriften III; "Studienausgabe.") Olten: Walter. pp. 121. Contents:
1. "Die Hysterielehre Freuds. Eine Erwiderung auf die Aschaffenburgsche Kritik." (7–14) GW 4,1 repub.

2. "Die Freudsche Hysterietheorie." (15–30) GW 4,2 repub.
3. "Die Traumanalyse." (31–40) GW 4,3 repub.
4. "Ein Beitrag zur Psychologie des Gerüchtes." (41–55) GW 4,4 repub.
5. "Ein Beitrag zur Kenntnis des Zahlentraumes." (56–64) GW 4,5 repub.
6. "Morton Prince M.D. *The Mechanism and Interpretation of Dreams*. Eine kritische Besprechung." (65–85) GW 4,6 repub.
7. "Zur Kritik über Psychoanalyse." (86–89) GW 4,7 repub.
8. "Zur Psychoanalyse." (90–93) GW 4,8 repub.
9. "Allgemeine Aspekte der Psychoanalyse." (94–108) GW 4,10 repub.
10. "Über Psychoanalyse." (109–18) GW 4,11 repub.

1973a *Briefe. Dritter Band, 1956–61.* pp. 431. Bibliographical information the same as for G. 1972a. The last of 3 vols. Cf. G. 1972a and G. 1972b. Contains 258 letters and a general index to the 3 vols. TR.— English: 1976a.

1973b *Versuch einer Darstellung der psychoanalytischen Theorie.* (Frühe Schriften IV; "Studienausgabe.") Olten: Walter. pp. 209. Contents:
1. "Versuch einer Darstellung der psychoanalytischen Theorie." (9–161) GW 4,9 repub.
2. "Psychotherapeutische Zeitfragen. Ein Briefwechsel zwischen C. G. Jung und R. Loÿ." (163–206) GW 4,12 repub.

1973c *Zum Wesen des Psychischen.* ("Studienausgabe.") Olten: Walter. pp. 149. Contents:
1. "Die transzendente Funktion." (7–36) GW 8,2 repub.
2. "Die Bedeutung von Konstitution und Vererbung für die Psychologie." (37–46) GW 8,4 repub.
3. "Psychologische Determinanten des menschlichen Verhaltens." (47–62) GW 8,5 repub.
4. "Theoretische Überlegungen zum Wesen des Psychischen." (63–145) GW 8,8 repub.

1973d *Zur Psychogenese der Geisteskrankheiten.* ("Studienausgabe.") Olten: Walter. pp. 100. Contents:
1. "Der Inhalt der Psychose." (7–49) GW 3,2 repub.
2. "Über das Problem der Psychogenese bei Geisteskrankheiten." (51–66) GW 3,5 repub.

3. "Über die Bedeutung des Unbewussten in der Psychopath-ologie." (67–74) GW 3,4 repub.

4. "Geisteskrankheit und Seele." (75–79) GW 3,6 repub.

5. "Die Schizophrenie." (81–98) GW 3,9 repub.

1974a With Sigmund Freud: *Briefwechsel*. Edited by William McGuire and Wolfgang Sauerländer. Frankfurt a. M.: S. Fischer. pp. 766. Contains 294 letters by Jung, dated 1906–1914 (+ 1 from 1923), of which 8 prev. appeared in G. 1972a. Editorial apparatus translated from E. 1974b by W. Sauerländer. TR.—English: 1974b // French: 1975a // Italian: 1974a.

1975a Address at the presentation of the Jung Codex and letters to G. Quispel. Gilles Quispel: "Jung en de Gnosis." pp. 85–146. *Jung— een mens voor deze tijd*. Rotterdam: Lemniscaat. Contains the fol-lowing works by Jung:
Letters to Quispel:
1. 18 Feb. 1953. (139)
2. 21 Apr. 1950. (140–41) Also pub. in G. 1972b. TR.—English: 1973b.
3. 22 July 1951. (142–43)
4. [Address at the presentation of the Jung Codex]. (144–46) Given in Zurich, 15 Nov. 1953. Dutch summary included. TR.—English: CW 18,97.

1907a "On Psychophysical Relations of the Associative Experiment."
J. abnorm. Psychol., 1:6 (Feb.), 247–55. Repub., slightly rev., with
slight title change as CW 2,12. TR.—GW 2,12.

1907b With F. Peterson: "Psycho-physical Investigations with the Galva-
nometer and Pneumograph in Normal and Insane Individuals."
Brain, XXX:2 (pt. 118) (July), 153–218. Repub., slightly rev., as
CW 2,13. TR.—GW 2,13.

1908a With Charles Ricksher: "Further Investigations on the Galvanic
Phenomenon and Respiration in Normal and Insane Individuals."
J. abnorm. Psychol., II:5 (Dec. 1907–Jan. 1908), 189–217. Repub.,
slightly rev., as CW 2,14. TR.—GW 2,14.

1909a *The Psychology of Dementia Praecox.* (Nervous and Mental Disease
Monograph Series No. 3.) New York: The Journal of Nervous and
Mental Disease Publishing Co. pp. 153. 1971: facsimile edn. New
York: Johnson Reprint Corp. pp. 150. Trans. from G. 1907a by
Frederick W. Peterson and A. A. Brill. Contents:
  Author's Preface. (xix–xx) Dated July 1906.
    I. Critical Presentation of Theoretical Views on the Psychology
       of Dementia Praecox.
    II. The Emotional Complex and Its General Action on the
        Psyche.
    III. The Influence of the Emotional Complex on Association.
    IV. Dementia Praecox and Hysteria, a Parallel.
    V. Analysis of a Case of Paranoid Dementia as a Paradigm.
  Pub. in dif. trans.'s as E. 1936b and CW 3,1.

1910a "The Association Method." *American Journal of Psychology*, XXI:2
(Apr.), 219–69. Trans. from a largely unpub. German text by A. A.
Brill. Contents:
    1. Lecture I. (Untitled) (219–40) Pub. in a dif. trans. as CW 2,10.
       Partially incorporates It. 1908a.

2. Lecture II. "Familial [printed as "Familiar"] Constellations. (240–51) Pub. in a dif. trans. as CW 2,11. Cf. Fr. 1907a.

3. Lecture III. "Experiences Concerning the Psychic Life of the Child." (251–69) German version pub. as G. 1910k. Cf. CW 17,1.

Repub. in *Lectures and Addresses Delivered before the Departments of Psychology and Pedagogy in Celebration of the Twentieth Anniversary of the Opening of Clark University—September, 1909.* Worcester, Mass.: The University. pp. 39–89. Pub. with stylistic alterations as E. 1916a,3.

1913a   "On the Doctrine of Complexes." *Australasian Medical Congress, Transactions of the 9th Session,* II, 835–39. Sydney: Wm. Applegate Gullick, Government Printer, under the direction of the Literary Committee. Repub., slightly rev., as CW 2,18. Paper contributed to the Congress, Sydney, Australia, Sept. 1911. TR.—GW 2,18.

1913b   "The Theory of Psychoanalysis." [1st section: Introduction and Chs. I–III.] *Psychoanal. Rev.,* I:1 (Nov.), 1–40. Trans. from G. 1913a by Edith and M. D. Eder and Mary Moltzer. The 1st of 5 sections. Repub., with E. 1914a and 1915b, as E. 1915a. Pub., together with E. 1914a and 1915b, with addns., in a dif. trans. as CW 4,9. First part of a series of 9 lectures given in English as an Extension Course at Fordham University, New York City, Sept. 1912.

1913c   "Letter from Dr. Jung." (To *The Psychoanalytic Review,* Nov. 1913.) *Psychoanal. Rev.,* I:1 (Nov.), 117–18. Repub. in E. 1973b. TR.—German: 1972a.

1913d   "Psycho-Analysis." *Transactions of the Psycho-Medical Society,* IV:2. pp. 19. Trans. (by ?) from the orig. German ms., a version of which was ultimately pub. as GW 4,10. Repub. with slight title change as E. 1915d. Read before the Psycho-Medical Society, London, 5 Aug. 1913. TR.—Dutch: 1914a.

1914a   "The Theory of Psychoanalysis." *Psychoanal. Rev.* [2d–4th sections: Chs. IV–VII: 1:2 (Feb.), 153–77; Ch. VIII: I:3 (July), 260–84; Ch. IX: 1:4 (Oct.), 415–30.] Trans. from G. 1913a by Edith and M. D. Eder and Mary Moltzer. The 2d, 3d, and 4th of 5 sections. Cf. E. 1913b and E. 1915b. Repub., with E. 1913b and 1915b, as E. 1915a.

Pub., with E. 1913b and 1915b, with addns, in a dif. trans. as CW 4,9. The middle portion of a series of 9 lectures. Cf. E. 1913b.

1914b "On the Importance of the Unconscious in Psychopathology." *British Medical Journal*, II (5 Dec.), 964–66. Repub. as E. 1916a,11. Paper read in the Section of Neurology and Psychological Medicine, 82d Annual Meeting of the British Medical Association, Aberdeen, 29–31 July 1914. (Discussion with Ernest Jones follows ?) Summary appeared in *The Lancet*, II (1914) (5 Sept.), 650.

1915a *The Theory of Psychoanalysis*. (Nervous and Mental Disease Monograph Series No. 19.) New York: Journal of Nervous and Mental Disease Publishing Co. pp. 135. 1971: Facsimile edn. New York: Johnson Reprint Corp. Contents:
Introduction. (1–3)
    I. Consideration of Early Hypotheses. (4–16)
    II. The Infantile Sexuality. (17–26)
    III. The Conception of Libido. (27–44)
    IV. The Etiological Significance of the Infantile Sexuality. (45–54)
    V. The Unconscious. (55–59)
    VI. The Dream. (60–66)
    VII. The Content of the Unconscious. (67–71)
    VIII. The Etiology of the Neuroses. (72–95)
    IX. The Therapeutical Principles of Psychoanalysis. (96–110)
    X. Some General Remarks on Psychoanalysis. (111–33)
E. 1913b, 1914a, and 1915b repub. as a monograph. Pub. in a dif. trans. as CW 4,9.

1915b "The Theory of Psychoanalysis." [5th section: Ch. X.] *Psychoanal. Rev.*, II:1 (Jan.), 29–51. Trans. from G. 1913a by Edith and M. D. Eder and Mary Moltzer. The last of 5 sections. Cf. E. 1913b and 1914a. Repub., with E. 1913b and 1914a, as E. 1915a. Pub., with E. 1913b and 1914a, with addns., in a dif. trans. as CW 4,9. The last of a series of lectures. Cf. E. 1913b.

1915c "On Psychological Understanding." *J. abnorm. Psychol.*, IX:6 (Feb.–Mar.), 385–99. German version, rev. and slightly exp., pub. as supplement in G. 1914a. ?Incorporated in E. 1916a,14. English version read before the Psycho-Medical Society, London, 24 July 1914.

1915d "Psychoanalysis." *Psychoanal. Rev.*, II:3 (July), 241–59. E. 1913d repub. with slight title change. Repub. as E. 1916a,8. Pub. in a dif. trans., with title change, as CW 4,10.

1916a *Collected Papers on Analytical Psychology.* Ed. by Constance E. Long. New York: Moffat, Yard; London: Bailliére, Tindall & Cox. pp. 392. Some copies bear the title: *Analytical Psychology.* Contents:

1. Author's Preface. (vii–x) Probably trans. from a German ms. by Constance E. Long. Dated Jan. 1916. Repub. as E. 1917a, 1, and in a dif. trans. as CW 4,13, "First Edition." TR.—German: GW 4,13,a.

2. "On the Psychology and Pathology of So-called Occult Phenomena." (1–93) Trans. from G. 1902a by M. D. Eder. Repub. as E. 1917a,2, and, in a dif. trans., as CW 1,1.

3. "The Association Method." (94–155) E. 1910a pub. with stylistic alterations. Consists of 3 lectures, the 1st 2 pub. in a dif. trans. as CW 2,10 and 11. In regard to the 3d, cf. CW 17,1. Repub. as E. 1917a,3.

4. "The Significance of the Father in the Destiny of the Individual." (156–75) Trans. from G. 1909c by M. D. Eder. Repub. as E. 1917a,4. Cf. CW 4,14.

5. "A Contribution to the Psychology of Rumour." (176–90) Trans. from G. 1910q. Repub. as E. 1917a,5. Pub. in a dif. trans. as CW 4,4.

6. "On the Significance of Number-Dreams." (191–99) Trans. from G. 1911e by M. D. Eder. Repub. as E. 1917a,6. Pub. in a dif. trans. as CW 4,5.

7. "A Criticism of Bleuler's 'Theory of Schizophrenic Negativism'." (200–05) Trans. from G. 1911c by M. D. Eder. Repub. as E. 1917a,7. Pub. in a dif. trans. as CW 3,4.

8. "Psychoanalysis." (206–25) E. 1915d repub. Repub. as E. 1917a,8. Pub. in a dif. trans., with title change, as CW 4,10.

9. "On Psychoanalysis." (226–35) Repub. as E. 1917a,9, and with minor revs. and title change as CW 4,11. Read in English before the New York Academy of Medicine, 8 Oct. 1912, and to the 17th International Medical Congress, London, 1913.

10. "On Some Crucial Points in Psychoanalysis." (236–77) Trans. from G. 1914b by Edith Eder. Repub. as E. 1917a,10. Pub. in a dif. trans. with minor title change as CW 4,12.

11. "On the Importance of the Unconscious in Psychopathology." (278–86) E. 1914b repub. Repub. as E. 1917a,11. Pub., slightly rev., as CW 3,5.

12. "A Contribution to the Study of Psychological Types." (287–98) Trans. from Fr. 1913a by Constance E. Long. Repub. as E. 1917a,12. Pub. in a dif. trans. as CW 6,5.

13. "The Psychology of Dreams." (299–311) Trans. from an unpub. ms. (greatly exp. and pub. as G. 1928b,2) by Dora Hecht. Repub. as E. 1917a,13. Cf. E. 1956b and CW 8,9 for dif. trans.'s of an exp. version.

14. "The Content of the Psychoses." (312–51) Trans. from G. 1914a by M. D. Eder. Repub. as E. 1917a,14. Pub. in a dif. trans. as CW 3,2. ?Incorporates E. 1915c.

15. "New Paths in Psychology." (352–77) Trans. from G. 1912d by Dora Hecht. Pub., rev. and exp., with title change, as E. 1917a,15. Pub. in a dif. trans. as CW 7,3.

TR.—Japanese: (7 articles only) 1926a.

1916b *Psychology of the Unconscious. A Study of the Transformation and Symbolisms of the Libido. A Contribution to the History of the Evolution of Thought.* New York: Moffat, Yard; London: Kegan Paul, Trench, Trubner. pp. lvi + 566. (Lengthy front matter contains intro. by the translator.) Trans. from G. 1912a by Beatrice M. Hinkle. The American edn. was imported, presumably as sheets, into Great Britain by Kegan Paul, who substituted their title page. Publication date for the London edn. is considered to be 1917, although copies bear only the 1916 copyright date by Moffat Yard. In 1919, Moffat Yard issued a "new edn.," xxxvi + 339 pp. Kegan Paul reprinted this last version in 1921, continuing to do so through the 6th impression, 1951. (In 1947, the imprint became Routledge & Kegan Paul.) Dodd Mead (New York) acquired the book from Moffat Yard in 1925, reprinting the 1916 edn. which was in print until 1972. Contents (the first pagination given is that of the 1916 edn., the second, that of the 1919 edn.):

1. Author's Note. (xlvii) (xxix) Cf. CW 5, 2d edn., 2d pr.

Part I.

2. Introduction. (3–7) (1–3)

3. Concerning the Two Kinds of Thinking. (8–41) (4–21)

4. The Miller Phantasies. (42–48) (22–25)

5. The Hymn of Creation. (49–86) (26–46)
6. The Song of the Moth. (87–126) (47–69)
Part II.
7. Aspects of the Libido. (127–38) (70–76)
8. The Conception and the Genetic Theory of Libido. (139–56) (77–86)
9. The Transformation of the Libido. A Possible Source of Primitive Human Discoveries. (157–90) (87–105)
10. The Unconscious Origin of the Hero. (191–232) (106–28)
11. Symbolism of the Mother and of Rebirth. (233–306) (129–168)
12. The Battle for Deliverance from the Mother. (307–40) (169–87)
13. The Dual Mother Role. (341–427) (188–236)
14. The Sacrifice. (428–83) (237–67)

Entire work pub., rev. and expanded, in a dif. trans. with change of title, as CW 5. TR.—Japanese: 1931b.

1917a *Collected Papers on Analytical Psychology.* Ed. by Constance E. Long. 2d edn. New York: Moffat, Yard; London: Bailliére, Tindall & Cox. pp. 492. Contents conform to those of the 1st edn. (cf. E. 1916a) with the following addns. and substitution:
1a. Author's Preface to the Second Edition. (ix–xii) Probably trans. from the German ms. by Constance E. Long. Dated June 1917. Repub. in a dif. trans. as CW 4,13,b.
15. "The Psychology of the Unconscious Processes." (352–444) Trans. from G. 1917a by Dora Hecht. Replaces E. 1916a,15, of which this is a rev. and exp. version. Cf. E. 1928b,1 and CW 7,1 for trans.'s of further rev. versions.
16. "The Conception of the Unconscious." (445–74) Trans. from a German ms. subsequently lost, a French trans. of which was pub. as Fr. 1916a. The orig. ms. was found posthumously and a dif. trans. pub. as CW 7,4 (2d edn.). Cf. E. 1928b,2 and CW 7,2 for trans. of further rev. versions. Delivered as a lecture to the Zurich School of Analytical Psychology, 1916.

1918a *Studies in Word-Association. Experiments in the Diagnosis of Psychopathological Conditions Carried Out at the Psychiatric Clinic of the University of Zurich, under the direction of C. G. Jung.* New York: Moffat, Yard; London: Heinemann, 1919. pp. 575. 1969:

New York: Russell & Russell; London: Routledge & Kegan Paul. Trans. by M. D. Eder. Contains the following works by Jung:

1. With F. Riklin: "The Associations of Normal Subjects." (8–172) Trans. from G. 1906a,1. Pub. in a dif. trans. as CW 2,1.

2. "Analysis of the Associations of an Epileptic." (206–26) Trans. from G. 1906a,2. Pub. in a dif. trans. as CW 2,2.

3. "Reaction-Time in Association Experiments." (227–65) Trans. from G. 1906a,3. Pub. in a dif. trans. as CW 2,3.

4. "Psycho-Analysis and Association Experiments." (297–321) Trans. from G. 1906a,4. Pub. in a dif. trans. with slight title change as CW 2,5.

5. "Association, Dream, and Hysterical Symptoms." (354–95) Trans. from G. 1909a,1. Pub. in a dif. trans. with slight title change as CW 2,7.

6. "On Disturbances in Reproduction in Association Experiments." (396–406) Trans. from G. 1909a,2. Pub. in a dif. trans. with slight title change as CW 2,9.

1919a   "On the Problem of Psychogenesis in Mental Diseases." *Proceedings of the Royal Society of Medicine* (Section of Psychiatry), XII:9 (Aug.), 63–76. Repub., slightly rev., as CW 3,6. Written in English and read to the Section of Psychiatry, The Society, Annual Meeting, London, 11 July 1919.

1919b   "Instinct and the Unconscious." *British Journal of Psychology*, X:1 (Nov.), 15–26. Trans. by H. G. Baynes from a German ms. subsequently pub. as G. 1928b,4. Repub. as E. 1928a,10. *Also issued as a pamphlet including other authors' papers, Cambridge, England: Cambridge University Press. Pub. in a dif. trans. as CW 8,6. A contribution to the Symposium of the same name, presented at the joint meeting of the British Psychological Society, the Aristotelian Society, and the Mind Association, London, 12 July 1919.

1920a   "Introduction." Elida Evans: *The Problem of the Nervous Child.* pp. v–viii. New York: Dodd Mead; London: Kegan Paul [1921]. Dated Oct. 1919. Repub. as CW 18,129.

1920b   "The Psychological Foundations of Belief in Spirits." *Proceedings of the Society for Psychical Research*, XXXI:79 (May), 75–93. Trans. by H. G. Baynes from a German ms. subsequently pub. as G. 1928b,

5. Repub. as E. 1928a,9. Pub. in a dif. trans. as CW 8,11. Read before a general meeting of the Society, London, 4 July 1919.

1921a "The Question of the Therapeutic Value of 'Abreaction'." *British Journal of Psychology* (Medical Section), II:1 (Oct.), 13–22. Pub., slightly rev., as E. 1928a,11. TR.—German: GW 16,11.

1923a *Psychological Types, or, The Psychology of Individuation.* New York: Harcourt Brace; London: Kegan Paul, Trench, Trubner. pp. 654. 1959: New York: Pantheon; London: Routledge & Kegan Paul. Trans. from G. 1921a by H. G. Baynes. Contents:
  1. Introduction. (9–14)
  2. The Problem of Types in the History of Classical and Medieval Thought. (15–86)
  3. Schiller's Ideas upon the Type Problem. (87–169)
  4. The Apollonian and the Dionysian. (170–83)
  5. The Type Problem in the Discernment of Human Character. (184–206)
  6. The Problem of Types in Poetry. (207–336)
  7. The Type Problem in Psychiatry. (337–57)
  8. The Problem of Typical Attitudes in Aesthetics. (358–71)
  9. The Problem of Types in Modern Philosophy. (372–400)
  10. The Type Problem in Biography. (401–11)
  11. General Description of the Types. (412–517)
  12. Definitions. (518–617)
  13. Conclusion. (618–28)
Repub., trans. rev., as CW 6. Items 1, 11, 12 pub. as E. 1959a,4.

1923b "On the Relation of Analytical Psychology to Poetic Art." *British Journal of Medical Psychology*, III:3, 213–31. Trans. from G. 1922a by H. G. Baynes. Repub. as E. 1928a,8. Pub. in a dif. trans. as CW 8,11.

1925a *VII Sermones ad Mortuos. The Seven Sermons to the Dead Written by Basilides in Alexandria, the City Where the East Toucheth the West.* Edinburgh: Neill. pp. 28. Trans. from G. 1916a by H. G. Baynes. Printed for private circulation. Repub. as E. 1966a,19 and E. 1967b. Cf. E. 1967a. Presentation copy examined inscribed "To R. F. C. Hull. C. G. Jung. June 1959. Translation by H. G. Baynes."

1925b "Psychological Types." *Problems of Personality. Studies Presented to Morton Prince, Pioneer in American Psychopathology.* pp. 289–302. Ed. by C. MacFie Campbell, et al. New York: Harcourt Brace; London: Kegan Paul, Trench, Trubner. Trans. from G. 1925c by H. G. Baynes. Pub. in dif. trans.'s as E. 1928a,12 and CW 6,6. Lecture delivered at the International Congress of Education, Territet, 1923.

1926a "Marriage as a Psychological Relationship." *The Book of Marriage.* pp. 348–62. Ed. by Hermann Keyserling. New York: Harcourt Brace. Trans. from G. 1925b by Therese Duerr. Pub. in dif. trans.'s as E. 1928a,6 and CW 17,8.

1927a "Introduction." Frances G. Wickes: *The Inner World of Childhood.* pp. xiii–xiv. New York: D. Appleton. Trans. from a ms. subsequently expanded into G. 1931e, of which the above comprises the 1st 3½ pars. Entire text of G. 1931e trans. and pub. as E. 1966c. Cf. CW 17,2.

1928a *Contributions to Analytical Psychology.* New York: Harcourt Brace; London: Kegan Paul, Trench, Trubner. pp. 410. Trans. by H. G. and Cary F. Baynes. Contents:
1. "On Psychical Energy." (1–76) Trans. from G. 1928b,2. Pub. in a dif. trans. with slight title change as CW 8,1.
2. "Spirit and Life." (77–98) Trans. from G. 1926c. Pub. in a dif. trans. as CW 8,12.
3. "Mind and the Earth." (99–140) Trans. from a German ms. subsequently pub. as G. 1931a,8. Pub. in a dif. trans. with minor title change as CW 10,2.
4. "Analytical Psychology and Weltanschauung." (141–63) Trans. from a German ms. subsequently rev. and exp. into G. 1931a,12. Cf. CW 8,14.
5. "Woman in Europe." (164–88) Trans. from G. 1927b. Pre-pub. as E. 1928c. Excerpt pub. as E. 1930d. Pub. in a dif. trans. as CW 10,6.
6. "Marriage as a Psychological Relationship." (189–203) Trans. from G. 1925b. Pub. in dif. trans.'s as E. 1926a and CW 17,8.
7. "The Love Problem of the Student." (204–24) Trans. from a German ms. subsequently pub. as G. 1971a,3. Pub. in a dif.

trans. with minor title change as CW 10,5. Lecture delivered to the student body, University of Zurich, 1924.

8. "On the Relation of Analytical Psychology to Poetic Art." (225–49) E. 1923b repub. Pub. in a dif. trans. with minor title change as CW 15,6.

9. "The Psychological Foundations of Belief in Spirits." (250–69) E. 1920b repub. Pub. in a dif. trans. as CW 8,11.

10. "Instinct and the Unconscious." (270–81) E. 1919b repub. Pub. in a dif. trans. as CW 8,6.

11. "The Question of the Therapeutic Value of 'Abreaction'." (282–94) E. 1921a, slightly rev. Repub., slightly rev. and with minor title change, as CW 16,11.

12. "Psychological Types." (295–312) Trans. from G. 1925c. Pub. in dif. trans.'s as E. 1925b and CW 6,6.

13. "Analytical Psychology and Education." (313–82) Consists of 4 lectures. Lecture I trans. from the unpub. German ms. subsequently pub. as G. 1971a,4. Repub., slightly rev., as CW 17,3. Delivered to the International Congress of Education, Territet, 1923. Lectures II–IV drafted in English and rev. by Roberts Aldrich. Cf. CW 17,4. Delivered to the International Congress of Education, London, May 1924.

14. "The Significance of the Unconscious in Individual Education." (383–402) Trans. from a German ms. subsequently pub. as G. 1971a,5. Delivered as a lecture to the International Congress of Education, Heidelberg, 1925. Pub. in a dif. trans. as CW 17,6. Excerpt pub. as "Analysis of Two Homosexual Dreams." pp. 286–93. *The Homosexuals as Seen by Themselves and Thirty Authorities.* Ed. by A. M. Krich. New York: Citadel Press., 1957.

1928b *Two Essays on Analytical Psychology.* New York: Dodd, Mead; London: Bailliére, Tindall & Cox. pp. 280. Trans. by H. G. and C. F. Baynes. Contents:

1. "The Unconscious in the Normal and Pathological Mind." (1–121) Trans. from G. 1926a. Cf. E. 1917a,15 and CW 7,1 for trans.'s of earlier and later versions. Extracts (Chs. V & VII; pt. of last par. omitted) pub. in *Classics in Psychology.* pp. 715–55. Ed. by Thorne Shipley. New York: Philosophical Library, 1961.

2. "The Relation of the Ego to the Unconscious." (125–269) Trans. from G. 1928a. Pub. in a dif. trans. with slight title change as CW 7,2.

1928c "Woman in Europe." *New Adelphi*, n.s. II:1 (Sept.), 19–35. E. 1928a,5 prepub.

1930a "Your Negroid and Indian Behavior." *Forum*, LXXXIII:4 (Apr.), 193–99. Repub., slightly rev. and with title change, as CW 10,22. Written in English.

1930b "Some Aspects of Modern Psychotherapy." *Journal of State Medicine*, XXXVIII:6 (June), 348–54. Repub. as CW 16,3. Written in English and delivered before the Congress of the Society of Public Health, Zurich, 1929. TR.—German: GW 16,4.

1930c "Psychology and Poetry." *transition*, no. 19/20 (June), 23–45. Trans. from G. 1930a by Eugene Jolas. Pub. in a dif. trans. with title change as E. 1933a,8. Cf. CW 15,7.

1930d "The Plight of Woman in Europe." *The 1930 European Scrap Book*. pp. 213–16. New York: Forum Press. Excerpted from E. 1928,5.

1931a With Richard Wilhelm: *The Secret of the Golden Flower*. New York: Harcourt Brace; London: Kegan Paul, Trench, Trubner. pp. 151. 1955: New York: Wehman Bros. pp. 151. Trans. by Cary F. Baynes. Pub., rev. and augmented, as E. 1962b. Contains the following works by Jung:

    1. "Commentary." (77–137) Trans. from G. 1929b,I,1–6. Cf. CW 13,1.

    2. "Examples of European Mandalas." (137–38 + 10 plates) Trans. from G. 1929b,I,7. Cf. CW 13,1, pp. 56 ff and CW 9,i,12.

    3. "In Memory of Richard Wilhelm." (139–51) Trans. from G. 1930c. Cf. E. 1958a,9 and CW 15,5.

1931b "Foreword." Charles Roberts Aldrich: *The Primitive Mind and Modern Civilization*. pp. xv–xvii. New York: Harcourt Brace; London: Kegan Paul, Trench, Trubner. Trans. by Aldrich from the German ms. Repub., trans. slightly rev., as CW 18,69.

1931c "The Spiritual Problem of Modern Man." *Prabuddha Bharata*, 36:8 (Aug.), 377–84; 36:9 (Sept.), 435–43. Trans. from G. 1928f by ? Also pub. as monograph: Mayavati Almora, Himalayas: Advaiti Ashrama. pp. 15. Cf. E. 1933a,10 and CW 10,4 for trans.'s of rev. version.

1931d "Problems of Modern Psychotherapy." *Schweizerisches Medizinisches Wochenschrift*, LXI:35 (29 Aug.) 810–32. Trans. from G. 1929d by Cary [F.] Baynes. Repub. as E. 1933a,2. Pub. in a dif. trans. as CW 16,6.

1932a "Introduction." W. M. Kranefeldt: *Secret Ways of the Mind*. pp. xxv–xl. New York: Henry Holt; London: Kegan Paul, Trench, Trubner, 1934. Trans. from G. 1930b by Ralph M. Eaton. Pub. in a dif. trans. as CW 4,15.

1932b "Sigmund Freud in His Historical Setting." *Character and Personality*, I:1 (Sept.), 48–55. Trans. from G. 1932f by Cary F. Baynes. English trans. issued simultaneously with the orig. German (cf. G. 1932f) which was pub. in the German edn. of this journal. Pub. in a dif. trans. as CW 15,3.

1932c "Crime and the Soul. The Mystery of Dual Personality in the Lawbreaker. Inoffensive People Who Become Criminals." *Sunday Referee* (London) (11 Dec.). For German version, see G. 1933a. Pub., with minor rev. in accordance with G. 1933a, as CW 18,13.

1933a *Modern Man in Search of a Soul*. New York: Harcourt Brace; London: Kegan Paul. pp. 282. 1955: Paperback edn. (Harvest Books) New York: Harcourt Brace Jovanovich. pp. 244. 1961: London: Routledge & Kegan Paul. pp. 282. Trans. by W. S. Dell and Cary F. Baynes. Contents:

    1. "Dream Analysis in Its Practical Application." (1–31) Trans. from G. 1931c. Pub. in a dif. trans. with title change as CW 16,12.

    2. "Problems of Modern Psychotherapy." (32–62) E. 1931d repub. Pub. in a dif. trans. as CW 16,6.

    3. "The Aims of Psychotherapy." (63–84) Trans. from G. 1931a, 5. Pub. in a dif. trans. as CW 16,5.

    4. "A Psychological Theory of Types." (85–108) Trans. from G. 1931a,6. Repub., trans. slightly rev., as CW 6,7.

5. "The Stages of Life." (109–31) Trans. from G. 1931a,10. Pub. in a dif. trans. as CW 8,16.

6. "Freud and Jung: Contrasts." (132–42) Trans. from G. 1931a, 4. Pub. in a dif. trans. as CW 4,16.

7. "Archaic Man." (143–74) Trans. from G. 1931a,9. Pub. in a dif. trans. as CW 10,3.

8. "Psychology and Literature." (175–99) Trans. from G. 1930a. Pub. in a dif. trans. with title change as E. 1930c. Cf. CW 15,7.

9. "The Basic Postulates of Analytical Psychology." (200–25) Trans. from G. 1931g. Pub., trans. slightly rev., as CW 8,13.

10. "The Spiritual Problem of Modern Man." (226–54) Trans. from G. 1931a,14. Pub. in a dif. trans. as CW 10,4. Cf. E. 1931c for a trans. of earlier version.

11. "Psychotherapists or the Clergy." (255–82) Trans. from G. 1932a. Repub. as E. 1956d. Pub. in a dif. trans. as CW 11,7.

1933b "Introduction." M. E. Harding: *The Way of All Women.* pp. ix–xiii. London: Longmans, Green. 1970: Rev. edn. New York: G. P. Putnam's Sons for the C. G. Jung Foundation for Analytical Psychology. pp. xv–xviii. Trans. by Cary F. Baynes from the German ms. subsequently pub. as G. 1935c. Repub., somewhat rev., as CW 18,130. Dated Feb. 1932. TR.—Italian: 1947c // Swedish: 1934b.

1936a *The Concept of the Collective Unconscious.* (Papers of the Analytical Psychology Club of New York.) New York: Analytical Psychology Club. pp. 20. Mimeographed for private circulation, Dec. 1936. Reissued in 2 pts. as E. 1936d and 1937b. Cf. CW 9,i,2. Text of lecture delivered to the Analytical Psychology Club, Plaza Hotel, New York, 2 Oct. 1936, and in London (cf. E. 1936d).

1936b *The Psychology of Dementia Praecox.* (Nervous and Mental Disease Monograph Series No. ?3.) New York and Washington: Journal of Nervous and Mental Disease Pub. Co. pp. 150. Trans. from G. 1907a by A. A. Brill. Pub. in dif. trans.'s as E. 1909a and CW 3,1. For contents, see E. 1909a.

1936c "Yoga and the West." *Prabuddha Bharata,* Section III, Sri Ramakrishna Centenary Number (Feb.), 170–77. Trans. from a German ms. by Cary F. Baynes. Pub. in a dif. trans. (based on this one) as CW 11,12. For German version, see GW 11,12. TR.—French: 1949a.

1936d "The Concept of the Collective Unconscious." (Pt. I.) *St. Bartholomew's Hospital Journal*, XLIV:3 (Dec.), 46–49. The 1st part of E. 1936a repub. The 1st of 2 pts. Cf. E. 1937b. Repub., slightly rev., with E. 1937b, as CW 9,i,2. Text of lecture previously delivered in New York (cf. E. 1936a) given before the Abernethian Society, St. Bartholomew's Hospital, London, 19 Oct. 1936.

1936e See 1968a.

1937a "Psychological Factors Determining Human Behavior." *Factors Determining Human Behavior*. pp. 49–63. (Harvard Tercentenary Publications.) Cambridge, Mass.: Harvard U. P.; London: Humphrey Milford/Oxford U. P. Pub., with slight alterations and title change, as E. 1942a, and with above title and slight alterations as CW 8,5. For German version based on the orig. ms., cf. GW 8,5. Paper delivered in English as contribution to the Harvard Tercentenary Conference of Arts and Sciences, September 1936.

1937aa Letter to the author (24 Sept. 1926). Louis London: *Mental Therapy: studies in fifty cases*. Vol. 2, p. 637. New York: Covici, Friede. Excerpts only. Written in English. Full text pub. in E. 1973b and trans. in G. 1972a.

1937b "The Concept of the Collective Unconscious." (Pt. II.) *St. Bartholomew's Hospital Journal*, XLIV:4 (Jan.), 64–66. The 2d pt. of E. 1936a repub. The 2d of 2 pts. Cf. E. 1936b. Repub., slightly rev., with E. 1936b, as CW 9,i,2.

1937c "Wotan." *Saturday Review of Literature*, XVI:25 (16 Oct.), 3–4, 18, 20. Trans. from G. 1936c by Barbara Hannah and altered by the editors. Pub. unaltered in dif. trans.'s, as E. 1947a,3 and CW 10,10.

1938a *Psychology and Religion*. (The Terry Lectures.) New Haven, Conn.: Yale U. P.; London: Oxford U. P. pp. 131. 1960: Paperback edn. (Yale Paperbound), New Haven: Yale U. P. Contents:
1. The Autonomy of the Unconscious Mind. (1–39)
2. Dogma and Natural Symbols. (40–77)
3. The History and Psychology of a Natural Symbol. (78–114)
Cf. CW 11,1. Written in English and delivered as the 15th series of

"Lectures on Religion in the Light of Science and Philosophy," Yale University, New Haven, Connecticut, 1937. Subsequently trans. into German, rev. by Toni Wolff and exp. by Jung, to form G. 1940a. TR.—Turkish: 1965a.

1938b "Presidential Address. Views Held in Common by the Different Schools of Psychotherapy Represented at the Congress, July, 1938." *Journal of Mental Science*, LXXXIV:353 (Nov.), 1055. Summary of Jung's address delivered to the Tenth International Medical Congress for Psychotherapy, Oxford, 29 July–2 Aug. 1938. Cf. CW 10,33.

1939a *The Integration of the Personality.* New York: Farrar and Rinehart; London: Kegan Paul, 1940. pp. 313. Trans. by Stanley M. (i.e., W. Stanley) Dell. Contents:

1. "The Meaning of Individuation." (3–29) Written in English for this volume, and pub. here with some addns. of material from other of Jung's writing by the translator. Subsequently rewritten in German, considerably rev., and pub., with the deletion of Dell's addns., as G. 1939e. Cf. CW 9,i,10, for a trans. of the rev. version.

2. "A Study in the Process of Individuation." (30–51) Trans. from G. 1934c. Cf. CW 9,i,11 for a trans. of the rev. version.

3. "Archetypes of the Collective Unconscious." (52–95) Trans. from G. 1935b. Cf. CW 9,i,1 for a trans. of the rev. version.

4. "Dream Symbols of the Process of Individuation." (96–204) Trans. from G. 1936a. Pub. in a dif. trans., with slight title change, as E. 1959d. Cf. CW 12,3, pt. II (2d edn.) for a trans. of the rev. version.

5. "The Idea of Redemption in Alchemy." (205–80) Trans. from G. 1937a. Cf. CW 12,3, pt. III (2d edn.) for a trans. of the rev. version.

6. "The Development of the Personality." (281–305) Trans. from G. 1934b,9. Pub. in a dif. trans. with slight title change as CW 17,7.

1939b "The Dreamlike World of India." *Asia*, XXXIX:1 (Jan.), 5–8. Repub. as CW 10,23. Written in English. TR.—German: GW 10,23.

1939c "What India Can Teach Us." *Asia*, XXXIX:2 (Feb.), 97–8. Repub. as CW 10,24. Written in English. TR.—German: GW 10,24.

1939d "On the Psychogenesis of Schizophrenia." *Journal of Mental Science*, LXXXV:358 (Sept.), 999–1011. Repub. as E. 1959a,8. Written in English and read at a meeting of the Section of Psychiatry, Royal Society of Medicine, London, 4 April 1939. TR.—German: GW 3,7.

1940a *Picasso.* (Papers of the Analytical Psychology Club.) New York: Analytical Psychology Club. pp. 8. Trans. from G. 1934b,8 by Alda F. Oertly. Printed for private circulation. Pub. in dif. trans.'s as E. 1953i and CW 15,9.

1942a "Human Behaviour." *Science and Man. Twenty-Four Original Essays* .... pp. 423–35. Ed. by Ruth Nanda Anshen. New York: Harcourt Brace. E. 1937a pub. with minor alterations, omission of last par., and title change. Pub. with slight alterations and reversion to title of E. 1937a as CW 8,5. Author given as "Charles Gustav Jung."

1942b "Psychotherapy Today." *Spring 1942.* pp. 1–12. New York: Analytical Psychology Club. Trans. by Hildegard Nagel from a German ms. pub. as G. 1945f. Printed for private circulation. Pub. in dif. trans.'s as E. 1947a,4 and CW 16,9.

1942c "Foreword." Jolande Jacobi: *The Psychology of C. G. Jung.* pp. vii–viii. London: Kegan Paul, Trench, Trubner. 1943: New Haven, Conn.: Yale U. P.; London: Kegan Paul, Trench, Trubner. pp. v–vi. Trans. from G. 1940c by K. W. Bash. Dated Aug. 1939. Pub. in a dif. trans. as E. 1962c. Repub., trans. rev., as CW 18,40.

1943a "The Psychological Aspects of the Mother Archetype." *Spring 1943.* pp. 1–31. New York: Analytical Psychology Club. Trans. from G. 1939b by Cary F. Baynes and Ximena de Angulo. Printed for private circulation. Cf. CW 9,i,4 for a trans. of a rev. version, which incorporates parts of the above.

1943b "An Interview with C. G. Jung." *Horizon*, VIII:48 (Dec.), 372–81. Trans. from G. 1943f by an unknown hand. Repub., trans. rev. and with title change, as E. 1969f and CW 18,131. Answers written by Jung to questions from Jolande Jacobi.

1944a "The Different Aspects of Rebirth." *Spring 1944.* pp. 1–25. New York: Analytical Psychology Club. Trans. from G. 1940b by Theodor Lorenz and Ximena de Angulo. Printed for private circulation. Cf. CW 9,i,5 for a trans. of the rev. version.

1944b "Introduction." Julius Spier: *The Hands of Children; An Introduction to Psychochirology.* pp. xv–xvi. London: Kegan Paul, Trench, Trubner. 1955: 2d edn. London: Routledge & Kegan Paul. Trans. from the German ms. by Victor Grove (who trans. the entire book). Repub., trans. rev., as CW 18,132.

1945a "The Soul and Death." *Spring 1945.* pp. 1–9. New York: Analytical Psychology Club. Trans. from G. 1934b,10 by Eugene H. Henley. Printed for private circulation. Repub., trans. slightly rev., as E. 1959c. Cf. CW 8,17.

1945b "Return to the Simple Life. Excerpts from a Swiss Newspaper Article." *Bull. APC*, 7:1 (Jan.), Supplement, 1–6. Excerpts of G. 1941e trans. by Eugene H. Henley. Printed for private circulation. Full text pub. in a dif. trans. as CW 18,72.

1946a "After the Catastrophe." *Spring 1946.* pp. 4–23. New York: Analytical Psychology Club. Trans. from G. 1945c by Elizabeth Welsh. Printed for private circulation. Repub. as E. 1947a,6. Pub. in a dif. trans. as CW 10,11.

1946b Foreword to K. A. Ziegler: "Alchemie II," List No. 17 (May). pp. 1–2. Bern. Written both in English and in German as a foreword to a bookseller's catalog. English text repub. as E. 1968d, and, slightly rev., as CW 18,104. Cf. G. 1946f for the German version.

1946c Contribution entitled "Jung's Commentary." pp. 372–77. Horace Gray: "Brother Klaus, With a Translation of Jung's Commentary." *Journal of Nervous and Mental Diseases*, CIII:4 (Apr.), 359–77. Trans. from G. 1933c by Horace Gray; title omitted. Pub. in a dif. trans. with inclusion of title as CW 11,6.

1946d Two letters. (1 Dec., and 26 May 1934) Ernest Harms: "Carl Gustav Jung—Defender of Freud and the Jews." *Psychiatric Quarterly*, 20:2 (Apr.), 199–233. Trans. by Ernest Harms.
    1. Circular letter to *Zentralblatt* subscribers (1 Dec. 1934). (222–23) Trans. from G. 1934j. Pub. in a dif. trans. as CW 10,27.

2. Excerpts from letter "to a Jewish pupil and friend" (James Kirsch, 26 May 1934) (227–30) Trans. from the German ms., parts of which are included here on pp. 225–27. Cf. G. 1946h. Repub. as E. 1972c,7, and, in a dif. trans., in E. 1973b. Cf. G. 1972a for text of the original letter.

1946e "The Fight with the Shadow." *Listener*, 37:930 (7 Nov.), 615–16, 641. Repub. with title change as E. 1947f and 1947a,2. Repub. slightly rev. and with reversion to above title as CW 10,12. Text of talk broadcast in the Third Programme, British Broadcasting Corp., 3 Nov. 1946.

1946f "The Bologna Enigma." *Ambix*, II:3/4 (Dec.), 182–91. Trans. from G. 1945b by Miss Marmorstein. Incorporated, in a dif. trans., into CW 14,II,3.

1947a *Essays on Contemporary Events*. London: Kegan Paul, Trench, Trubner. pp. 90. Contents:
  1. Preface. (vii–viii) Trans. from G. 1946a,1 by Elizabeth Welsh. Pub. in a dif. trans. as CW 10,9.
  2. Introduction: "Individual and Mass Psychology." (ix–xviii) E. 1946e repub. with title change. Repub. with title above as E. 1947f, and, slightly rev. and with reversion to title of E. 1946e, as CW 10,12.
  3. "Wotan." (1–16) Trans. from G. 1946a,2 by Barbara Hannah. Pub. in dif. trans.'s as E. 1937c and CW 10,10.
  4. "Psychotherapy Today." (17–35) Trans. from G. 1946a,3 by Mary Briner. Pub. in dif. trans.'s as E. 1942b and CW 16,9.
  5. "Psychotherapy and a Philosophy of Life." (36–44) Trans. from G. 1946a,4 by Mary Briner. Pub. in a dif. trans. as CW 16,7.
  6. "After the Catastrophe." (45–72) E. 1946a,5 repub. Pub. in a dif. trans. as CW 10,11.
  7. "Epilogue." (73–90) Trans. from G. 1946a,6 by Elizabeth Welsh. Pub. in a dif. trans. as CW 10,13.

1947b "On the Psychology of Eastern Meditation." *Art and Thought*. (Issued in honor of Dr. Ananda K. Coomaraswamy.) pp. 169–79. Ed. by K. Bharatha Iyer. London: Luzac. Trans. from G. 1943c by Carol Baumann. Reprint issued, dated Feb. 1948. Repub. as E. 1949b. Pub. in a dif. trans. with slight title change as CW 11,14.

1947c   "An Alchemistic Text Interpreted As If It Were a Dream." *Spring 1947.* pp. 3–10. New York: Analytical Psychology Club. Trans. and slightly condensed from G. 1955a,III,3 by Carol Baumann. Printed for private circulation.

1947d   "Jungian Method of Dream Analysis." *World of Dreams. An Anthology.* pp. 634–59. Ed. by Ralph L. Woods. New York: Random House. Extracts compiled from E. 1916a,8&13; E. 1939a,3; E. 1928b,2 and E. 1933a,1.

1947e   "Foreword." M. Esther Harding: *Psychic Energy: Its Source and Goal.* pp. xi–xii. (B. S. 10.) New York: Pantheon. 1963: 2d edn., rev. & enl. pp. xix–xx. Retitled *Psychic Energy: Its Source and Its Transformation.* pp. xix–xx. 1973: (Princeton/Bollingen Paperback.) Princeton University Press. Trans. by Hildegard Nagel from a German ms. pub. as G. 1948d. Dated 8 July 1947. Repub., trans. sl. rev., as CW 18,42. TR.—French: 1952b.

1947f   "Individual and Mass Psychology." *Chimera*, V:3 (Spring), 3–11. E. 1946e repub. Repub. with title change as E. 1947a,2.

1948a   "On the Nature of Dreams." *Spring 1948.* pp. 1–12. New York: Analytical Psychology Club. Trans. from G. 1945d by Ethel Kirkham. Also issued separately for private circulation as mimeographed pamphlet: (Papers of the Analytical Psychology Club of New York, 6.) New York: The Club. 12 pp. Cf. CW 8,10 for trans. of rev. & exp. version.

1948b   "Address Given at the Opening Meeting of the C. G. Jung Institute of Zurich, April 24, 1948." *Bull. APC*, 10:7 (Oct.), Suppl., 1–7. Trans. by Hildegard Nagel from the unpub. German ms. Pub. in a dif. trans. as CW 18,43.

1948c   "Letter to Miss Pinckney." *Bull. APC*, 10:7 (Oct.), 3. Written in English at the request of the editor, Sally M. Pinckney; dated 30 Sept. 1948. Repub. in E. 1973b. TR.—German: 1972b.

1948d   *On the Psychology of the Spirit.* (Papers of the Analytical Psychology Club of New York, 6.) New York: The Club. 43 pp. Trans. from G. 1946e by Hildegard Nagel. Printed for private circulation.

1949a With C. Kerényi: *Essays on a Science of Mythology. The Myth of the Divine Child and the Mysteries of Eleusis.* (B. S. 22.) New York: Pantheon. pp. 289. 1950: British edn. *Introduction to a Science of Mythology.* London: Routledge & Kegan Paul. pp. 289. Trans. from G. 1941c by R. F. C. Hull. Repub., trans. rev., as E. 1963a. Contains the following works by Jung:

    1. "The Psychology of the Child Archetype." (95–138) Repub. as E. 1958a,4, and, trans. rev., as CW 9,i,6.

    2. "The Psychological Aspects of the Kore." (215–56) Repub., trans. rev., as CW 9,i,7.

1949b *On the Psychology of Eastern Meditation.* New York: Analytical Psychology Club. pp. 19. E. 1947b repub. Printed for private circulation. Pub. in a dif. trans. with slight title change as CW 11,14.

1949c "Ulysses, a Monologue." *Spring 1949.* pp. 1–20. New York: Analytical Psychology Club. Trans. from G. 1934b,7 by W. Stanley Dell. Printed for private circulation. Repub. as E. 1953h. Pub. in a dif. trans. as CW 15,8. Unauthorized facsimile of this edn. without indication of source pub. 1972: Folcroft, Pa.: Folcroft Library Editions. pp. 22.

1949d "Foreword." Daisetz Suzuki: *An Introduction to Zen Buddhism.* pp. 9–29. New York: Philosophical Library; London: Rider. *1959: Paperback edn. London: Arrow Books. 1964: Paperback edn. (Evergreen Black Cat) New York: Grove Press. Trans. from G. 1939c by Constance Rolfe. Pub. in a dif. trans. as CW 11,13. (1st edn.—Kyoto, 1934—lacks Foreword.) TR.—Dutch: 1958b.

1950a "Shadow, Animus and Anima." *Spring 1950.* pp. 1–11. New York: Analytical Psychology Club. Trans. from G. 1948f by William H. Kennedy. Incorporated, in a dif. trans., into CW 9,ii, Chs. II–III.

1950b "Foreword." H. G. Baynes: *Analytical Psychology and the English Mind and Other Papers.* p. v. London: Methuen. Written in English. Repub. as CW 18,78.

1950c "Foreword." Linda Fierz-David: *The Dream of Poliphilo.* pp. xiii–xv. (B. S. 25.) New York: Pantheon. Trans. from G. 1947b by Mary Hottinger. Repub., trans. rev., as CW 18,118.

1950d   "Foreword." *The I Ching, or Book of Changes*. The Richard Wilhelm translation . . . p. i–xx. New York: Pantheon (B. S. 19); London: Routledge & Kegan Paul. (In 2 vols.) 1961: 2d edn. (In 1 vol.) pp. i–xx. 1967: 3d edn. (In 1 vol.) Princeton University Press. pp. xxi–xxxix. Trans. from the German ms. by Cary F. Baynes. Written for the English edn. and dated 1949. Repub. as E. 1958a,6 and, trans. slightly rev., as CW 11,16. Cf. GW 11,16 for original German version. TR.—Dutch: 1953b.

1950e   "Introductions by C. G. Jung." *Bull. APC*, 12:5 (May), 10–13. Excerpts from G. 1935e and G. 1949e trans. by Hildegard Nagel. Entire text of G. 1935e pub. in dif. trans.'s as E. 1967d and CW 18,45. Entire text of G. 1949e pub. in a dif. trans. as CW 18,45.

1951a   "Concerning the Self." *Spring 1951*. pp. 1–20. New York: Analytical Psychology Club. Trans. from G. 1949b by Hildegard Nagel. Also issued for private circulation as mimeographed pamphlet. (Papers of the APC of NY, 7.) 20 pp. Cf. CW 9,ii, Chs. IV–V for trans. of exp. version.

1951b   "Foreword to the English Edition." *Paracelsus: Selected Writings*. pp. 23–24. Ed. by Jolande Jacobi. (B. S. 28.) New York: Pantheon. 1958: 2d edn. pp. xxi–xxii. Trans. from the German ms. by Norbert Guterman. Dated May 1949. Repub., slightly rev., as CW 18,120.

1952a   "Preface." John Custance: *Wisdom, Madness and Folly. The Philosophy of a Lunatic*. pp. [1–4]. New York: Pellegrini and Cudahy. Trans. by an unknown hand from a German ms. pub. as G. 1954d. Written in 1951. Repub., trans. rev., as CW 18,15. (British edn., 1951, lacks this Preface.) TR.—French: 1954a.

1952b   "Introduction." R. J. Zwi Werblowsky: *Lucifer and Prometheus. A Study of Milton's Satan*. pp. ix–xii. London: Routledge & Kegan Paul. Trans. from a German ms. pub. as GW 11,5 by R.F.C. Hull. Dated March 1951. Repub., trans. slightly rev., as CW 11,5.

1952c   "Foreword." Victor White: *God and the Unconscious*. pp. xiii–xxv. London: Harvill Press; Chicago: Henry Regnery, 1953. Trans. by Victor White from a German ms. pub. as G. 1957h. Dated May 1952. Pub. slightly rev. as CW 11,4. Also contains extracts from letters to Gebhard Frei (13 Jan. 1948 and 17 Jan. 1949), Appendix, pp. 235–62, the full texts of which appear in G. 1972b and are trans. in E. 1973b. TR.—Portuguese: 1964a // Spanish: 1955b.

1953a *Psychological Reflections. An Anthology of the Writings of C. G. Jung.* Selected and ed. by Jolande Jacobi. New York: Pantheon (B. S. 31); London: Routledge & Kegan Paul. pp. 342. 1961: Paperback edn. (Harper Torchbooks: The Bollingen Library.) New York: Harper. pp. 340. In effect, a trans. of G. 1945a: "R.F.C. Hull's translations for the *Collected Works* have been drawn upon insofar as possible . . . (supplemented by those of S. Dell, H. G. and C. F. Baynes and others; see p. xxi). . . . The passages for which no English translation is cited have been translated especially . . . by J. Verzar and revised by Elizabeth Welsh." Pub., rev. and exp., as E. 1970b.

1953b *The Spirit Mercury.* New York: Analytical Psychology Club. pp. 63. Trans. from G. 1948a,3 by Gladys Phelan and Hildegard Nagel. Printed for private circulation. Pub. in a dif. trans. with slight title change as CW 13,4.

1953c "Concerning Synchronicity." *Spring 1953.* pp. 1–10. New York: Analytical Psychology Club. Trans. from G. 1952f by Alice H. Dunn. Printed for private circulation. Pub. in a dif. trans. with title change as E. 1957b.

1953d "Foreword." Frieda Fordham: *An Introduction to Jung's Psychology.* p. 10. Harmondsworth, England and Baltimore, Md.: Penguin. 1966: 3d edn. p. 11. Written in English and dated Sept. 1952. Repub. as CW 18,46. TR.—Dutch: 1961a // German: 1959c // Italian: 1961b // Norwegian: 1964a.

1953e "Foreword." John Weir Perry: *The Self in Psychotic Process; Its Symbolization in Schizophrenia.* pp. v–viii. Berkeley and Los Angeles: University of California Press; London: Cambridge University Press. Apparently written in English. Repub. as CW 18,16.

1953f "Preface by C. G. Jung. *Ostasien Denkt Anders. . . .*" *Bull. APC,* 15:3 (Mar.), Supplement, 1–3. Trans. from G. 1950d by Hildegard Nagel and Ellen Thayer. Printed for private circulation. Repub. with title change as E. 1955j.

1953g "The Challenge of the Christian Enigma. A Letter . . . to Upton Sinclair." (3 Nov. 1952) *New Repub.*, 128:17 (27 Apr.), 18–19. Repub., with omission of some minor changes, in E. 1976a. Written in English. TR.—German: 1972b.

1953h "Ulysses: A Monologue." *Nimbus*, II:1 (June–Aug.), 7–20. E. 1949c repub. Pub. in a dif. trans. as CW 15,8.

1953i "Picasso." *Nimbus*, II:2 (Autumn), 25–27. Trans. from G. 1932g by Ivo Jarosy. Pub. in dif. trans.'s as E. 1940a and CW 15,9.

1954a *Answer to Job.* London: Routledge & Kegan Paul; Great Neck, N.Y.: Pastoral Psychology Book Club, 1955. pp. 194. Trans. from G. 1952a by R.F.C. Hull. Repub. with the addn. of E. 1956c sl. rev. and titled "Prefatory Note," as CW 11,9.

1954b *Spirit and Nature.* (Papers from the Eranos Yearbooks, 1.) New York: Pantheon (B. S. 30); London: Routledge & Kegan Paul, 1955. Trans. by R.F.C. Hull. Contains the following works by Jung:
  1. "The Phenomenology of the Spirit in Fairy Tales." (3–48) Trans. from G. 1948a,2. Repub. as E. 1958a,3, and, trans. slightly rev., as CW 9,i,8.
  2. "The Spirit of Psychology." (371–444) Trans. from G. 1947a. Pub., slightly abbreviated, as E. 1957e. Cf. CW 8,8 for trans. of the rev. and exp. version.

1954c *The Symbolic Life.* (Guild Lecture No. 80.) London: Guild of Pastoral Psychology. pp. 30. Pub. in abbrev. form as E. 1961d. Printed for private circulation. Repub., sl. rev., as CW 18,3. Transcript from the shorthand notes of Derek Kitchin of a seminar talk given to the Guild, London, 5 April 1939.

1954d "Foreword to *Symbols of Transformation.*" *Spring 1954.* pp. 13–15. New York: Analytical Psychology Club. Trans. from G. 1952e, Pt. I,I by R.F.C. Hull. Repub. as CW 5,4, I,I.

1954e "Psychological Commentary." *The Tibetan Book of the Great Liberation.* . . . . pp. xxix–lxiv. Ed. by W. Y. Evans-Wentz. London, New York: Oxford University Press. Repub., slightly rev., as CW 11,10. 1st 21 pp. of the commentary pub., very slightly rev. and with title change, as E. 1955k. Written in English in 1939. TR.—French: 1960a // German: 1955d.

1954f "Foreword." Erich Neumann: *The Origins and History of Consciousness*. pp. xiii–xiv. New York: Pantheon (B. S. 42.); London: Routledge & Kegan Paul, 1955. 1962: Paperback edn. (Harper Torchbooks: The Bollingen Library.) New York: Harper. 2 vols. Trans. from G. 1949f by R.F.C. Hull. Repub. as CW 18,54.

1954g "Preface by C. G. Jung." *Bull. APC*, 16:2 (Feb.), 7–8. Trans. from G. 1953b by Ethel D. Kirkham. Printed for private circulation. Pub. in a dif. trans. as CW 18,57.

1954h "C. G. Jung on Flying Saucers." *Bull. APC*, 16:7 (Oct.), 7–14. Trans. from G. 1954e by Ellen Thayer with the help of Hildegard Nagel. Printed for private circulation. Pub. in dif. trans.'s as E. 1959i,3 and CW 18,80. Extracts pub. in a dif. trans. as E. 1955i.

1955a With W. Pauli: *The Interpretation of Nature and the Psyche*. New York: Pantheon (B. S. 51.); London: Routledge & Kegan Paul. pp. 247. Contains the following work by Jung:
"Synchronicity: An Acausal Connecting Principle." (5–146) G. 1952b, rev. and exp. by the author, and trans. by R.F.C. Hull. Dated August 1950. Repub., trans. slightly rev., as CW 8,18.

1955b "Transformation Symbolism in the Mass." *The Mysteries*. (Papers from the Eranos Yearbooks, 2.) pp. 274–336. New York: Pantheon (B. S. 30.); London: Routledge & Kegan Paul, 1956. Trans. from G. 1942c by R.F.C. Hull. Includes certain of the rev.'s of G. 1954b,6. Repub. as E. 1958a,5 and in a slightly dif. trans. as CW 11,3. Cf. E. 1955l.

1955c "Memorial to J. S." *Spring 1955*. p. 63. New York: Analytical Psychology Club. Written in English and delivered in 1927. (J. S. = Jerome Schloss.—Ed. note.) Repub. as CW 18,107.

1955d "On the Psychology of the Trickster." *Spring 1955*. pp. 1–14. New York: Analytical Psychology Club. Trans. from G. 1954a by Hildegard Nagel. Pub. in a dif. trans., with slight title change, as E. 1956a. Cf. CW 9,i,9.

84

1955e   "Introduction." M. Esther Harding: *Woman's Mysteries*. pp. ix–xii. New and rev. edn. New York: Pantheon. Trans. from G. 1949d by Edward Whitmont. Repub., trans. rev., as CW 18,53. (1st edn.— London, 1935—pub. without this introduction, which was written for the Swiss edn.) TR.—French: 1953d.

1955f   "The Christian Legend. An Interpretation." (Letter to Upton Sinclair, 7 Jan. 1955.) *New Repub.*, 132:8 (21 Feb.), 30–31. Written in English. Letter pub. with minor changes and some omissions. Full text pub. in E. 1976a. Title appears thus on cover only. Titled "A Communication." on p. 30. TR.—German: 1972b.

1955g   "Mandalas." *Du*, Jhg. XV:4 (Apr.), 1 p. Trans. from G. 1955e by E. W. [Elizabeth Welsh]. This English trans. accompanied the pub. of the German original in the same issue. Pub. in a dif. trans. as CW 9,i,13. TR.—Turkish: 1954a.

1955h   "Human Nature Does Not Yield Easily to Idealistic Advice." *New Repub.*, 132:20 (16 May), 18–19. Written in English as an invited comment on a previous article. Repub. as CW 18,83.

1955i   *"C. G. Jung on the Question of Flying Saucers." *Flying Saucer Review*, May–June. Extracts trans. from G. 1954e. (Extracts selected give misleading impression of Jung's views.) Repub. as E. 1958f. Entire text pub. in dif. trans.'s as E. 1954h, E. 1959i,3 and CW 18,81.

1955j   "The Mind of East and West." *Inward Light*, no. 49 (Fall), 3–4. E. 1953f repub. with title change. Repub. with title change as CW 18,92.

1955k   "Psychology, East and West." *Tomorrow*, IV:1 (Autumn), 5–23. The 1st 21 pp. of E. 1954e pub., very slightly rev. and with title change.

1955l   "The Mass and the Individuation Process." *The Black Mountain Review* (Bañalbufar, Mallorca), no. 5 (Summer), 90–147. Trans. from G. 1942c, last part, by Elizabeth Welsh. Cf. E. 1955b.

1956a   "On the Psychology of the Trickster Figure." Paul Radin and Karl Kerényi: *The Trickster. A Study of American Indian Mythology.*

pp. 193–211. New York: Philosophical Library; London: Routledge & Kegan Paul. Trans. from G. 1954a by R.F.C. Hull. Repub., trans. slightly rev., as CW 9,i,9, and in a dif. trans. with slight title change as E. 1955d.

1956aa *Answer to Job*. Great Neck, N.Y.: Pastoral Psychology Book Club. pp. ?194. E. 1954a pub. with new title page. Repub. as CW 11,9.

1956b "General Aspects of the Psychology of the Dream." *Spring 1956*. pp. 1–25. New York: Analytical Psychology Club. Trans. from G. 1948b,4 by Robert A. Clark. Pub. in a dif. trans. with slight title change as CW 8,9. Cf. E. 1916a,13 for trans. of an earlier version.

1956c "Why and How I Wrote My 'Answer to Job'." *Pastoral Psychology*, VI:60 (Jan.), 80–81. Written in English as a letter to the ed., Simon Doniger (Nov. 1955). Repub. in *Bull. APC*, 18:4 (Apr.), 1–3. Included as "Prefatory Note," with minor stylistic rev., in CW 11,9. Pub. with the restoration of "an important phrase" in E. 1973a. Original letter pub. in E. 1976a. TR.—German: 1961a ("Nachwort") / 1972b (text of letter).

1956d "Psychotherapists or the Clergy." *Pastoral Psychology*, VII:63 (Apr.), 27–42. E. 1933a,11 repub. Pub. in a dif. trans. as CW 11,7.

1956e "Preface." *Psychotherapy*, I:1 (Apr.), 1 p. Typescript written in English and dated 7 Sept. 1955. Inaugural issue of Calcutta journal devoted to Analytical Psychology. Repub. as CW 18,127.

1957a *The Transcendent Function*. Zurich: Students' Association, C. G. Jung-Institut. pp. 23. Trans. by A. R. Pope from a German ms. written in 1916 and pub., rev. and exp., as G. 1958b. Printed for private circulation. Cf. CW 8,2 for a trans. of the rev. version.

1957b "On Synchronicity." *Man and Time*. (Papers from the Eranos Yearbooks, 3.) pp. 201–11. New York: Pantheon (B. S. 30); London: Routledge & Kegan Paul, 1958. Trans. from G. 1952f by R.F.C. Hull. Repub., trans. slightly rev., as CW 8,19. Pub. in a dif. trans. with title change as E. 1953c.

1957c "The Mind of Man Reaches Out." *New Frontiers of Knowledge: A Symposium*. pp. 53–55. Ed. by M. B. Schnapper. Washington: Public Affairs Press. E. 1957h condensed and re-edited, with title change.

1957d "Answer to Buber." *Spring 1957.* pp. 1–9. New York: Analytical Psychology Club. Trans. from G. 1952j by Robert A. Clark. Printed for private circulation. Pub. in a dif. trans. with title change as E. 1973e.

1957e "The Spirit of Psychology." *This Is My Philosophy.* pp. 115–67. Ed. by Whit Burnett. New York: Harper; London: Allen and Unwin. E. 1954b,2, slightly abbreviated. TR.—Italian: 1959b.

1957f "Psychological Commentary." *The Tibetan Book of the Dead . . .* pp. xxxv–lii. Ed. by W. Y. Evans-Wentz. 3d edn. London: Oxford University Press. Trans. from G. 1935f by R.F.C. Hull. Repub. with slight title change as E. 1958a,8, and, with minor alterations, as CW 11,11. (1st and 2d edn.'s lack commentary.)

1957g "Foreword." Michael Fordham: *New Developments in Analytical Psychology.* pp. xi–xiv. London: Routledge & Kegan Paul. Written in English and dated June 1957. Repub. as CW 18,47.

1957h "Dr. Jung's Contribution to the Voice of America Symposium 'The Frontiers of Knowledge and Humanity's Hopes for the Future'." *Bull. APC,* 19:4 (Apr.), Supplement, 1–8. Text of contribution, written in English, to the United States Information Agency broadcast in 30 languages the week of the 16th Dec. 1956. Printed for private circulation. Repub. as E. 1959f. Pub., slightly rev. in accordance with the German version (G. 1959f) and with title change, as CW 3,9. Pub., condensed and re-edited, with title change, as E. 1957c. TR.—German: 1959f.

1957i Letters to the author (26 Jan. and 10 Feb. 1955). Hans A. Illing: "C. G. Jung on the Present Trends in Group Psychotherapy." *Human Relations,* X:1, 78ff. Trans. from the orig. German mss. by Hans A. Illing. Letter of 10 Feb. repub., with slight deletions, on p. 394, in Illing's "Jung's Theory of the Group as a Tool in Psychotherapy." *International Journal of Group Psychotherapy,* VII:4 (Oct.), 392–97. Letters pub. in a dif. trans. in E. 1976a. German originals pub. in full in G. 1972b, and with deletions as G. 1956d (both letters), and G. 1955f (letter of 10 Feb. only).

1957j Excerpt of letter to the author. Patricia Hutchins: *James Joyce's World.* pp. 184–85, ftnote i. London: Methuen. Written in English to Patricia Graecen (Hutchins) (29 June 1955). Repub. as E. 1959l,2. Entire letter pub. in E. 1976a.

1958a *Psyche and Symbol. A Selection from the Writings of C. G. Jung.*
Ed. by Violet S. de Laszlo. Paperback. (Anchor Books.) Garden
City, N.Y.: Doubleday. pp. 363. Contents:

1. "Preface." (xi–xvii) Dated August 1957. Repub., slightly rev.,
   as CW 18,62.
2. "Five Chapters from: *Aion*." (1–60) CW 9,ii, Chs. I–V prepub.
3. "The Phenomenology of the Spirit in Fairy Tales." (61–112)
   E. 1954b,1 repub. Repub., trans. slightly rev., as CW 9,i,8.
4. "The Psychology of the Child Archetype." (113–47) E. 1949a,
   1 repub. Repub., trans. rev., as CW 9,i,6 (1st edn.).
5. "Transformation Symbolism in the Mass." (148–224) E. 1955b
   repub. Repub., trans. slightly rev., as CW 11,3.
6. "Foreword to the *I Ching*." (225–44) E. 1950d repub. Repub.,
   trans. slightly rev., as CW 11,16.
7. "Two Chapters from: *The Interpretation of Nature and the
   Psyche*." (245–82) E. 1955a, Chs. III–IV repub. Repub., along
   with rest of text, trans. slightly rev., as CW 8,18.
8. "Psychological Commentary on *The Tibetan Book of the
   Dead*." (283–301) E. 1957f repub. Repub., trans. slightly rev.,
   as CW 11,11.
9. "Commentary on The Secret of the Golden Flower." (302–51)
   E. 1962b,2 prepub. Pub. in a dif. trans. as CW 13,1.

1958b *The Undiscovered Self.* (Atlantic Monthly Press Book.) Boston:
Little, Brown; London: Routledge & Kegan Paul. pp. 113. 1959:
Paperback edn. New York: Mentor Books/New American Library.
pp. 125. 1971: (Atlantic Monthly Press Book.) Boston: Little,
Brown. pp. 113. Trans. from G. 1957i by R.F.C. Hull, and rev. by
the American editors. Repub., trans. further rev., as CW 10,14.
Extract prepub. as "God, the Devil, and the Human Soul." *Atlantic
Monthly*, CC:5 (Nov.), 57–63. ". . . prompted by conversations be-
tween Dr. Jung and Dr. Carleton Smith, Director of the National
Arts Foundation, which brought it to the attention of the editors
of the Atlantic Monthly Press." TR.—Portuguese: 1961a.

1958c Answers to questions of, and correspondence with, the author and
David Cox. Howard L. Philp: *Jung and the Problem of Evil.* pp. 5–
21, 209–54. London: Rockliff. Repub., with minor stylistic rev. and
addn. of title, as CW 18,103. Letter of 11 June 1957 repub. in E.
1976a.

1958d "Message of the Honorary President." *Chemical Concepts of Psychosis.* p. xxi. Ed. by Max Rinkel with Herman C. B. Denber. New York: McDowell/Obolensky. Letter to Max Rinkel (Apr. 1957), chairman of a Symposium on Chemical Concepts of Psychosis, pub. in the volume above, which comprises the "Proceedings of the Symposium . . . held at the Second International Congress of Psychiatry in Zurich . . . 1 to 7 September 1957." Repub. with title change as CW 3,11. TR.—German: 1973a.

1958e "Foreword." Eleanor Bertine: *Human Relationships: In the Family, in Friendship, in Love.* pp. v–vii. New York, London: Longmans, Green. 1963: New York: David MacKay. Trans. from G. 1957d by Barbara Hannah. Repub., trans. slightly rev., as CW 18,61.

1958f "Dr. Carl Jung on Unconventional Aerial Objects." *A.P.R.O. Bulletin* (July), 1,5. E. 1955i repub. Repub. in E. 1959i,3. Cf. E. 1954h and CW 18,81.

1958g "Dr. Jung Sets the Record Straight." *UFO Investigator,* I:5 (Aug.–Sept.), 1 p. Letter written (in English) to Major Keyhoe (NICAP) (16 Aug. 1958). Repub. with title change as E. 1959g. Pub. condensed as E. 1959i,2.

1958h "Released to United Press from Dr. Jung." *Bull. APC,* 20:6 (Oct.), 10. Trans. from G. 1958h by Henny Carioba. Pub. in dif. trans.'s as E. 1958j, 1959i,1 and CW 18,81. Repudiates statement attributed to him in an *A.P.R.O. Bulletin* article. Cf. E. 1955i.

1958i "Banalized beyond Endurance." Contribution to symposium, "If Christ Walked the Earth Today." *Cosmopolitan,* CXLV:6 (Dec.), 30. Title added by editors. Repub. under title of the symposium as CW 18,86.

1958j Statement to United Press International. *A.P.R.O. Bulletin* (Sept.), 7. Trans. from G. 1958h. Repub. in dif. trans.'s as E. 1958h, 1959i,1 and CW 18,81.

1959a *The Basic Writings of C. G. Jung.* Ed. by Violet Staub de Laszlo. New York: Modern Library (Div. of Random House). pp. 552. Contents:
> 1. from *Symbols of Transformation.* (3–36) CW 5,1&4, Pt. I, Ch. I–II repub.

2. from "On the Nature of the Psyche." (37–104) CW 8,8 repub. with some omissions.

3. from "The Relations between the Ego and the Unconscious." (105–82) CW 7,2: Preface to 2d edn.; Pt. I, Chs. 1–3; Pt. II, Chs. 1–2, repub.

4. from *Psychological Types.* (183–285) E. 1923a: Introduction, and Chs. 10–11 (abridged), repub. Cf. CW 6.

5. "Archetypes of the Collective Unconscious." (286–326) CW 9,i,1 repub.

6. "Psychological Aspects of the Mother Archetype." (327–60) CW 9,i,4 repub.

7. "On the Nature of Dreams." (363–79) CW 8,10 prepub.

8. "On the Psychogenesis of Schizophrenia." (380–97) E. 1939d repub. Repub. as CW 3,8.

9. from "The Psychology of the Transference." (398–429) CW 16,13 (1st edn.): Introduction, repub.

10. "Introduction to the Religious and Psychological Problems of Alchemy." (433–68) CW 12,2, Pt. I (1st edn.) repub.

11. "Psychology and Religion." (469–528) CW 11,1 repub.

12. "Marriage as a Psychological Relationship." (531–44) CW 17,8 repub.

1959b   *Flying Saucers. A Modern Myth of Things Seen in the Skies.* New York: Harcourt Brace; London: Routledge & Kegan Paul. pp. 184. 1969: Paperback edn. New York: Signet Books/New American Library. pp. 144. Trans. from G. 1958a by R.F.C. Hull. Pts. 1 & 9 below not included in the text of G. 1958a. Repub., trans. slightly rev., as CW 10,15. Much abbreviated version pub. with title change as E. 1959h. Contents:

1. Preface to the English Edition. (ix–x) Dated Sept. 1958. TR.— German: GW 10,15.

2. Introductory. (xi–xiv)

3. Ufos as Rumours. (1–24)

4. Ufos in Dreams. (25–101)

5. Ufos in Modern Painting. (102–27)

6. Previous History of the Ufo Phenomenon. (128–45)

7. Ufos Considered in a Non-Psychological Light. (146–53)

8. Epilogue. (154–74)

9. Supplement. (174–76) Added to the English edition. TR.— German: GW 10,15, pp. 471–73.

1959c "The Soul and Death." *The Meaning of Death.* pp. 3–15. Ed. by Herman Feifel. New York: McGraw-Hill, Blakiston Division. E. 1945a repub., trans. slightly rev. by R.F.C. Hull. Repub. as CW 8,17.

1959d "Dream Symbols of the Individuation Process." *Spiritual Disciplines.* (Papers from the Eranos Yearbooks, 4.) pp. 341–423. New York: Pantheon (B. S. 30); London: Routledge & Kegan Paul. Trans. from G. 1936a by R.F.C. Hull. Pub. in a dif. trans. with slight title change as E. 1939a,4. Cf. CW 12,3, Pt. II (2d edn.) for a trans. of the rev. version.

1959e "Foreword." Jolande Jacobi: *Complex/Archetype/Symbol in the Psychology of C. G. Jung.* pp. ix–xi. New York: Pantheon (B. S. 57); London: Routledge & Kegan Paul. 1971: Paperback edn. (Princeton/Bollingen Paperback.) Princeton University Press. Trans. from G. 1957g by R.F.C. Hull. Repub. as CW 18,60.

1959f "New Thoughts on Schizophrenie." *Universitas*, III:1 (Jan.), 53–58. E. 1957h repub. with title change. Repub., slightly rev., with title change, as CW 3,9. Cf. E. 1957c for condensed version. Pub. simultaneously with the German trans. Cf. G. 1959f.

1959g "UFO." *Bull. APC*, 21:2 (Feb.), 6–8. E. 1958g repub. with title change. Printed for private circulation. Repub. with title change as CW 18,83. Pub. condensed as E. 1959i,2.

1959h "A Visionary Rumour." *Journal of Analytical Psychology*, IV:1 (Apr.), 5–19. E. 1959b much abbreviated.

1959i "Jung on the UFO . . ." *CSI of New York*, No. 27 (July), var. pp. Contains the following works by Jung:
   1. Statement on UFO's to UPI (13 Aug. 1958). (4) Trans. from G. 1958h by "CSI." Pub. in dif. trans.'s as E. 1958h, 1958j and CW 18,81.
   2. Letter to Maj. Donald Keyhoe (NICAP), (16 Aug. 1958). (5) E. 1959g pub. condensed. Full text pub. as E. 1958g, 1959g and CW 18,82.
   3. "C. G. Jung on the Question of Flying Saucers." (Appendix 1: 1–5) Consists of a trans. by "CSI" of G. 1954e together with

E. 1955i repub. for purpose of comparison. Includes in brackets "material omitted [from E. 1955i]. When [these translations] differ appreciably, the CSI version appears [on left, the other] in the right-hand column." Pub. in dif. trans.'s as E. 1954h and CW 18,80.

1959j "'National Character' and Behavior in Traffic. A Letter from Dr. Jung." *Bull. APC*, 21:8 (Dec.), Supplement, 1–4. Trans. from G. 1958j by Hildegard Nagel. Printed for private circulation. Letter to F. von Tischendorf (19 April 1958). Pub. in a dif. trans. in E. 1976a.

1959k "The Swiss National Character." *Adam*, 275 (27th year), 13–16. Trans. from G. 1928e by Gwen Mountford and Miron Grindea. Pub. in a dif. trans. with title change as CW 10,19. A retort to Keyserling's *Das Spectrum Europa*.

1959l Two letters. Richard Ellmann: *James Joyce*. New York: Oxford University Press. Contains the following letters from Jung:
1. To James Joyce (27 Sept. 1932) (642) Repub. as E. 1966d.
2. To Patricia Graecen (Hutchins) (29 June 1955) (692) E. 1957 repub. Entire letter pub. in E. 1975a and trans. in G. 1972b.

1960a *Answer to Job*. Paperback edn. New York: Meridian. pp. 223. CW 11,9 repub. (reset) with omission of "Prefatory Note."

1960b "Foreword." Miguel Serrano: *The Visits of the Queen of Sheba*. 2 pp. Bombay: Asia Publishing House. 1972: London: Routledge & Kegan Paul. Paperback edn. New York: Harper. Written in English as letter to Serrano (14 Jan. 1960) and pub. here slightly rev. Repub., somewhat rev., as CW 18,122. Entire letter pub. in full as E. 1966b,1. TR.—Spanish: 1960a.

1960c Letter to the Editor (Jan. 1960). *Listener*, XLIII:1608 (21 Jan.), 133. Written in English in response to reaction to his interview on the B.B.C. program "Face to Face," 22 Oct. 1959. Cf. E. 1975a, letters to Hugh Burnett (5 Dec. 1959) and M. Leonard (5 Dec. 1959). TR.—German: GW 11,25 / 1973a.

1960d "Preface by Dr. Jung." *Bull. APC*, 22:5 (May), 20–28. Trans. from G. 1959e by Edith Wallace. Pub. in a dif. trans. with title change as CW 10,18.

1960e "Good and Evil in Analytical Psychology." *Journal of Analytical Psychology*, V:2 (July), 91–99. Trans. from G. 1959b by R.F.C. Hull. Repub., trans. rev., as CW 10,17.

1961a "A Letter on Parapsychology and Synchronicity. Dr. Jung's Response to an Inquiry." *Spring 1961*. pp. 50-57. New York: Analytical Psychology Club. Trans. from G. 1961b by Hildegard Nagel. Written in English to A. D. Cornell (9 Feb. 1960) and trans., with addns. and corrections by Jung, as G. 1961c, from which the above has been trans. in turn. Repub., slightly rev., in E. 1976a. (In lieu of the orig. English ms., which had been lost.) *Spring 1961* reissued, photocopied and bound as one with *Spring 1960* and *Spring 1962*, in 1973.

1961b "Foreword." *Hugh Crichton-Miller, 1877–1959, A Personal Memoir by His Friends and Family*. pp. 1–2. Dorchester (England): Longmans Ltd. Written in English and dated Jan. 1960. Repub., slightly rev., as CW 18,87.

1961c "Yoga, Zen, and Koestler." *Encounter*, XVI:2 (Feb.), 56–58. Letter written in English to the editor, Melvin J. Lasky (19 Oct. 1960) in response to 2 articles by Koestler. Repub. as E. 1963f. TR.—German: 1961b / 1973a.

1961d "The Symbolic Life." *Darshana*, I:3 (Aug.) (C. G. Jung memorial issue.) 11–22. E. 1954c abbrev. Cf. CW 18,3.

1962a *Memories, Dreams, Reflections*. Recorded and ed. by Aniela Jaffé. New York: Pantheon (Div. of Random House). pp. 398. London: Collins and Routledge & Kegan Paul, 1963. pp. 383. 1965: Paperback edn. New York: Vintage (Div. of Random House). pp. 398 (index added). 1973: Rev. edn., with corrections. Trans. from G. 1962a by Richard and Clara Winston. Pub. with addn. as E. 1966a. Contents (2d pagination refers to London edn.):
  1. Prologue. (3–5) (17–19) Extracts prepub. as pt. of "Jung on Freud." *Atlantic Monthly*, CCX:5 (Nov.), 47–56. Cf. no. 6 below.
  2. First Years. (6–23) (21–36)
  3. School Years. (24–83) (37–89)
  4. Student Years. (84–113) (90–115)
  5. Psychiatric Activities. (114–45) (116–43)

6. Sigmund Freud. (146–69) (144–64) Extracts pub. as pt. of "Jung on Freud." Cf. no. 1 above.

7. Confrontation with the Unconscious. (170–99) (165–91)

8. The Work. (200–22) (192–211)

9. The Tower. (223–37) (212–24)

10. Travels. (238–88) (224–69)

11. Visions. (289–98) (270–77)

12. On Life after Death. (299–326) (278–301) Extracts pub. as "Jung on Life after Death." *Atlantic Monthly*, CCX:6 (Dec.), 39–44.

13. Late Thoughts. (327–54) (302–26) 1st par. and Pt. I pub. as "Jung's View of Christianity." *Atlantic Monthly*, CCXI:1 (Jan. '63), 61–66.

14. Retrospect. (355–59) (327–30)

Appendixes (contents differ somewhat from Anhang of G. 1962a):

15. Freud to Jung. (Letters: 16 Apr. 1909; 12 May 1911; 15 June 1911) (361–64) (333–35) Cf. E. 1974b.

16. Letters to Emma Jung from America (1909). (365–70) (336–40)

17. Letters to Emma Jung from North Africa (1920). (371–72) (340–41)

18. "Richard Wilhelm." (373–77) (342–45)

Also contains pts. of letter to Gustav Steiner (30 Dec. 1957). (viii–ix) (11–12) Cf. E. 1975a. TR.—Danish: 1965/66a // Italian: 1965c // ?Japanese: 1972a and 1973a.

1962b   With Richard Wilhelm: *The Secret of the Golden Flower. A Chinese Book of Life*. New York: Harcourt Brace. pp. 149. 1962: Paperback edn. New York: Harvest Books. Trans. from G. 1938a by Cary F. Baynes. E. 1931a, rev. and augmented by the addn. of "part of the Chinese meditation text 'The Book of Consciousness and Life' with a Foreword by Salomé Wilhelm." Cf. G. 1957b. Contains the following works by Jung:

1. "Foreword to the Second German Edition." (xiii–xiv) Trans. from G. 1938a,1. Pub. in a dif. trans. as pp. 3–5, CW 13,1.

2. "Commentary." (81–137) Trans. from G. 1938a,3&4, here combined. Pub. in a dif. trans. as CW 13,1. Prepub. as E. 1958a,9.

3. "In Memory of Richard Wilhelm." (138–49) Trans. from G. 1938a,2. Pub. in a dif. trans. with title change as CW 15,5.

1962c "Foreword." Jolande Jacobi: *The Psychology of C. G. Jung.* p. vii. New Haven: Yale University Press. Trans. from G. 1940c by Ralph Manheim. Repub., trans. rev., as CW 18,40. Pub. in a dif. trans. as E. 1942c.

1963a With C. Kerényi: *Essays on a Science of Mythology: The Myth of the Divine Child and The Mysteries of Eleusis.* Paperback edn. (Harper Torchbooks/Bollingen Library.) New York: Harper & Row. pp. 200. E. 1949a, trans. rev. Cf. E. 1969a. Contains the following works by Jung:

    1. "The Psychology of the Child Archetype." (70–100) CW 9,i,6 (1st edn.) repub. Repub., trans. further slightly rev., as CW 9,i,6 (2d edn.).

    2. "The Psychological Aspects of the Kore." (156–77) CW 9,i,7 (1st edn.) repub. Repub., trans. further slightly rev., as CW 9,i,7 (2d edn.).

1963b "Foreword." Aniela Jaffé: *Apparitions and Precognition; A Study from the Point of View of C. G. Jung's Analytical Psychology.* pp. v–viii. New Hyde Park, N.Y.: University Books. Trans. from G. 1958e by R.F.C. Hull. Repub., trans. sl. rev., as CW 18,8.

1963c Letter to Emanuel Maier (24 March 1950). Benjamin Nelson: "Hesse and Jung. Two Newly Recovered Letters." p. 15. *Psychoanal. Rev.*, 50:3 (Fall), 11–16. Repub. in E. 1973b. TR.—German: 1972b.

1963d Letter to Wm. G. Wilson (30 Jan. 1961), pp. 6–7, "The Bill W.– Carl Jung Letters." *AA Grapevine*, XIX:8 (Jan.), 2–7. Also pub. in *Bull. APC*, 25:3 (Mar.), 6–13. Repub. as E. 1968e. TR.—German: 1973a.

1963e Answers to questionnaire, "The Future of Parapsychology," added as "Appendix," pp. 450–51, to Martin Ebon, "The Second Soul of C. G. Jung." *International Journal of Parapsychology*, V:4 (Autumn), 427–58. Dated 23 June 1960. Repub. with addn. of title as CW 18,50.

1963f Letter to Melvin Lasky, editor of *Encounter, Bull. APC*, 25:6 (Oct.), 16–20. Dated 19 Oct. 1960. E. 1961c repub. without title. Repub. in *Bull. APC*, 25:6 (Oct.), 16–20, and in E. 1976a.

1964a "Approaching the Unconscious." *Man and His Symbols*. pp. 18–103. Ed. by Carl G. Jung and after his death M.-L. von Franz. Co-ordinating ed., John Freeman. London: Aldus Books; Garden City, N.Y.: Doubleday. 1968: Paperback edn. New York: Dell. pp. 1–94. Written in English in 1961 and extensively rev. and rearranged under the supervision of John Freeman in collaboration with Marie-Louise von Franz. Jung's original text pub. with title change as CW 18,2. "The remaining chapters were written by the various authors to Jung's direction and under his supervision." TR.—Dutch: 1966a // French: 1964c // German: 1968a // Italian: 1967a // Spanish: 1966c // Swedish: 1966a.

1964b Letters to Richard Evans. Richard I. Evans: *Conversations with Carl Jung and Reactions from Ernest Jones*. Princeton, N.J.: D. Van Nostrand. pp. 173. Contains the following letters:
    1. April 1957. (7)
    2. April 1957. (9)
    3. 30 May 1957. (10)
Also contains a lengthy interview, rev. by Evans. Repub. 1976: *Jung on Elementary Psychology: A Discussion between Carl Jung and Richard Evans*. New York: Dutton. A verbatim transcript of the interview added in appendix. TR.—French: 1964e. German: 1967c.

1965aa *Answer to Job*. Paperback edn. London: Hodder and Stoughton. pp. 192. E. 1954a repub. (offset). Repub. with the addn. of "Prefatory Note" as E. 1971a,15.

1965a Letter to the author (7 July 1958), pp. 141–42. Edward Thornton: "Jungian Psychology and the Vedanta." pp. 131–42. *Spectrum Psychologiae. Eine Freundesgabe*. Festschrift zum 60. Geburtstag C. A. Meier. Ed. by C. T. Frey-Wehrlin. Zurich: Rascher. Written in English.

1966a *Memories, Dreams, Reflections*. Recorded and ed. by Aniela Jaffé. Paperback edn. New York: Vintage Books (Div. of Random House). pp. 430. E. 1962a (New York edn., 1965 paperback) repub. with the following addn.:
    19. "Septem Sermones ad Mortuos." (378–90) E. 1925a repub.
Cf. hardcover, E. 1967a.

96

1966b Letters to the author. Miguel Serrano: *C. G. Jung and Hermann Hesse. A Record of Two Friendships*. London: Routledge & Kegan Paul. pp. 112. 1968: Paperback edn. New York: Schocken. pp. 112. Written in English. Letters repub. along with Spanish trans. in Sp. 1965a. Contains the following letters by Jung, with minor corrections:

    1. 14 January 1960. (68) Pub. with minor deletions and alteration as E. 1960b.

    2. 16 June 1960. (69–70)

    3. 31 March 1960. (74–75) Repub. in E. 1975a. TR.—German: 1973a.

    4. 14 September 1960. (83–88) Repub. in E. 1975a. TR.—German: 1973a.

    TR.—Spanish: 1965a.

1966c "Introduction." Frances G. Wickes: *The Inner World of Childhood. A Study in Analytical Psychology*. pp. xvii–xxv. Rev. edn. New York: Appleton-Century. 1968: Paperback edn. (Signet) New York: New American Library. pp. 304. CW 17,2 repub. Original brief version pub. as E. 1927a.

1966d Letter to James Joyce (27 Sept. 1932)† *Letters of James Joyce*. Ed. by Richard Ellmann. Vol. 3, pp. 253–54. New York: Viking. E. 1959l,1 repub. Repub. in CW 15,8, pp. 133–34 and E. 1973b.
† Date given as "? August 1932."

1966e "Foreword." Gerhard Adler: *Studies in Analytical Psychology*. pp. 3–5. New edn. London: Hodder & Stoughton. 1967: New York: G. P. Putnam's Sons for the C. G. Jung Foundation for Analytical Psychology. 1969: Paperback edn. New York: Capricorn. Trans. from G. 1952g by R.F.C. Hull. Repub. as CW 18,55. (1st edn.— London & New York, 1948—lacks Foreword.)

1967a *Memories, Dreams, Reflections*. Recorded and ed. by Aniela Jaffé. 4th ptg. New York: Pantheon (Div. of Random House). pp. 430. E. 1962a repub. with same addn. as E. 1966a. TR.—Japanese: 1972a and 1973a.

1967b *VII Sermones ad Mortuos. The Seven Sermons to the Dead Written by Basilides in Alexandria*. . . . London: Stuart & Watkins. pp. 34. E. 1925a repub. Cf. 1966a,19.

1967d "Foreword to Studies from the C. G. Jung Institute, Zurich." *Evil.* pp. xi–xii. Ed. by the Curatorium of the C. G. Jung Institute, Zurich. (Studies in Jungian Thought.) Evanston, Ill.: Northwestern University Press. Trans. from G. 1949e by Ralph Manheim. Also pub. in C. A. Meier: *Ancient Incubation and Modern Psychotherapy.* pp. ix–x. (Studies in Jungian Thought.) Evanston, Ill.: Northwestern University Press. Pub. in a dif. trans. with slight title change as CW 18,45. Excerpt pub. in a dif. trans. as pt. of E. 1950e.

1967e "Preface." John Trinick: *The Fire-Tried Stone.* pp. [8–11]. Marazion, Cornwall: Wordens of Cornwall, in association with London: Stuart & Watkins. Two letters to the author, written in English (13 Oct. 1956 and 15 Oct. 1957), pub. as Preface. Letter of 15 Oct. 1957 repub. in E. 1975a.

1967f Letter to the author (1 Dec. 1960). Edward Thornton: *Diary of a Mystic.* p. 14. London: George Allen & Unwin. Written in English. Repub. in E. 1975a. TR.—German: 1973a.

1968a *Analytical Psychology; Its Theory and Practice. The Tavistock Lectures.* New York: Pantheon (Div. of Random House); London: Routledge & Kegan Paul. pp. 224. 1970: Paperback edn. New York: Vintage Books (Div. of Random House). pp. 224. 5 lectures, each with transcript of ensuing discussion, given for the Institute of Medical Psychology, London, 30 Sept.–4 Oct. 1935. Stenographic transcript ed. by Mary Barker and Margaret Game, mimeographed for private circulation by the Analytical Psychology Club of London, 1936, entitled *Fundmental Psychological Conceptions: A Report of Five Lectures . . .* and here slightly rev. by R.F.C. Hull. Repub. as CW 18,1. TR.—French: (excerpts only, from 1936 version) 1944a,3,4&8 // German: 1969a.

1968b Letter to the author (27 April 1959). Joseph F. Rychlak: *A Philosophy of Science for Personality Theory.* pp. 342–43. Boston: Houghton Mifflin. Written in English. Repub. in E. 1975a. TR.—German: 1973a.

1968c "Letter of Professor C. G. Jung to the Author." Josef Rudin: *Psychotherapy and Religion.* pp. xi–xiii. Notre Dame, Ind.: Notre Dame University Press. Trans. from G. 1964a by Elisabeth Reinecke and Paul C. Bailey. Dated 30 Apr. 1960. Pub. in a dif. trans. in E. 1976a.

1968d Prefatory note. *Alchemy and the Occult. A Catalogue of Books and Manuscripts from the Collection of Paul and Mary Mellon Given to Yale University Library.* Vol. I, 1 p. Compiled by Ian MacPhail. New Haven, Conn.: Yale University Library. (In 2 vols.) E. 1946b repub. Repub., slightly rev. and with addn. of title, as CW 18,104.

1968e Letter to Wm. G. Wilson (30 Jan. 1961), pp. 20–21, "The Bill W.– Carl Jung Letters." *AA Grapevine*, XXIV:8 (Jan.), 16–21. E. 1963d repub. Repub. in E. 1975a.

1968f "Answers to Questions on Freud." *Spring 1968.* pp. 46–48. New York: Analytical Psychology Club. Written in English in reply to questions sent by Michael L. Hoffman, Geneva representative of the *New York Times*, and dated 7 Aug. 1953. Repub. as CW 18,32.

1968g "A 1937 Letter from C. G. Jung." *Journal of Religion and Health,* V:3 (July), 275. Written in English to the Rev. Kendig Cully (25 Sept. 1937). Repub. in E. 1973b. TR.—German: 1972a.

1969a With C. Kerényi: *Essays on a Science of Mythology* . . . Rev. edn. (Princeton/Bollingen Paperback.) Princeton University Press. pp. 200. CW 9,i,6 and 7 (2d edn.) repub.

1969b *On the Nature of the Psyche.* (Princeton/Bollingen Paperback.) Princeton University Press. pp. 175. Contents:
    1. "On Psychic Energy." (3–66) CW 8,1 repub.
    2. "On the Nature of the Psyche." (67–144) CW 8,8 repub.

1969c *Psychology and Education.* (Princeton/Bollingen Paperback.) Princeton University Press. pp. 161. Contents:
    1. "Psychic Conflicts in a Child." (1–35) CW 17,1 repub.
    2. "Child Development and Education." (37–52) CW 17,3 repub.
    3. "Analytical Psychology and Education." (53–122) CW 17,4 repub.
    4. "The Gifted Child." (123–35) CW 17,5 repub.

1969d *The Psychology of the Transference.* (Princeton/Bollingen Paperback.) Princeton University Press. pp. 207. CW 16,13 (2d edn.) repub.

1969e "Foreword." Erich Neumann: *Depth Psychology and a New Ethic.* pp. 11–18. New York: G. P. Putnam's Sons for the C. G. Jung Foundation for Analytical Psychology. Trans. from the German ms. by R.F.C. Hull. Written for a proposed English edn. not pub. until 1969. Dated March 1949. Repub., trans. slightly rev., as CW 18,77. German edn. lacks this Foreword.

1969f "Depth Psychology and Self-Knowledge. Dr. Jung's Answers to Questions Asked by Dr. Jolande Jacobi." *Spring 1969.* pp. 129–39. New York: Analytical Psychology Club. E. 1943b repub. with title change; trans. rev. by R.F.C. Hull. Repub. as CW 18,131.

1970a *Four Archetypes: Mother, Rebirth, Spirit, Trickster.* (Princeton/Bollingen Paperback.) Princeton University Press. pp. 173. 1972, London: Routledge & Kegan Paul. Contents:
  1. "Psychological Aspects of the Mother Archetype." (7–44) CW 9,i,4 repub.
  2. "Concerning Rebirth." (45–81) CW 9,i,5 repub.
  3. "The Phenomenology of the Spirit in Fairytales." (83–132) CW 9,i,8 repub.
  4. "On the Psychology of the Trickster-Figure." (133–52) CW 9,i,9 repub.

1970b *Psychological Reflections. A New Anthology of His Writings 1905–1961.* Selected and ed. by Jolande Jacobi in collaboration with R.F.C. Hull. Princeton University Press (B. S. 31); London: Routledge & Kegan Paul. pp. 391. 1973: (Princeton/Bollingen Paperback.) Princeton University Press. pp. 379. Trans. by R.F.C. Hull. (". . . all but relatively few of the quotations are taken from the Collected Works. . . ." This revision, prepared in English, adds passages from 1945–61 and omits some older material. The Swiss edn. [G. 1971b] is based on this one.) E. 1953a rev. and exp. Extracts pub. as E. 1972e.

1970c "Two Posthumous Papers. 1916." *Spring 1970.* pp. 170–76. Zurich: Analytical Psychology Club of New York. Trans. by R.F.C. Hull from the unpub. German typescripts found posthumously. Dated Oct. 1916. Contents:
  1. "Adaptation." (170–73)
  2. "Individuation and Collectivity." (174–76)
Repub. as CW 18,35.

1970d *Letter to André Barbault (26 May 1954). Aquarian Agent, I:13 (Dec.). Trans. from Fr. 1954b by an unknown hand. Pub. in a dif. trans. in E. 1976a.

1971a *The Portable Jung.* Ed. with an intro. by Joseph Campbell. New York: Viking. pp. 650. (Published simultaneously in paperback.) Trans. by R.F.C. Hull. Contents:

    Part I.

       1. "The Stages of Life." (3–22) CW 8,16 repub.
       2. "The Structure of the Psyche." (23–46) CW 8,7 repub.
       3. "Instinct and the Unconscious." (47–58) CW 8,6 repub.
       4. "The Concept of the Collective Unconscious." (59–69) CW 9,i,2 repub.
       5. "The Relations between the Ego and the Unconscious." (70–138) CW 7,2 repub.
       6. "Aion: Phenomenology of the Self." (139–62) CW 9,ii, Chs. I–III, repub.
       7. "Marriage as a Psychological Relationship." (163–77) CW 17,8 repub.
       8. "Psychological Types." (178–269) CW 6, Ch. X, repub.

    Part II.

       9. "The Transcendent Function." (273–300) CW 8,2 repub.
     10. "On the Relation of Analytical Psychology to Poetry." (301–22) CW 15,6 repub.
     11. "Individual Dream Symbolism in Relation to Alchemy." (323–455) CW 12,3, Pt. II (2d edn.) repub.
     12. "The Spiritual Problem of Modern Man." (456–79) CW 10,4 repub.
     13. "The Difference between Eastern and Western Thinking." (480–502) CW 11,10, pars. 759–87, repub.

    Part III.

     14. "On Synchronicity." (505–18) CW 8,19 repub.
     15. "Answer to Job." (519–650) CW 11,9 repub. Cf. E. 1973a.

1971b "Excerpts from Selected Letters." *Spring 1971.* pp. 121–35. Zurich: Analytical Psychology Club of New York. Excerpts from E. 1973b and 1976a prepub. Contents:

    †1. ". . . to a little daughter." (1 July 1919) To Marianne Jung.
    †2. "to a solicitous colleague." (6 Nov. 1926) To Frances G. Wickes.

† Prepub. from E. 1973b.

†3. ". . . to Freud." (5 Oct. 1906) Also prepub. from E. 1974b.

†4. "Recollections of . . . the U. S." (23 July 1949) To Virginia Payne.

‡5. "On Einstein and Synchronicity." (25 Feb. 1953) To Carl Seelig.

‡6. "On Mescalin." (15 Feb. 1955) To A. M. Hubbard.

‡7. "On the Shadow and Protestantism." (9 Nov. 1955) To Theodor Bovet.

†8. "To a Colleague on Suicide." (25 July 1946) To Eleanor Bertine.

†9. "On Suicide." (19 Nov. 1955) To an anonymous recipient.

‡10. "In Old Age." (10 Aug. 1960) To the Earl of Sandwich.

† Prepub. from E. 1973b.   ‡ Prepub. from E. 1976a.

1972a *Mandala Symbolism.* (Princeton/Bollingen Paperback.) Princeton University Press. pp. 121. Contents:

    1. "Mandalas." (3–5) CW 9,i,13 repub.

    2. "A Study in the Process of Individuation." (6–70) CW 9,i,11 repub.

    3. "Concerning Mandala Symbolism." (71–100) CW 9,i,12 repub.

1972b Letters to the author (4 Mar. and 3 Dec. 1957). Frederic Spiegelberg: *Images from Tibetan Art.* pp. [4–5]. A folio collection of eight reproductions for coloring and meditation with an essay and commentaries by Frederic Spiegelberg and additional commentaries by C. G. Jung. San Francisco: Lodestar Press. Trans. by Frederic Spiegelberg from the German letters.

1972c "Letters to a Friend: Part I." *Psychological Perspectives,* III:1 (Spring), 9–18. To James Kirsch. Trans. by James Kirsch from the German mss. except as otherwise noted. The 1st of 2 pts. Cf. E. 1972d. Contents:

    1. 19 Aug. 1929. Pub. in a dif. trans. in E. 1976a. German letter pub. in G. 1973a.

    2. 15 Aug. 1930.

    3. 12 Aug. 1931.

    4. 12 Mar. 1932.

    5. 20 Jan. 1933.

    6. 20 Feb. 1934.

7. 26 May 1934. E. 1946d,2 repub. Trans. by Ernest Harms. Pub. in a dif. trans. in E. 1973b. German letter pub. in G. 1972a.

8. 16 Aug. 1934.

9. 29 Sept. 1934. Last par. only. Entire letter pub. in a dif. trans. in E. 1973b. German letter pub. in G. 1972a.

10. 17 Feb. 1935.

11. 25 July 1946. Written in English.

12. 12 July 1951.

13. 18 Nov. 1952. Written in English. Repub. in E. 1976a. TR.— German: 1972b.

14. 23 Nov. 1952.

15. 28 Nov. 1952. Written in English.

1972d "Letters to a Friend: Part II." *Psychological Perspectives*, III:2 (Fall), 167–78. To James Kirsch, except no. 15 below, to Hildegard Kirsch. Trans. by James Kirsch from the German mss. except as otherwise noted. The last of 2 pts. Cf. E. 1972c. Contents:

1. 29 Jan. 1953. Pub. in a dif. trans. in E. 1976a. German letter pub. in G. 1972b.

2. 28 May 1953. Pub. in a dif. trans. in E. 1976a. German letter pub. in G. 1972b.

3. 6 Aug. 1953.

4. 2 Oct. 1953.

5. 16 Feb. 1954. Pub. in a dif. trans. in E. 1976a. German letter pub. in G. 1972b.

6. 5 Mar. 1954. Pub. in a dif. trans. in E. 1976a. German letter pub. in G. 1972b.

7. 23 June 1954.

8. 11 Sept. 1954.

9. Summer 1957.

10. 29 Apr. 1958. Pub. in a dif. trans. in E. 1976a. German letter pub. in G. 1973a.

11. 3 Nov. 1958.

12. 10 Dec. 1958. Pub. in a dif. trans. in E. 1976a. German letter pub. in G. 1973a.

13. 12 Nov. 1959. Pub. in a dif. trans. in E. 1976a. German letter pub. in G. 1973a.

14. 10 Jan. 1960.

15. 2 Nov. 1960. To Hildegard Kirsch.

1972e " 'Psychological Reflections' on Youth and Age." *University*, 51 (Winter), 18–22. Extracts of E. 1970b.

1973a *Answer to Job.* (Princeton/Bollingen Paperback.) Princeton University Press. pp. 121. CW 11,9, 2d edn., 2d ptg. (1973) repub.

1973b *Letters. 1: 1906–1950.* Selected and ed. by Gerhard Adler in collaboration with Aniela Jaffé. Princeton University Press (B. S. 95); London: Routledge & Kegan Paul. pp. 596. German letters trans. by R.F.C. Hull, French letters by Jane A. Pratt. The 1st of 2 vols. Cf. E. 1976a. Contains 522 letters, of which 152 are in the orig. English. Contents arranged chronologically. "With a very few exceptions . . . the selection of letters in the Swiss and American editions is identical." Cf. G. 1972a and 1972b for the German version. TR.— (English originals) German: 1972a/1972b.

1973c *Synchronicity: An Acausal Connecting Principle.* (Princeton/Bollingen Paperback.) Princeton University Press; London: Routledge & Kegan Paul. pp. 135. Contents:
  1. "Synchronicity: An Acausal Connecting Principle." (1–103) CW 8,18 repub.
  2. "On Synchronicity." (104–15) E. 1971a,14 repub.

1973d "Three Early Papers." *Spring 1973.* pp. 171–87. Zurich: Analytical Psychology Club of New York. Trans. by R.F.C. Hull. Contents:
  1. "Sigmund Freud: *On Dreams* (1901)." (171–79) Trans. from a typescript apparently of a report given at Burghölzli and dated 25 Jan. 1901. CW 18,18 prepub.
  2. "Marginal Note on F. Wittels: *Die sexuelle Not.* (1910)." (179–82) Trans. from G. 1910l. CW 18,24 prepub.
  3. "A Comment on Tausk's Criticism of Nelken (1913)." (182–87) Trans. from G. 1913d. CW 18,31 prepub.

1973e "Religion and Psychology: A Reply to Martin Buber." *Spring 1973.* pp. 196–203. Zurich: Analytical Psychology Club of New York. Trans. from G. 1952j by R.F.C. Hull. Repub. as CW 18,96. Pub. in a dif. trans. with title change as E. 1957d.

1974a *Dreams.* (Princeton/Bollingen Paperback.) Princeton University Press. pp. 337. Contents:
  Part I: Dreams and Psychoanalysis.

    1. "The Analysis of Dreams." (3–12) CW 4,3 repub.

    2. "On the Significance of Number Dreams." (13–20) CW 4,5 repub.

Part II: Dreams and Psychic Energy.

    3. "General Aspects of Dream Psychology." (23–66) CW 8,9 repub.

    4. "On the Nature of Dreams." (67–83) CW 8,10 repub.

Part III: The Practical Use of Dream-Analysis.

    5. "The Practical Use of Dream-Analysis." (87–109) CW 16,12 repub.

Part IV: Individual Dream Symbolism in Relation to Alchemy.

    6. "Individual Dream Symbolism in Relation to Alchemy." (111–297) CW 12,3, Part II (2d edn.) repub.

1974b With Sigmund Freud: *The Freud/Jung Letters. The Correspondence between Sigmund Freud and C. G. Jung.* Ed. by William McGuire. Princeton University Press (B. S. 94); London: Hogarth Press and Routledge & Kegan Paul. pp. 650. Freud letters trans. by Ralph Manheim, Jung letters trans. by R.F.C. Hull, from the German mss. (pub. simultaneously as G. 1974a). Contains 196 letters by Jung to Freud written 1906–1914 (+ 1 from 1923); 8 were prepub. in E. 1973b, 8 in E. 1974d, and 1 as E. 1971b,3. Intro. includes 2 letters to Ernest Jones (22 Feb. 1952) p. xxi and (19 Dec. 1953) p. xxiii, and 1 to K. R. Eissler (20 July 1958) pp. xxvii–xxviii, the full texts of which appear in E. 1976a.

1974c *The Psychology of Dementia Praecox.* (Princeton/Bollingen Paperback.) Princeton University Press. pp. 222. CW 3,1 repub.

1974d Letters to Freud. pp. 40–42, 86–94. "The Freud/Jung Letters." Ed. by William McGuire. *Psychology Today,* VII:9 (Feb.), 37–42, 86–94. Extracts of E. 1974b prepub. 8 letters dated 18 Jan. 1911– 6 Jan. 1913, selected and ed. by Elizabeth Hall, with an introduction by William McGuire.

1974e Letters to Mary Foote. pp. 259–66. Edward Foote: "Who Was Mary Foote?" *Spring 1974.* pp. 256–68. Zurich: Analytical Psychology Club of New York. Contents:

    1. 19 Mar. 1927. Prepub. from E. 1976a.

    2. 12 Dec. 1929.

3. 18 Dec. 1929. Prepub. from E. 1976a.
4. 29 Mar. 1933. Prepub. from E. 1976a.
5. 12 July 1937. Prepub. from E. 1976a.
6. 22 July 1939.
7. 28 July 1942.
8. 11 May 1944.

1975a "To Oskar Schmitz (1921–1931)" *Psychological Perspectives*, 6:1 (Spring), 79–95. Trans. from the German, with the aid of an anon. trans., by James Kirsch, except as noted below. Contains the following letters from Jung to Schmitz:

1. 15 Mar. 1921 (80)
2. 26 May 1923 (80–83) †Repub. from E. 1973b. For orig. German, see G. 1972a.
3. 2 Nov. 1926 (83–84)
4. 13 Nov. 1926 (84–85)
5. 7 Jan. 1927 (85–86) †Prepub. from E. 1976a.
6. 21 July 1927 (86–87) †Prepub. from E. 1976a.
7. 3 Mar. 1928 (87)
8. 20 Sept. 1928 (89–90) †Repub. from E. 1973b.
9. 5 Apr. 1929 (91)
10. 5 Apr. 1929 (92)
11. 8 Sept. 1929 (92)
12. 24 Sept. 1929 (93)

Also contains a letter from Jung to Keyserling (25 Aug. 1928), pp. 87–88, †repub. from E. 1973b, as well as letters to Schmitz from Emma Jung, pp. 90–91, 93–95.
† Trans. by R.F.C. Hull.

1976a *Letters. 2: 1951–1961*. Selected and ed. by Gerhard Adler in collaboration with Aniela Jaffé. Princeton University Press (B. S. 95); London: Routledge & Kegan Paul. pp. 716. German letters trans. by R.F.C. Hull (8 trans. by Hildegard Nagel), French letters by Jane A. Pratt. The 2d of 2 vols. Cf. E. 1973b. Contains 463 letters, of which 214 are in the orig. English. In addition, the 1914–50 Addenda consist of 16 letters, of which 9 are in the orig. English. Contents arranged chronologically. Cf. G. 1972b and 1973a for the German version. TR.— (English originals) G. 1972b/1973a.

DANISH

1957a "Menneskets sjaeleliv." *Perspektiv*, IV:6 (Mar.), 34–37. Trans. from the German ms. by Hans Reitzel. Written as contribution to a series of articles entitled "Mennesket og fremtiden—En international enquete" (Man and the Future—An international symposium), ed. through the agency of the American Cultural Attaché in Copenhagen.

1959a *Nutid og fremtid*. Copenhagen: Gyldendal. pp. 100. Trans. from G. 1957i by Mogens Boisen.

1961a *Det ubevidste*. Copenhagen: Gyldendal. pp. 160. Trans. from G. 1943a by Mogens Boisen.

1962a *Jeget og det ubevidste*. Copenhagen: Gyldendal. pp. 160. Trans. from G. 1935a by Mogens Boisen.

1963a Foreword to Jolande Jacobi: *C. G. Jungs psykologi*. pp. 7–8. Copenhagen: Gyldendal. Trans. from G. 1940c by Mogens Boisen.

1964a "Af den analytiske psykologis forhold til det digteriske kunstvaerk." *Vindrosen*, XI:3, 13–24. Trans. from G. 1931d,3 by Erik Nielsen.

1965–66a *Erindringer, drømme og tanker*. Recorded and ed. by Aniela Jaffé. Copenhagen: Biilmann og Eriksen. Vol. I, pp. 198. 1966: Vol. 2, pp. 319. Trans. from E. 1962a by Jon Kilje.

1968a *Psykologi og religion*. (Uglebøger, 213.) Copenhagen: Gyldendal. pp. 156. Trans. from G. 1940a by Christian Kock.

1969a *Den psykiske energetik og drømmenes vaesen*. (Uglebøger.) Copenhagen: Gyldendal. pp. 220. Trans. from G. 1948b by Christian Kock.

DUTCH

1908a "De theorie van Freud over hysterie." *Geneeskundige Courant,* XLII, 225–58. Trans. from G. 1908m by ?.

1914a "Over Psychoanalyse." *Nederlandsch Tijdschrift voor Geneeskunde,* II:19 (7 Nov.), 1512–23. Trans. from E. 1913d by J. H. van der Hoop.

1928a *Analytische psychologie en opvoeding. Drie voordrachten gehouden te Londen in Mei 1924.* Zutphen: W. J. Thieme. pp. 87. Trans. from G. 1926b by J. L. Gunning. Cf. Du. 1948a,1–3, for trans. of rev. version.

1935a *De banden tussen het ik en het onbewuste.* (Psychologische bibliotheek, 5.) Hague: Servire. pp. 179. 1960, paperback edn. *Het ik en het onbewuste.* (Luxe-pockets, 92.) pp. 135. Trans. from G. 1928a by A. M. Meerlo.

1935b *Theoloog of medicus?* Zutphen: G.J.A. Ruys. pp. 44. Trans. from G. 1932a by ?.

1938a Foreword to Esther Harding: *Vrouwen Lewensweg.* pp. xi–xiv. Leiden: E. J. Brill. Trans. from G. 1949d by W.E.D. Sterek.

1940a *Zielsproblemen van deze tijd.* Amsterdam: Meulenhoff. pp. 202. Trans. from G. 1931a and 1934b by Frank de Vries. Cf. Du. 1956a. Contents:
    1. "De ziel als probleem voor den modernen mens." (1–33) Trans. from G. 1931a,14. Cf. Du. 1956a,13.
    2. "Het huwelijk als psychologische verhouding." (34–52) Trans. from G. 1931a,11. Cf. Du. 1956a,10.
    3. "Het leven op een keerpunt." (53–78) Trans. from G. 1931a,10. Cf. Du. 1956a,9.
    4. "Over de wording der persoonlijkheid." (79–109) Trans. from G. 1934b,9. Cf. Du. 1957a.

5. "De archaïsche mens." (110–45) Trans. from G. 1931a,9. Cf. Du. 1956a,8.

6. "De ziel en de dood." (146–163) Trans. from G. 1934b,10. Cf. Du. 1957a.

7. "Analytische psychologie en wereldbeschouwing." (164–202) Trans. from G. 1931a,12. Cf. Du. 1956a,11.

1947a *De catastrophe. Psychologische beschouwingen over Europa's jongste geschiedenis.* Arnhem: Van Loghum Slaterus. pp. 152. Trans. from G. 1946a by C. L. de Ligt-van Rossem.

1947b "De betekenis der Dromen." *Ciba-Tijdschrift,* 22 (Mar.), 714–26. Trans. from G. 1945d by M. C. Schoute.

1948a *Psychologie en opvoeding* . . . Arnhem: Van Loghum Slaterus. pp. 187. Trans. from G. 1946b by G. Ringeling. Contents:

1–3. "Drie Voordrachten." Cf. Du. 1928a for trans. of earlier version.

4. "Conflicten in de Kinderziel."

5. "Het begaafde Kind."

1948b "Voorwoord" and essay: "Over de Indische heilige." Heinrich Zimmer: *De weg tot het zelf.* p. 5, and pp. 225–37. Hague: De Driehoek. Trans. from G. 1944b by Madelon de Man.

1949a *Psychologische beschouwingen. Een keur uit zijn werken.* Comp. and ed. by Jólan Jacobi. Antwerp: Het Kompas; Amsterdam: L. J. Veen, 1950. pp. 362. Trans. from G. 1945a by Elisabeth Camerling.

1949b *Psychologische typen.* Hague: Servire. pp. 473. Trans. from G. 1921a by Rob Limburg.

1949c *De vrouw in Europa.* Lochem: H. Buys. Trans. from G. 1929a by ?.

1949d "Woord ten geleide." Jólan Jacobi: *De psychologie van C. G. Jung.* p. 7. Amsterdam: Contact. pp. 198. 1963: Antwerp: Zeist. p. 7. Trans. from G. 1940c by M. Drukker.

1950a *De mens op weg naar zelf-ontdekking. Structuur en functie van het onbewuste geestesleven.* Amsterdam: Meulenhoff. pp. 298. Trans. from Fr. 1944a by J. Kassies.

1950b *De psychologie van het onbewuste.* Arnhem: Van Loghum Slaterus. pp. 192. Trans. from G. 1943a by G. Ringeling.

1951a *Psychologie en godsdienst. De Terry Lectures 1937 gehouden aan de Yale University.* Amsterdam: L. J. Veen; Antwerp: Het Kompas. pp. 151. Trans. from G. 1940a by Elisabeth Camerling.

1953a With Richard Wilhelm: *Het geheim van de gouden bloem. Een Chinees levensboek.* Amsterdam: L. J. Veen. pp. 159. 1975: Deventer: Ankh-Hermes. Trans. from G. 1938a by J. M. Hondius and R. de Jong-Belinfante.

1953b "Voorwoord." *I Tjing: Het boek der veranderingen.* Vol. I, pp. vi–xxiii. Amsterdam: L. J. Veen. 2 vols. Trans. from E. 1950d by A. Hochberg-van Wallinga.

1954a *Synchroniciteit als beginsel van acausale samenhangen.* Amsterdam: L. J. Veen. pp. 141. Trans. from G. 1952b by J. M. Hondius.

1955a *De symboliek van de geest.* Amsterdam: L. J. Veen. pp. 361. Trans. from G. 1948a by Elisabeth Camerling.

1955b *De wereld der ziel.* Arnhem: Van Loghum Slaterus. pp. 188. Trans. from G. 1954c by G. Ringeling.

1956a *Zielsproblemen van onze tijd.* Amsterdam: L. J. Veen. pp. 272. Trans. from G. 1931a by Elisabeth Camerling and Fr. de Vries. Cf. Du. 1940a. Contents:
1. "Problemen der moderne psychotherapie." (9–31)
2. "Over de relaties van de analytische psychologie tot het kunstwerk van de dichter. (32–52)
3. "De tegenstelling Freud en Jung." (53–60)
4. "Doelstellingen van de psychotherapie." (61–77)
5. "Psychologische typologie." (78–95)
6. "De structuur van de ziel." (96–115)
7. "Ziel en aarde." (116–136)
8. "De archaïsche mens." (137–158) Cf. Du. 1940a,5.
9. "Het leven op een keerpunt." (159–174) Cf. Du. 1940a,3.
10. "Het huwelijk als psychologische verhouding." (175–86) Cf. Du. 1940a,2.

11. "Analytische psychologie en wereldbeschouwing." (187–230) Cf. Du. 1940a,7.

12. "Geest en leven." (231–249)

13. "Het zielsprobleem van de moderne mens." (250–?72) Cf. Du. 1940a,1.

1957a *De werkelijkheid van de ziel.* Amsterdam: L. J. Veen. pp. 247. Trans. from G. 1934b by Elisabeth Camerling and Frank de Vries. Cf. Du. 1940a,4&6.

1957b Foreword to Frances G. Wickes: *De innerlijke wereld van het kind.* pp. 13–19. Amsterdam: L. J. Veen. Trans. from G. 1931e by Elisabeth Camerling and Frank de Vries.

1958a *Onze tijd en zijn toekomst.* Amsterdam: L. J. Veen. pp. 86. Trans. from G. 1957i by Elisabeth Camerling.

1958b "Voorwoord." D. T. Suzuki: *Inleiding tot het Zen-Boeddhisme.* pp. 1–27. Deventer: N. Kluwer. pp. 162. 1972: Deventer: Ankh-Hermes. Trans. from E. 1949d by William B. Moens.

1961a Foreword to Frieda Fordham: *Inleiding tot de psychologie van Jung.* pp. 5–6. Amsterdam: Wereldbibliotheek. Trans. from E. 1953d by Annie J. Blits.

1962a *Archetypen.* (Luxe-pockets, 93.) Hague: Servire. pp. 240. Trans. from G. 1954b,1–4,8 by Elisabeth Camerling. Contents:

1. "Voorwoord." (7–8)

2. "Over de archetypen van het collectieve onbewuste." (9–56)

3. "Over het archetype met speciale belichting van het begrip 'anima.'" (57–78)

4. "De psychologische aspecten van het moederarchetype." (79–118)

5. "Over het wezen van het psychische." (119–205)

6. Appendices (226–240)

1963a *Herinneringen, dromen, gedachten.* Recorded and ed. by Aniela Jaffé. Arnhem: Van Loghum Slaterus. pp. 356. Trans. from G. 1962a by Agaath van Ree. Contents conform to those of G. 1962a, with the exception of those of the appendix, which are as follows:

1. "Uit brieven van Freud aan Jung." (329–31)
2. "Uit brieven aan Emma Jung." (333–37)
3. "Richard Wilhelm." (338–42)
4. "Heinrich Zimmer." (343–56)

1966a "Die benadering van het onbewuste." *De mens en zijn symbolen.* pp. 17–111. With M.-L. von Franz, Joseph L. Henderson, Jolande Jacobi, and Aniela Jaffé. Rotterdam: Lemniscaat. pp. 368. Trans. from E. 1964a by Elisabeth Camerling and Annie J. Blits.

FINNISH

1960a *Nykyhetki ja tulevaisuus.* Helsinki: Kirjayhtymä. pp. 102. Trans. from G. 1957i by Kaj Kauhanen.

1966a *Piilotajunnan psykologiaa.* (Forum Kirjaston, 13.) Helsinki: Tammi. pp. 158. Trans. from G. 1943a by Erkki Rutanen.

1974a *Job saa Vastauksen.* Helsinki: Kustannusosakeyhtiö Otava. pp. 159. Trans. from G. ?1961a by Sinikka Kallio.

FRENCH

1907a "Associations d'idées familiales." *Archs. psychol.*, VII:26 (Oct.), 160–68. The content of this paper considerably overlaps that of E. 1910a,2; in addition, "some material reused in ETH lectures, *Modern Psychology*, April 1934–July 1935."

1908a A summary of *Diagnostische Associationsstudien*, Vol. I. *Année psychologique*, XIV, 453–55. Summarized from G. 1906a. Each article summarized individually in 1 or 2 paragraphs.

1909a "L'Analyse des rêves." *Année psychologique*, XV, 160–67. TR.—English: CW 4,3.

1913a "Contribution à l'étude des types psychologiques." *Archs. psychol.*, XIII:52 (Dec.), 289–99. Lecture delivered to the Fourth Psychoanalytic Congress, Munich, 7–8 Sept. 1913, in German and then rev. into French by the author. Cf. GW 6,4 for the German version. TR.—English: 1916a,12.

1913b "La Psycho-analyse." *Encéphale*, VIII, 263–66. Summary of a report read in English to the 17th International Congress of Medicine, London, August 1913. Cf. E. 1916a,9.

1916a "La Structure de l'inconscient." *Archs. psychol.*, XVI:62 (Dec.), 152–79. Trans. by M. Marsen from a German ms. subsequently pub. as GW 7,4. Cf. Fr. 1938a for a trans. of a rev. version. Delivered in German as a lecture to the Zurich School of Analytical Psychology, 1916. TR.—English: CW 7,4 (1st edn.).

1928a *L'Inconscient dans la vie psychique normale et anormale*. Paris: Payot. pp. 190. Trans. from G. 1926a by E. Grandjean-Bayard. Cf. Fr. 1952a for trans. of rev. version.

1931a   *Essais de psychologie analytique.* Paris: Stock, Delamain et Boutel- leau. pp. 198. Trans. by Yves Le Lay. Cf. Fr. 1961b for a rev. and exp. version. Contents:

     1. "Les problèmes psychiques des différents âges de l'homme." (1–26) Trans. from G. 1930d. Cf. Fr. 1961b,8.

     2. "Le problème psychique de l'homme moderne." (27–59) Trans. from G. 1928f. Repub. as Fr. 1961b,6.

     3. "Le conditionnement terrestre de l'âme." (60–114) Trans. from G. 1927a. Repub. as Fr. 1961b,2 with title change.

     4. "La psychologie analytique dans ses rapports avec l'œuvre poétique." (115–46) Trans. from G. 1922a. Repub. as Fr. 1961b,13.

     5. "Le mariage, relation psychologique." (147–66) Trans. from G. 1925b. Repub. as Fr. 1961b,11.

     6. "La femme en Europe." (167–98) Trans. from G. 1929a. Re- pub. as Fr. 1961b,10.

1931b   **Métamorphoses et symboles de la libido.* Paris: Montaigne (Au- bier); Geneva: Kundig. pp. 488. Trans. from G. 1925a by Louis de Vos. Cf. Fr. 1953c for trans. of a rev. and exp. version.

1932a   **La théorie psychanalytique.* Paris: Montaigne (Aubier); Geneva: Kundig. pp. 125. Trans. from G. 1913a by Marthe Schmid-Guisan.

1932b   "La psychanalyse devant la poésie. Existe-t-il une poésie de signe 'freudien'?" *Journal des poètes,* III:5 (11 Dec.), 1. Written in Ger- man in reply to the question in the title and trans. by ?. Cf. CW 18,111.

1933a   "Sur la psychologie." *Revue d'Allemagne,* VII:70 (15 Aug.: "No. spécial sur C. G. Jung"), 690–708. Parts of G. 1933b trans. by —— Decourdemanche. Cf. Fr. 1944a,2.

1935a   *Conflits de l'âme enfantine. La rumeur.—L'influence du père.* Paris: Montaigne (Aubier). pp. 77. Trans. by L. de Vos and Olga Raesvsky. Cf. Fr. 1963a for trans. of rev. and exp. version. Contents:

     1. "Conflits de l'âme enfantine." (9–42) Trans. from G. 1916b by L. DeVos. Cf. Fr. 1963a,2.

     2. "Contribution à la psychologie de la 'rumeur publique'." (43– 58) Trans. from G. 1910g by Olga Raesvsky. Repub. as Fr. 1963a,3 with title change.

3. "L'influence du père sur la destinée de ses enfants." (59–77) Trans. from G. 1909c by Olga Raesvsky. Cf. Fr. 1963,4.

1938a *Le moi et l'inconscient.* (Psychologie, 5.) Paris: Gallimard. pp. 254. Trans. from G. 1935a by A. Adamov. Pub. in a dif. trans. with title change as Fr. 1964a. Cf. Fr. 1916a for trans. of earlier version.

1939a *Phénomènes occultes.* Paris: Montaigne (Aubier). pp. 122. Trans. by E. Godet and Yves Le Lay. Contents:
    1. Préface. (v–vii) Trans. from the German ms., written for this edn. Dated 1938. Cf. CW 18,5.
    2. "A propos de certains phénomènes dits occultes." (1–94) Trans. from G. 1902a. Cf. Fr. 1956a,4.
    3. "Âme et mort." (95–106) Trans. from G. 1934b,10. Cf. Fr. 1956a,5.
    4. "Croyance aux esprits." (107–22) Trans. from G. 1928b,5. Cf. Fr. 1956a,6.

1943a *L'homme à la découverte de son âme. Structure et fonctionnement de l'inconscient.* (Action et Pensée, 10.) Geneva: Éditions du Mont-Blanc. pp. 403. 1946: 2d edn., rev. & corrected. pp. 354. Trans. by R. Cahen-Salabelle. Pub., rev. & exp., as Fr. 1962a. Extract prepub. as Fr. 1944a. Contents:
    1. "Le problème fondamental de la psychologie contemporaine." (3–31) Trans. from G. 1934b,2. Cf. Fr. 1962a,1 for rev. version with title change.
    2. "La psychologie et le temps présent." (33–67) Trans. from G. 1934b,3. Cf. Fr. 1962a,2 for rev. version with title change and Fr. 1933a for trans. of extracts.
    †3. Conférence I: "Introduction à la psychologie analytique. Notions fondamentales, Pt. 1. Psychologie générale." (71–134) The 1st of 6 seminars given to the "Société de Psychologie," Basel, 1934, and at the Institute of Medical Psychology, London, 1935. The remainder follow as noted. Trans. from a lecture later pub. in E. 1968a. Cf. Fr. 1962a,3 for rev. version with title change.
    †4. Conférence II: "Introduction à la psychologie analytique. Notions fondamentales, Pt. II. Les complexes." (135–87) Trans. from a lecture later pub. in E. 1968a. Cf. Fr. 1962a,4 for rev. version with title change.

5. "Considérations générales sur la théorie des complexes." (189–211) Trans. from G. 1934a. Cf. Fr. 1962a,5 for trans. of rev. version.

6. "La psychologie du rêve." (215–80) Trans. from G. 1928b,3. Cf. Fr. 1962a,6 for trans. of rev. version.

7. "L'utilisation pratique de l'analyse onirique." (281–314) Trans. from G. 1934b,4. Repub., trans. rev., as Fr. 1962a,7.

†8. Conférences IV–VI: "Introduction à la psychologie analytique. Notions fondamentales, Pt. III. Les rêves." (315–400) Trans. from a lecture later pub. in E. 1968a. Cf. Fr. 1962a,8 for rev. version with title change.

9. "Epilogue." (401–03) Written for this edn. and dated Jan. 1944. Repub., trans. rev., as Fr. 1962a,9. TR.—English: CW 18,72.

TR.—Dutch: 1950a // Portuguese: 1962a.

† Items marked are composed of a seminar report edited by Dr. Cahen, who takes responsibility for the contents of these chapters.—M. F. (Cf. details above under item no. 3.)

1944a "L'expérience des associations." *Action et Pensée*, XX:1 (Feb.), 1–11. A prepub. extract of Fr. 1943a.

1945a "De la nature des rêves." *Revue Ciba* (Basel), 46 (Sept.), 1602–13. Trans. from G. 1945d by René Kaech. Pub. in a dif. trans., with title change, as Fr. 1953a,4.

1948a *Aspects du drame contemporain*. Geneva: Georg. pp. 233. Trans. from the German by Roland Cahen-Salabelle. Pub., exp. and trans. rev., as Fr. 1971a. Contents:

1. "Avertissement de l'auteur." (69–74) Written for this edn.

2. "Wotan." (75–106) Trans. from G. 1946a,2.

3. "Signification de la ligne suisse dans l'analyse spectrale de l'Europe." (107–32) Trans. from G. 1928e.

4. "Après la catastrophe." (133–90) Trans. from G. 1946a,5 in collaboration with M. B. Besson. Extracts pub. in Henri Stierlin, "Les solutions de Bertrand Russell et de Carl Gustav Jung." *Tribune de Genève* (19 July 1955). 1 p.

5. "Epilogue." (191–233) Trans. from G. 1946a,6.

1949a "Le yoga et l'occident." *Approches de l'Inde. Textes et études.* pp. 320–29. Ed. by Jacques Masui. Paris: Cahiers du Sud. Trans. from E. 1936c by ?.

1950a   *Types psychologiques.* Geneva: Georg; Paris: Albin Michel. pp. 523. 1958: 2d edn. Geneva: Georg; Paris: Buchet/Chastel. pp. 507. Trans. from G. 1921a by Yves Le Lay. Contents (paging of 1st edn.):

    1. Avant-propos. (1–2)
    2. Avant-propos de la 7e édition allemande. (3)
    3. Introduction. (5–9)
    4. Le problème des types dans l'histoire de la pensée antique et médiévale. (11–69)
    5. Les idées de Schiller sur le problème des types. (70–136)
    6. L'Apollinien et le Dionysien. (137–48)
    7. Le problème des types dans la connaissance des hommes. (149–68)
    8. Le problème des types dans la poésie. (169–277)
    9. Le problème des types dans la psychiatrie. (278–93)
    10. Le problème de l'attitude typique dans l'esthétique. (294–304)
    11. Le problème des types dans la philosophie moderne. (305–27)
    12. Le problème des types dans la biographie. (328–36)
    13. Description générale des types. (337–419)
    14. Définitions. (420–500)
    15. Epilogue. (501–510)

1950b   "Introduction." Jolan Jacobi: *La psychologie de C. G. Jung.* p. 12. Neuchâtel: Delachaux et Niestlé. 1964: Rev. and enl. edn. Geneva: Editions du Mont-Blanc. pp. 19–20. Trans. from G. 1940c by V. Baillods.

1952a   *Psychologie de l'inconscient.* Geneva: Georg; Paris: Buchet/Chastel. pp. 235. 1963: 2d edn. pp. 228. 1973: new edn. pp. 220. Trans. from G. 1943a by Roland Cahen. Cf. Fr. 1928a for trans. of earlier version.

1952b   "Préface." M. Esther Harding: *Réalité de l'âme. L'énergie psychique, son origine et son but.* pp. 7–8. Neuchâtel: La Baconnière. Trans. from E. 1947e by Elisabeth Huguenin.

1952c   "Psychothérapie pratique. Fondements généraux." *Encéphale,* XL, 407–30. A prepub. extract of Fr. 1953a,5.

1953a   *La guérison psychologique.* Geneva: Georg. pp. 337. 1970: Rev. edn. Geneva: Georg; Paris: Buchet/Chastel. pp. 342. Trans. by Roland Cahen. Contents:

    1. "Qu'est-ce que la psychothérapie?" (3–13) Trans. from G. 1935g.

2. "Médecine et psychothérapie." (14–28) Trans. from G. 1945e.

3. "Les problèmes de la psychothérapie moderne." (29–59) Trans. from G. 1931a,2.

4. "De la nature des rêves." (60–79) Trans. from G. 1945d. Pub. in a dif. trans. as Fr. 1945a.

5. "Psychothérapie pratique." (80–104) Trans. from G. 1935l. Excerpt prepub. as Fr. 1952c.

6. "Moyens et buts de la psychothérapie." (105–26) Trans. from G. 1931a,5.

7. "Des méthodes suggestives à la psychanalyse." (129–76) Trans. from G. 1914b.

8. "L'opposition entre Freud et Jung." (177–87) Trans. from G. 1931a,4.

9. "La névrose et l'auto-régulation psychologique." (188–208) Trans. from G. 1934k.

10. "Des images parentales au totalitarisme étatique." (209–30) Trans. from G. 1946a,3.

11. "Le relativisme essentiel de la psychothérapie." (231–51) Trans. from G. 1951d.

12. "Conscience, inconscient et individuation." (255–72) Trans. from G. 1939e.

13. "Des rapports de la psychothérapie et de la direction de conscience." (273–300) Trans. from G. 1932a.

14. "Psychothérapie et conception du monde." (301–11) Trans. from G. 1946a,4.

1953b With Charles Kerényi: *Introduction à l'essence de la mythologie. L'enfant divin.—La jeune fille divine.* Paris: Payot. pp. 221. Trans. from G. 1951b by Henri E. Del Medico.

1953c *Métamorphoses de l'âme et ses symboles.* . . . Geneva: Georg. pp. 770. 1967: Repr. Geneva: Georg; Paris: Buchet/Chastel. pp. 770. Trans. from G. 1952e by Yves Le Lay. Cf. Fr. 1931b for trans. of earlier version.

1953d "Introduction." M. Esther Harding: *Les mystères de la femme dans les temps anciens et modernes.* pp. 5–7. Paris: Payot. Trans. from G. 1949d by Eveline Mahyere.

1954a "Avant-propos." John Custance: *Le livre de la sagesse et de la folie.* pp. 7-11. Paris: Plon. Trans. from E. 1952a by Michel Tournier.

1954b "C. G. Jung et l'astrologie." *Astrologie moderne*. Pub. here in the form of an "Interview du 26 Mai 1954 de André Barbault et Jean Carteret" but actually taken from a letter in French to André Barbault (26 May 1954), written in response to a questionnaire. Letter trans. as E. 1970d and in E. 1976a.

1955a "Psychologie et poésie." *Le Disque vert: C. G. Jung*. pp. 9–39. Brussels: Le Disque vert. 1964: Facsimile. (Les Cahiers pensée et action, 23/24, Jan.–May.) Paris, Brussels: Editions "Pensée et Action." Trans. from G. 1950a,2 by Roland Cahen. Repub. as Fr. 1961b,12. TR.—Turkish: 1964a.

1955b "Devenir de la personnalité." *Synthèses: Revue Européenne* (Brussels), 10th yr: 115 (Dec.), 354–72. Trans. from G. 1934b,9 by Yves Le Lay. Repub. as Fr. 1961b,9.

1956a *L'Énergétique psychique*. Geneva: Georg; Paris: Albin Michel?. pp. 253. Trans. by Yves Le Lay. Contents:
   1. "Énergétique psychique." (17–93) Trans. from G. 1948b,2.
   2. "Instinct et inconscient." (94–105) Trans. from G. 1948b,6.
   3. "Contribution à la connaissance du rêve de nombres." (107–17) Trans. from G. 1911e.
   4. "Psychologie et pathologie des phénomènes dits occultes." (118–218) Trans. from G. 1902a. Cf. Fr. 1939a,2.
   5. "Âme et mort." (219–31) Trans. from G. 1934b,10. Cf. Fr. 1939a,3.
   6. "Fondements psychologiques de la croyance aux esprits." (232–52) Trans. from G. 1948b. Cf. Fr. 1939a,4.

1956b Letters to Père Bruno. Père Bruno de Jésus-Marie, with the collaboration of Ch. Baudouin, C. G. Jung, and R. Laforgue: "Puissance de l'archétype." pp. 13–18. *Élie le prophète*. Vol. II, pp. 11–33. Ed. by Père Bruno de Jésus-Marie. (Les Études Carmélitaines.) Paris: Desclée de Brouwer. Written in French to Père Bruno and dated 5 Nov. 1953 (pp. 13–17) and 22 Dec. 1953 (error for 1954) (pp. 17–18). TR.—English: CW 18,98.

1957a "Préface." Gerhard Adler: *Essais sur la théorie et pratique de l'analyse jungienne*. pp. 3–6. Geneva: Georg. Trans. from G. 1952g by Liliane Fearn and Jenny Leclerq.

1957b   "Le problème du quatrième." *La Table Ronde*, 120 (Dec.), 183–96. Trans., slightly abridged, from G. 1948a,4, "Das Problem des Vierten," by Yves Le Lay. The 1st of 2 pts. Cf. Fr. 1958c.

1958a   With Paul Radin and Charles Kerényi: *Le fripon divin. Un mythe indien.* (Analyse et Synthèse, 3.) Geneva: Georg; Paris: Buchet/ Chastel. pp. 205. Trans. from G. 1954a by Arthur Reiss. Contains the following work by Jung:
    1. "Contribution à l'étude de la psychologie du fripon." (175–99)

1958b   *Psychologie et religion.* Paris: Buchet/Chastel, Corrêa. pp. 220. Trans. from G. 1940a by Marthe Bernson and Gilbert Cahen.

1958c   "Le problème du quatrième." (Pt. 2.) *La Table Ronde*, 121 (Jan.), 89–101. Trans., slightly abridged, from G. 1948a,4, "Das Problem des Vierten," by Yves Le Lay. The 2d of 2 pts. Cf. Fr. 1957b.

1958d   "Hors des lieux communs." *Le Jura libre*, 8 Aug. 1 p.

1959a   "Préface." Georges Duplain: *Aux frontières de la connaissance. Entretien avec le professeur C.-G. Jung à propos d'une étude sur les "soucoupes volantes."* Lausanne: Gazette de Lausanne. 1 p. (t.p. verso) Reprint ("separatum") of interview by Duplain, pub. in the *Gazette*, Aug. 24, Sept. 1 and 8, 1959, with addition of Jung's "Préface," which appears only in this reprint, not in the original articles. TR.—English: *C. G. Jung Speaking* (1977), pp. 410–11.

1960a   "Commentaire psychologique." *Le livre tibétain de la grande libération.* pp. 15–49. Ed. by W. Y. Evans-Wentz. Paris: Adyar. Trans. from E. 1957e by Margurite La Fuente, with the assistance of Constance Lounsbery.

1960b   *"Psychoanalyse d'une réalité: l'âme." Arts, Lettres, Spectacles, Musique*, 790 (5–11 Oct.), 1–2. An excerpt of Fr. 1961b, prepub. TR.—Slovenian: 1961a.

1961a   *Un mythe moderne. Des "signes du ciel."* (Les Essais, XCVIII.) Paris: Gallimard. pp. 306. Trans. from G. 1958a by Roland Cahen, with the collaboration of René and Françoise Baumann.

1961b *Problèmes de l'âme moderne.* Paris: Buchet/Chastel, Corrêa. pp. 466. Trans. by Yves Le Lay, with the exception of no. 12 below, as noted. Fr. 1931a, rev. and exp. Excerpt prepub. as Fr. 1960b. Contents:

Pt. I: L'Âme et l'esprit.
1. "La structure de l'âme." (11–38) Trans. from G. 1931a,7.
2. "Âme et terre." (39–67) Fr. 1931a,3 repub. with title change.
3. "L'esprit et la vie." (69–94) Trans. from G. 1931a,13.
4. "Psychologie analytique et conception du monde (Weltanschauung)." (95–129) Trans. from G. 1931a,12.

Pt. II: L'Homme et l'existence.
5. "L'homme archaïque." (133–64) Trans. from G. 1931a,9.
6. "Le problème psychique de l'homme moderne." (165–93) Fr. 1931a,2 repub.
7. "Typologie psychologique." (195–219) Trans. from G. 1931a,6.
8. "Au solstice de la vie." (221–43) Trans. from G. 1931a,10. Cf. Fr. 1931a,1.
9. "Le devenir de la personnalité." (245–70) Fr. 1955b repub.

Pt. III: La Femme et le couple.
10. "La femme en Europe." (273–300) Fr. 1931a,6 repub.
11. "Le mariage, relation psychologique." (301–17) Fr. 1931a,5 repub.

Pt. IV: La Poésie et l'art.
12. "Psychologie et poésie." (321–52) Trans. by Roland Cahen. Fr. 1955a repub. Repub. as Fr. 1964d.
13. "La psychologie analytique dans ses rapports avec l'oeuvre poétique." (353–80) Fr. 1931a,4 repub.
14. "Paracelse." (381–93) Trans. from G. 1934b,5.
15. "Freud." (395–405) Trans. from G. 1934b,6.
16. "Ulysse." (407–39) Trans. from G. 1934b,7.
17. "Picasso." (441–49) Trans. from G. 1934b,8.

1961c "Préface." Jolande Jacobi: *Complexe, archétype, symbole.* pp. 5–6. Neuchâtel: Delachaux et Niestlé. Trans. from G. 1957g by Jacques Chavy.

1961d **"Réponse à la question du bilinguisme." Flinker Almanac 1961.* pp. 21. Paris: Librairie Française et Etrangère. Letter to the editor, Martin Flinker, written in response to a question. TR.—English: CW 18,123.

1962a *L'homme à la découverte de son âme. Structure et fonctionnement de l'inconscient.* (Action et Pensée, 10.) 6th edn., rev. and exp. Geneva: Éditions du Mont-Blanc. pp. 354. 1963: Reset. (Petite Bibliothèque Payot, 53.) Paris: Payot. pp. 341. (Lacks index.) Trans. by Roland Cahen. Fr. 1943a, rev. and exp. Contents (pagination of 1962 and 1963 edns. respectively):

Livre I: Exposition.

1. "Visages de l'âme contemporaine." (49–68) (35–56) Fr. 1944a,1, trans. rev. and with title change.
2. "Reconquête de la conscience." (69–93) (57–83) Fr. 1944a,2, trans. rev. and with title change.

Livre II: Les Complexes.

3. "Fonctions et structures du conscient et de l'inconscient." (97–142) (85–133) Fr. 1944a,3, rev. and with title change.
4. "L'expérience des associations." (143–80) (135–74) Fr. 1944a,4, rev. and with title change.
5. "Théorie des complexes." (181–97) (175–92) Trans. from G. 1948b,3. Cf. Fr. 1944a,5 for trans. of earlier version.

Livre III: Les Rêves.

6. "Les enseignements du rêve." (201–46) (193–243) Trans. from G. 1948b,4. Cf. Fr. 1944a,6 for trans. of earlier version.
7. "Signification individuelle du rêve." (247–71) (245–71) Fr. 1944a,7 repub., trans. rev., with title change.
8. "Du rêve au mythe." (273–332) (273–337) Fr. 1944a,8 rev., with title change.
9. "Épilogue." (333–34) (339–40) Fr. 1944a,9 repub., trans. rev.

TR.—Spanish: 1969a.

1962b *Présent et avenir.* Paris: Buchet/Chastel. pp. 213. 1970: Paris: Denoël, Gonthier. pp. 189. Trans. from G. 1957i by Roland Cahen, with the collaboration of René and Françoise Baumann. Extract prepub. as "Malheur à l'homme normal dans le monde moderne." *Arts, Lettres, Spectacles, Musique,* 881 (12–18 Sept.), 9.

1963a *Psychologie et éducation.* Paris: Buchet/Chastel. pp. 266. Trans. by Yves Le Lay, with the collaboration of L. de Vos and Olga Raesvski. Cf. Fr. 1935a for trans. of earlier version. Contents:

1. "Psychologie analytique et éducation." (11–117) Trans. from G. 1946b,1 by Yves Le Lay.
2. "Conflits de l'âme enfantine." (119–77) Trans. from G. 1946b,2 by L. de Vos. Cf. Fr. 1935a,1.

3. "La rumeur." (179–204) Fr. 1935a,2 repub. with title change.

4. "De l'importance du père pour la destinée de l'individu." (205–40) Trans. from G. 1949a by Olga Raesvski; trans. rev. and completed by Yves Le Lay. Cf. Fr. 1935a,3.

5. "L'enfant doué." (241–59) Trans. from G. 1946b,3 by Yves Le Lay.

1963b *L'âme et la vie. Ouvrages de C.-G. Jung.* Compiled and ed. by Jolande Jacobi. Paris: Buchet/Chastel. pp. 534. Trans. from G. 1945a by Roland Cahen and Yves Le Lay.

1964a *Dialectique du moi et de l'inconscient.* (Les Essais, CXIII.) Paris: Gallimard. pp. 334. 1973: rev. and corr. edn. pp. 274. Trans. from G. 1935a by Roland Cahen. Pub. in a dif. trans. with title change as Fr. 1938a.

1964b *Réponse à Job.* Paris: Buchet/Chastel. pp. 301. 1971: new edn. Trans. from G. 1952a by Roland Cahen.

1964c * "Essai d'exploration de l'inconscient." *L'Homme et ses symboles.* pp. 18–103. Conceived and realized by C. G. Jung and M.-L. von Franz, Joseph L. Henderson, Jolande Jacobi, Aniela Jaffé. Paris: Editions Laffont. pp. 320. Also pub. as paperback monograph: *Essai d'exploration de l'inconscient.* Paris: Editions Gonthier. pp. 155. Trans. from E. 1964a by Laure Deutschmeister.

1964d "Psychologie et poésie." *Le Disque Vert: C. G. Jung.* pp. 9–39. (Les cahiers Pensée et Action, 23–24.) Brussels, Paris: Le Disque Vert. Fr. 1961b,12 repub.

1964e Letters to Richard Evans. Richard I. Evans: *Entretiens avec Jung.* Paris: Payot. pp. 144. Trans. from E. 1964b by Philip Coussy. Contains 2 letters dated April 1957 and one dated 30 May 1957 (and a lengthy interview).

1966a "Ma vie." *Souvenirs, rêves et pensées.* Recorded and ed. by Aniela Jaffé. (Collection "Témoins.") Paris: Gallimard. pp. 464. 1973: new edn. with index. (Coll. Vécu.) pp. 528. Trans. from G. 1962a by Roland Cahen and Yves Le Lay, with the collaboration of Salomé Burckhardt. Contents conform to those of G. 1962a with the omission of G. 1962a,15, x: "Septem sermones ad mortuos."

1970a *Psychologie et alchimie.* Paris: Buchet/Chastel. pp. 705. Trans. from G. 1952d by Henry Pernet and Roland Cahen.

1971a *Aspects du drame contemporain.* Geneva: Georg; Paris: Buchet/ Chastel. pp. 270. Trans. by Roland Cahen. Fr. 1948a, exp. and trans. rev. Contents:

    1–3 as in Fr. 1948a with the addition of:

        4. "La Conscience morale d'un point de vue psychologique." Trans. from G. 1958c.

1971b *Racines de la conscience.* Paris: Buchet/Chastel. pp. 630. Trans. from G. 1954b by Yves Le Lay and Etienne Perrot.

1975a With Sigmund Freud: *Correspondance.* Edited by William Mc-Guire. (Collection "Connaissance de l'inconscient," directed by J.-B. Pontalis.) Paris: Gallimard. Vol. I, pp. 365; Vol. II, pp. 409. Trans. from G. 1974a and E. 1974b by Ruth Fivaz-Silbermann.

GREEK

1935a   *Charakteres e Psychologikoi Typoi.* Athens: Embo Tinos oinos . . . pp. ? Trans. from G. 1921a by ? Cf. Gr. 1954a.

1949a   *To Themeliōdes Problēma tēs Synchrones Psychologias.* Athens: Avgi. pp. 72. Trans. from G. ?1931a,14 by K. L. Méranaios.

1950a   *Eisagōgē stēn Analytikē Psychologia.* Athens: Avgi. pp. 160. Trans. from G. ? by K. L. Méranaios and Minas Zographou.

1954a   *Psychologikoi Typoi.* Athens: Maris. pp. 480. Trans. from G. 1921a by Minas Zographou and K. L. Méranaios. Cf. Gr. 1935a.

1956a   *E Psychologia tou Asyneidetou.* Athens: Karavia. pp. 160. Trans. from ?G. 1943a by K. B. Nikolaou. Pub. in a dif. trans. as Gr. 1962a,1.

1962a   *Analytike Psychologia.* Athens: Kovostes. pp. 288. Trans. by Pen Ieromnemonos. Contents:
1. "E. Psychologia tou Asyneidetou." Trans. from G. ?1943a. Pub. in a dif. trans. as Gr. 1956a.
2. "Scheseis Metaxy tou 'Ego' kai tou Asyneidetou." Trans. from G. ? 1935a.

1962b   *Psychologia kai Threskeia.* Athens: Maris. pp. 160. Trans. from G. 1940a by K. L. Méranaios.

1962c   *Ta Problemata tes Synchrones Psyches.* Athens: Bibliotheke ïia Olous. pp. ? Trans. from ?G. 1931a by E. Androvliake.

HEBREW

1950/51a "Alkhimiah we-psykhologiah." *Encyclopaedia Hebraica*. Vol. 3, pp. 606–08. Jerusalem: Encyclopedia Publishing Co. Written especially for this volume and trans. by a member of the editorial board from the English text pub., slightly rev., as CW 18,106.

1958a *Psykhologiah analytit we-khinukh.* Tel Aviv: Dvir. pp. 143. Trans. from G. 1946b by Netta Blech. Contains a foreword dated 1955 especially written for this edition. TR.—English: (foreword only) CW 18,133.

1973a *Ha-any we-ha-lo-muda.* Tel Aviv: Dvir. pp. 140. Trans. from G. 1935a by Haym Yzak.

1973b *Ha-psykhologiah shel ha-lo-muda.* Tel Aviv: Dvir. pp. 115. Trans. from G. 1943a by Haym Yzak.

1974a "Ma-amar Jung le-ktav Mishmar be-shweits lifnei 29 shanim." *Al Hamishmar*, 15 Nov. [What did Jung say to *Mishmar*'s correspondent in Switzerland 29 years ago?] Trans. by an unknown hand from a letter written in German to Eugen Kolb (14 Sept. 1945), Swiss correspondent for *Al Hamishmar*, in response to questions on Hitler. Cf. CW 18,74.

HUNGARIAN

1948a *Bevezetés a tudattalan pszichológiájába.* Budapest: Bibliotheca. pp. 177. Trans. from G. 1943a by Peter Nagy. Contains a foreword written especially for the Hungarian edn., dated Jan. 1944. Cf. CW 18,36.

ITALIAN

1908a "Le nuove vedute della psicologia criminale. Contributo al metodo della 'Diagnosi della conoscenza del fatto' (Tatbestandsdiagnose)." *Rivista di psicologia applicata*, IV:4 (July–Aug.), 285–304. Trans. from a German ms. by L. Baroncini. Partially incorporated into E. 1910a,1. TR.—English: CW 2,16 // German: GW 2,16.

1936a With Richard Wilhelm: *Il mistero del fiore d'oro*. Bari: Laterza. pp. 154. Trans. from G. 1929b by Mario Gabrieli.

1942a *Il problema dell'inconscio nella psicologia moderna*. (La cultura, 51.) Turin: Einaudi. pp. 297. Trans. from G. 1931a by Arrigo Vita and Giovanni Bollea. Pub. with the addn. of a foreword as It. 1959c.

1946a "Picasso alla luce della psicologia analitica." *Lettere ed arti*, II:6, 8–13. Trans. from G. 1934b,8 by C. L. Musatti.

1947a *Psicologia e educazione*. (Psiche e coscienza, 8.) Rome: Astrolabio. pp. 147. Trans. from G. 1946b by Roberto Bazlen.

1947b *Sulla psicologia dell'inconscio*. (Psiche e coscienza, 3.) Rome: Astrolabio. pp. 153. Trans. from G. 1943a by B. Veneziani and M. Vivarelli. Pub. in a dif. trans., with title change, as It. 1968a.

1947c Introduction to M. Esther Harding: *La strada della donna*. pp. 12–15. (Psiche e coscienza, 7.) Rome: Astrolabio. Trans. from E. 1933b by Adriana and Tomaso Carini.

1948a *L'io e l'inconscio*. Turin: Einaudi. pp. 156. Repub. 1967, Turin: Boringhieri. Trans. from G. 1935a by Arrigo De Vita.

1948b With K. Kerényi: *Prolegomeni allo studio scientifico della mitologia*. Turin: Einaudi. pp. 250. 1964, Turin: Boringhieri. pp. 257. Trans. from G. 1941c by Angelo Brelich.

1948c   *Psicologia e religione.* Milan: Edizioni di Comunità. pp. 151. Trans. from G. 1940a by Bruno Veneziani.

1948d   *Tipi psicologici.* (Psiche e coscienza, 5.) Rome: Astrolabio. pp. 523. Trans. from G. 1921a by Cesare L. Musatti. Pub., trans. rev., as It. 1969a.

1948e   Introduction to Frances G. Wickes: *Il mondo psichico dell'infanzia.* pp. 15–22. Rome: Astrolabio. Trans. from G. 1931e by Olga Aquarone.

1949a   *Psicologia e alchimia.* (Psiche e coscienza, 12.) Rome: Astrolabio. pp. 535. Trans. from G. 1944a by Roberto Bazlen.

1949b   *La realtà dell'anima.* (Psiche e coscienza, 4.) Rome: Astrolabio. pp. 210. Trans. from G. 1934b by Paolo Santarcangeli. Repub. with additions as It. 1963a. Excerpts pub. as It. 1961c.

1949c   Foreword to Jolande Jacobi: *La psicologia di Carl G. Jung.* pp. [11–12]. Turin: Einaudi. Trans. from G. 1940c by Arrigo Vita.

1950a   "Prefazione alla traduzione inglese . . ." *I King.* pp. 11–28. Rome: Astrolabio. Trans. by Bruno Veneziani from the German ms. pub. as GW 11,16.

1959a   *La simbolica dello spirito.* Turin: Einaudi. pp. 349. Trans. from G. 1948a by Olga Bovero Caporali.

1959b   "Lo spirito della psicologia." *Questa è la mia filosofia.* Ed. by Whit Burnett. pp. 163–229. Milan: Bompiani. Trans. from E. 1957e by Gianni Di Benedetto.

1959c   *Il problema dell'inconscio nella psicologia moderna.* Turin: Einaudi. It. 1942a repub. with the addn. of a foreword to this Italian repr. dated March 1959. Only Jung's typescript has been seen. Poss. reissued 1964. pp. 307. TR.—(Foreword only) English: CW 18,68.

1960a   *Su cose che si vedono nel cielo.* Milan: Bompiani. pp. 193. Trans. from G. 1958a by Silvano Daniele.

1961a "Presentazione." Eleanor Bertine: *Le relazioni tra le persone.* pp. 7–9. Milan: Ed. di Comunità. Trans. from G. 1957d by Margherita Allievi Clerici.

1961b "Premessa." Frieda Fordham: *Introduzione a Carl Gustav Jung.* pp. 19–20. Florence: Ed. Universitaria. Trans. from E. 1959d by Vera Nozzoli.

1961c "L'individuo e la massa nel pensiero di Carl G. Jung. Il rischio della personalità." *Espresso* (18 June), 4 pp. Excerpts of It. 1949b.

?1962a *La psicologia del transfert.* Rome: Mondadori. pp. 184. 1962: Milan: Il Saggiatore. 1963: Milan: Club degli Editori. pp. 188. 1968: New edn. Milan: Il Saggiatore. pp. 236. Trans. from G. 1946c by Silvano Daniele.

1963a *Realtà dell'anima.* (Biblioteca de cultura scientifica. Serie viola, 36.) Turin: Boringhieri. pp. 262. Trans. by Paolo Santarcangeli. It. 1949b repub. with addns. Contents:
   1. "Il problema fondamentale della psicologia contemporanea." (10–35) Repub. from It. 1949b.
   2. "Il significato della psicologia per i tempi moderni." (36–63) Repub. from It. 1949b.
   3. "L'applicabilità pratica dell'analisi dei sogni." (64–92) Repub. from It. 1949b.
   4. "La donna in Europa." (93–118) Trans. from G. 1929a.
   5. "Paracelso." (119–30) Repub. from It. 1949b.
   6. "Sigmund Freud come fenomeno culturale." (131–40) Repub. from It. 1949b.
   7. "Ulisse—Monolog." (141–71) Repub. from It. 1949b.
   8. "Picasso." (172–79) Repub. from It. 1949b.
   9. "Anima e morte." (180–93) Repub. from It. 1949b.
   10. "Presente e futuro." (194–262) Trans. from G. 1957i.
   Note: Omits a trans. of G. 1934b,9.

1965a With Paul Radin and Karl Kerényi: *Il briccone divino.* Milan: Bompiani. pp. 234. Trans. from G. 1954a by Nini Dalmasso and Silvano Daniele. Contains the following work by Jung:
   1. "Contributo allo studio psicologico della figura del Briccone." (175–201)

1965b *La libido. Simboli e trasformazioni.* (Opere di C. G. Jung, 5.) Turin: Boringhieri. pp. 602. Trans. from G. 1952e by Renato Raho. Cf. It. 1970a and 1975d.

1965c *Ricordi, sogni, riflessioni.* Recorded and ed. by Aniela Jaffé. (La cultura, 104.) Milan: Il Saggiatore. pp. 432. Trans. from E. 1962a by Guido Russo. Contents conform to those of E. 1962a with the omission of E. 1962a,18, "Richard Wilhelm."

1965d *Risposta a Giobbe.* Milan: Il Saggiatore. pp. 188. Trans. from G. 1952a by Alfredo Viz.

1967a "Introduzione all'inconscio." *L'uomo e i suoi simboli.* pp. 18–103. Ed. by C. G. Jung, and after his death M.-L. von Franz. Florence: Casini. pp. 320. Trans. from E. 1964a by Roberto Tatucci.

1968a *Psicologia dell'inconscio.* Turin: Boringhieri. pp. 185. Trans. from G. 1943a by Silvano Daniele. Also pub. in a dif. trans. with change of title as It. 1947b.

1969a *Tipi psicologici.* (Opere di C. G. Jung, 6.) Turin: Boringhieri. pp. 606. Trans. from GW 6 by Cesare Luigi Musatti and Luigi Aurigemma. It. 1948d repub., trans. rev. Cf. It. 1972d,8.

1970a *Simboli della trasformazione.* (Opere di C. G. Jung, 5.) Turin: Boringhieri. pp. 581. Trans. from G. 1952e by Renato Raho. Cf. It. 1965b and 1975d.

1970b *Studi psichiatrici.* (Opere di C. G. Jung, 1.) Turin: Boringhieri. pp. 258. Trans. from GW 1 by Guido Bistolfi.

1971a *Psicogenesi delle malattie mentali.* (Opere di C. G. Jung, 3.) Turin: Boringhieri. pp. 307. Trans. from GW 3 by Lucia Personeni and Luigi Aurigemma.

1972a With Károly Kerényi: *Prolegomeni allo studio scientifico della mitologia.* (Universale scientifica, 74.) Turin: Boringhieri. pp. 267. Trans. from G. 1951b by Angelo Brelich. Contains the following works by Jung:
   1. "Psicologia dell'archetipo del Fanciullo."
   2. "Aspetto psicologico della figura di Kore."

1972b "Prefazione." Jolande Jacobi: *Complesso archetipo simbolo.* pp. 7–9. Turin: Boringhieri. pp. 201. Trans. from G. 1957g by Giuseppe Zappone.

1973a *Freud e la psicoanalisi.* (Opere di C. G. Jung, 4.) Turin: Boringhieri. pp. 397. Trans. from GW 4 by Lucia Personeni and Silvano Daniele. Pts. pub. in a dif. trans. as It. 1971d.

1974a With Sigmund Freud: *Lettere tra Freud e Jung.* Ed. by William McGuire with the collaboration of Wolfgang Sauerländer. Turin: Boringhieri. pp. 645. Jung's letters trans. from G. 1974a by Silvano Daniele. Conforms to G. 1974a and E. 1974b with the following omissions: "Acknowledgments," "Appendix 1," the Freud and Jung entries in the index, and 1 photo and 2 facsimiles. Additions consist of the last appendix (6) and a chronological table.

See addenda at the end of this volume.

JAPANESE

Entries marked † are taken from photocopies of title pages and tables of contents collected, transliterated, and identified by Mihoko Okamura.

1926a *Jung ronbunshu, renso jikkenho sonota.* (Kinsei hentai. Shinrigaku taikan, 10.) Tokyo: Nihon seishin igakkai and Nihon hentai shinrigaku taikan. pp. 302. 7 articles trans. from E. 1916a by Kokyo Nakamura.

1931b *Seimeiryoku no hatten.* (Sekai dai-shiso zenshu, 44.) Tokyo: Shunjusha. pp. 298. Trans. from E. 1916b by Kokyo Nakamura.

1955a † *Gendaijin no tamashii.* (Jung chosakushu, 2.) Tokyo: Nihon kyobun-sha. pp. 307. Trans. from G. 1931a by Yoshitaka Takahashi and Senjirō Eno. Consists of 1–3,7–9,11,13, and 14.

1955b *Kokoro no kôzô—kindai shinrigaku no oyo to shinpo.* (Jung chosakushu, 3.) Tokyo: Nihon kyōbun-sha. pp. 254. Trans. from G. 1934b,1–4,6–10 by Senjirō Eno.

1956a † *Ningen shinri to kyōiku.* (Jung chosakushu, 5.) Tokyo: Nihon kyōbun-sha. pp. 253. Trans. from G. 1946b and 1948a,2 by Shihō Nishimaru. Contains the following works by Jung:
   1. "Bunsekiteki shinrigaku to kyoiku." Trans. from G. 1946b,1.
   2. "Kodomo no kokoro no katto ni tsuite." Trans. from G. 1946b,2.
   3. "Shusai." Trans. from G. 1946b,3.
   4. "Otogo-banashi no seishin no gensho-gaku." Trans. from G. 1948a,2.

1956b †*Ningen shinri to shūkyō.* (Jung chosakushu, 4.) Tokyo: Nihon kyōbun-sha. pp. 306. Trans. by Sakae Hamakawa. Contains the following works by Jung:
   1. "Ningen shinri to shūkyō." Trans. from G. 1940a.
   2. "Toyo-teki meiso no shinri." Trans. from G. 1948a,5.
   3. "Yoroppa no josei." Trans. from G. 1929a.

1957a † *Ningen no taipu.* (Jung chosakushu, 1.) Tokyo: Nihon kyōbun-sha. pp. 305. Trans. from G. 1921a,X–XII, by Yoshitaka Takahashi.

1972a *Yungu Jiden: Omoide, Yume, Shiso.* Vol. 1. Tokyo: Misuzo Shobo. pp. 290. Trans. from E. 1967a and/or G. 1962a by Hayao Kawai, Akira Fujinawa, and Yoshiko Idei.

1973a *Yungu Jiden: Omoide, Yume, Shiso.* Vol. 2. Tokyo: Misuzu Shobo. pp. 284. Trans. from E. 1967a and/or G. 1962a by Hayao Kawai, Akira Fujinawa, and Yoshiko Idei.

NORWEGIAN

1956a "Om Sigmund Freud." *Horisont*, 2:7 (Oct.), 225–29. Trans. from G. 1939d by André Bjerke.

1963a *Det ubevisste.* (Cappelens realbøker, 4.) Oslo: Cappelen. pp. 140. Trans. from G. 1943a by Carl-Martin Borgen.

1964a Foreword to Frieda Fordham: *Innføring i Jungs psykologi.* pp. 5–6. Oslo: Gyldendal. Trans. from E. 1953d by Jan Brøgger.

1965a *Psykologi og religion.* Oslo: Cappelen. pp. 140. Trans. from G. 1940a by Hedvig Wergeland.

1966a *Jeg'et og det ubevisste.* Oslo: Cappelen. pp. 144. Trans. from G. 1935a by Hedvig Wergeland.

1966b *Mitt liv. Minner, drømmer, tanker.* Recorded and ed. by Aniela Jaffé. (Fakkel-bok, 88.) Oslo: Gyldendal. pp. 280. Trans. from G. 1962a by Ole Grepp. Contents conform to those of G. 1962a, except that G. 1962a,9–11 are combined into one chapter. "Drømmer og visjoner," and the appendix consists solely of G. 1962a,15,ii.

1966c *Nåtid og fremtid.* Oslo: Cappelen. pp. 88. Trans. from G. 1957i by Hedvig Wergeland.

1967a *Psykologi og oppdragelse.* (Ugle-bøkene, 2.) Oslo: Cappelen. pp. 132. Trans. from G. 1946b by Trond Winje.

1968a *Psykisk energi.* (Ugle-bøkene, 15.) Oslo: Cappelen. pp. 195. Trans. from G. 1948b by Hedvig Wergeland.

1969a *Psykens Verden.* (Ugle-bøkene, 22.) Oslo: Cappelen. pp. 116. Trans. from G. 1954c by Hedvig Wergeland.

1969b *Svar på Job.* (Ugle-bøkene, 35.) Oslo: Cappelen. pp. 116. Trans. from G. 1952a by Hedvig Wergeland.

1972a *Analytisk psykologi.* Oslo: Cappelen. pp. 234. Trans. from G. 1969a by Trond Winje.

PORTUGUESE

1947a "A natureza dos sonhos." *Actas Ciba* (Rio de Janeiro), XIV:2/3 (Feb.–Mar.), 51–63. Trans. from G. 1945d. Repub. as Port. 1948a in a trans. identical save for minor verbal differences.

1948a "Da natureza dos sonhos." *Actas Ciba* (Lisbon), IV (Jan.), 132–43. Trans. from G. 1945d by Teresa Bandara. Port. 1947a repub. in a trans. identical save for minor verbal differences.

1956a *Psicologia e religião*. Rio de Janeiro: Zahar. pp. 119. Trans. from G. 1940a by Fausto Guimarães.

1961a *O eu desconhecido*. Rio de Janeiro: Editora Fundo de Cultura. pp. 131. Trans. from E. 1958b by Fausto Cunha.

1962a *O homem à descoberta da alma*. (Filosofia e religiao [new series], 15.) Porto: Livraria Tavares Martins. pp. 507. Trans. from Fr. 1944a by Camilo Alves Pais.

?1962b *Um mito moderno*. Lisbon: Minotauro. pp. 293. Trans. from G. 1958a by José Blanc de Portugal. Book lacks date.

1962c *Psicologia e educação*. Rio de Janeiro: Fundo de Cultura. pp. ?. Trans. from ?G. 1946b by ?.

1964a "Prologo." Victor White: *Deus e a psicanálise*. pp. 15–32. (Circulo de humanismo cristão. Pessoa e cultura, 7.) Lisbon: Morais. Trans. from E. 1952c by Belmiro Masino Figueiro. Frei's appendix also contains extracts from letters written by Jung to the author.

1967a *Acerca da psicologia do inconsciente*. Lisbon: Ediçöes Delfos. pp. 206. Trans. from G. 1943a by Ingrid Bauner Trigo Trinidade.

1967b *Tipos psicológicos*. Rio de Janeiro: Zahar. pp. 567. Trans. from G. 1921a by Álvaro Cabral.

1967c *Sobre a psicologia do inconsciente.* Lisbon: Delfos. pp. ??. Trans. from G. 19?? by ?.

1972a *Fundamentos de psicologia analitica.* Petropolis, Brazil: Vozes. pp. 239. Trans. from E. 1968a by Araceli Elman.

1975a *Memórias, Sonhos, Reflexões.* Rio de Janeiro: Nova Frontiera. pp. 360. Trans. from 1962a by Dora Ferreira da Silva.

RUSSIAN

1909a *Psikhoz i ego soderzhanie.* St. Petersburg: Obshchestvennaia Pol'za. pp. 32. Trans. from G. 1908a by Vera Epelbaum. Cf. Rus. 1939a for trans. of later version (G. 1914a).

1924a *Psikhologicheskie tipy.* Moscow: Moskovskoie Gosudarstvennoie Izdatel'stvo. pp. 96. Trans. from a part of G. 1921a by E. I. Ruzer. Entire work pub. in a dif. trans. as Rus. 1929a.

1929a *Psikhologicheskie tipy.* Ed. by Emil Medtner. (Izbrannye trudy po analititcheskoi psikhologii, 1.) Berlin: Petropolis ("Musaget"). pp. 475. Trans. from G. 1921a by Sophia Lorie. Parts of G. 1921a pub. in a dif. trans. as Rus. 1924a.

1939a *Psikhologiya dementia praecox; Konflikty dietskoi dushi; Psikhoz i ego soderzhianie, i drugiia stat'i.* Ed. by Emil Medtner. (Izbrannye trudy po analititcheskoi psikhologii.) Paris: Les Éditeurs Réunis. pp. 365. Trans. from G. 1907a, 1910k, 1914a, 1902a, and "4 short papers (mainly on diagnostic methods) originally published between 1902 and 1914" by Olga Raevskaia, et al. "A Publication of the Psychology Club, Zurich." Cf. Rus. 1909a for trans. of an earlier version of G. 1914a.

SERBO-CROATIAN

1938a *Psihološki tipovi.* (Karijatide. Filozofska Biblioteka, 5.) Belgrade: Kosmos. pp. 411. 1963: 2d edn. (Karijatide. Filozofska Biblioteka, 12.) pp. 425. Trans. from G. 1921a by Miloš Djuric.

1969a *Lavirint u čoveku.* (Biblioteka "Zodijak," 16.) Belgrade: Vuk Karadžić. pp. 188. Trans. from the German by Slobodan Janković. Contents:
1. "Predgovor." (7–46)
2. "Primena energetskog stanovišta." (47–61)
3. "Osnovni pojmovi teorije o libidu." (62–75)
4. "Arhaični čovek." (76–98)
5. "O biću sna." (99–109)
6. "Prilozi simbolici Jastva." (110–128)
7. "Ciljevi psihoterapije." (129–145)
8. "O odnosima analitičke psihologije prema umetničkom delu." (146–165) Trans. from G. 1931a,3.
9. "Psihologija i poezija." (166–186) Trans. from G. ?1950a,2.
Except as indicated, sources have not been ascertained.

SLOVENIAN

1961a "Psihoanaliza neke realnosti. Duševnost." *Naši Razgledi,* X:12 (June), 280–81. Trans from Fr. 1960b by Vladimir Bartol.

SPANISH

1925a "Tipos psicológicos." *Revta. Occid.*, 10 (Nov.), 161–83. Trans. from ?G. 1925c by an unknown hand.

1927a *Lo inconsciente en la vida psíquica normal y patólogica.* Madrid: Revista de Occidente. pp ?. 1938: Buenos Aires: Losada. pp. 136. 1965: pp. 142. Trans. from G. 1926a by E. Rodriguez Sadia.

1931a "El hombre arcaico." *Revta. Occid.*, 32 (Apr.), 1–36. Trans. from G. 1931f by an unknown hand.

1932a "El problema psíquico del hombre moderno." *Revta. Occid.*, 36 (May), 202–34. Trans. from G. 1931a,14 by an unknown hand.

1933a "Ulises." *Revta. Occid.*, 39 (Feb.), 113–49. Trans. from G. 1932e by an unknown hand. Cf. Sp. 1944a.

1933b "Picasso." *Atenea*, XXIV:99, 105–10. Trans. from G. 1932g by Luisa Frey and Juán Uribe Echevarría. Cf. Sp. 1934b.

1934a *Tipos psicológicos.* (Col. Piragra, 23.) Buenos Aires: Sudamericana. pp. 566. Trans. from G. 1921a by Ramón Gómez de la Serna. In later edns., paging and format vary. 1945: pp. 552; 1960: pp. 483; 1964: pp. 659; 1965: 2 vols. Contains a foreword written for this edn. and dated October 1934. TR.—(Foreword only) English: CW 6,3.

1934b "Picasso." *Revta. Occid.*, 44 (Apr.), 113–22. Trans. from G. 1932g, by an unknown hand. Cf. Sp. 1933b.

1935a *La psique y sus problemas actuales.* Madrid and Buenos Aires: Poblet. pp. 376. Trans. from G. 1934b by Eugenio Imaz. 1944: 2nd edn. Cf. Sp. 1940a.

1935b *Teoría del psicoanálisis.* Barcelona: Apolo. pp. 240. 1961: Barcelona: Plaza Janés. pp. 194. Trans. from G. 1913a by F. Oliver Brachfeld.

1935c "Ubicación histórica de Sigmund Freud." Abraham Meyer: *Crítica de la teoría sexual de Freud*. pp. 7–18. Buenos Aires: Inman. Trans. from G. 1932f by ?.

1936a *El yo y el inconsciente*. (Biblioteca de psicoanálisis y caracterólogia, 3.) Barcelona: Luis Miracle. pp. 255. Trans. from G. 1935a by S. Montserrat Esteve.

1936b "Los arquetipos del inconsciente colectivo." *Revta. Occid.*, 54 (July), 1–56. Trans. from G. 1935b by ?.

1938a *Lo inconsciente*. (Colección Biblioteca Contemporánea.) Buenos Aires: Losada. pp. 142. Trans. from G. 1926a by Emilio Rodríguez Sadia.

1940a *Realidad del alma*. (Colección Cristal del Tiempo.) Buenos Aires: Losada. pp. 200. Trans. from G. 1929a and 1934b by Fernando Vela and Felipe Jiménez de Asúa. Cf. Sp. 1935a.

1944a *¿Quién es Ulises?* Buenos Aires: Santiago Rueda. pp. 91. Trans. from G. ?1934b,7 by an unknown hand. Cf. Sp. 1933a.

1945a *Conflictos del alma infantil*. Buenos Aires: Paidós. pp. 123. 1972: 5th ptg. or edn. pp. 126. Trans. from G. 1939a by Ida Germán de Butelman.

1946a "La naturaleza de los sueños." *Actas Ciba* (Buenos Aires), 10 (Oct.), 279–93. Trans. from G. 1945d by Antonio Hernández.

1947a "Prefacio" and "Prólogo . . . a la edición española." Jolande Jacobi: *La psicología de C. G. Jung*. pp. 25–26 and p. 27. Madrid: Espasa-Calpe. Preface trans. from G. 1940c and the prologue (written especially for this edn.) from the German ms. by José M. Sacristán. TR.—English: (Prologue only) CW 18,41.

1949a *Psicología y educación*. Buenos Aires: Paidós. pp. 111. 1974: 5th ptg. or edn. Trans. from G. 1946b by Ludovico Rosenthal.

1949b *Psicología y religión*. Buenos Aires: Paidós. 1972: 5th ptg. or edn. pp. 168. Trans. from G. 1940a by Enrique Butelman.

1953a Psicología y alquimia. Buenos Aires: Santiago Rueda. pp. 501. Trans. from G. 1952d by Alberto Luis Bixio.

1953b Transformaciones y símbolos de la libido. Buenos Aires: Paidós. pp. 441. Trans. from G. 1925a by Ludovico Rosenthal. Rev. version pub. as Sp. 1962b.

1954a La psicología de la transferencia. Buenos Aires: Paidós. pp. 198. 1972: 3d ptg. or edn. pp. 200. Trans. from G. 1946c by J. Kogan Albert.

1954b Energética psíquica y esencia del sueño. (Biblioteca de Psicología Profunda.) Buenos Aires: Paidós. pp. 218. 1973: 3d edn. or ptg. pp. 238. Trans. from G. 1948b by Ludovico Rosenthal and Blas Sosa.

1955a With Richard Wilhelm: El secreto de la flor de oro. (Biblioteca de Psicología Profunda, 10.) Buenos Aires: Paidós. pp. 136. 1972: 3d ptg. or edn. Trans. from G. 1938a by Roberto Pope.

1955b "Prólogo." Victor White: Dios y el inconsciente. pp. 19–34. Madrid: Gredos. Trans. from E. 1952c by Fr. Acacio Fernández.

1957a Presente y futuro. (Otras Publicaciones, Ensayos, 23.) Buenos Aires: Sur. pp. 104. Trans. from G. 1957i by Pablo Simon.

1960a "Prólogo." Miguel Serrano: Las visitas de la reina de Saba. p. vii. Santiago: Nascimiento. Trans. from E. 1960b by Miguel Serrano. Written as letter to the author. Cf. Sp. 1965a,1 for trans. of whole letter.

1961a Sobre cosas que se ven en el cielo. Buenos Aires: Sur. pp. 206. Trans. from G. 1958a by Alberto Luis Bixio.

1962a Simbología del espíritu. (Biblioteca de Psicología y Psicoanálisis.) Mexico: Fondo de Cultura Económica. pp. 325. Trans. from G. 1948a by Matilde Rodríguez Cabo.

1962b Símbolos de transformación. Buenos Aires: Paidós. pp. 444. Trans. from G. 1952e by Enrique Butelman. A rev. version of Sp. 1953b.

1964a *Respuesta a Job.* Mexico: Fondo de Cultura Económica. pp. 132. Trans. from G. 1952a by Andrés Pedro Sánchez Pascual.

1964b *La interpretación de la naturaleza y la psique.* (Biblioteca de Psicología Profunda, 12.) Buenos Aires: Paidós. pp. 130. Contains the following work by Jung:
"La sincronicidad como principio de conexión acausal." Trans. from G. 1952b by Haraldo Kanemann.

1964c "Prólogo." D. T. Suzuki: *Introducción al Budismo zen.* pp. ?. Buenos Aires: Paidós. Trans. from ?G. 1939c by ?.

1965a Letters to the author. Miguel Serrano: *El círculo hermetico, de Hermann Hesse a C. G. Jung.* Santiago: Zig-Zag. Letters trans. from the English by Miguel Serrano. Contains the following letters from Jung (pp. of facsimiles follow those of trans. text):
  1. 14 Jan. 1960 (139, 143–44) (141) English letter pub., sl. rev., as E. 1960b, and in orig. form as E. 1966c,1. Spanish trans. pub., sl. rev., as Sp. 1960a.
  2. 16 June 1960 (145, 149) (147) English letter repub. as E. 1966c,2.
  3. 31 Mar. 1960 (159–60) (157) English letter repub. as E. 1966c,3.
  4. 14 Sept. 1960 (175, 187–96) (177–86) English letter repub. as E. 1966c,4.

1966a *Paracelsica.* Buenos Aires: Sur. pp. 138. Trans. from G. 1942a by Eduardo García Belsunce.

1966b *Recuerdos, sueños y pensamientos.* Ed. by Aniela Jaffé. (Biblioteca Breve, Ciencias Humanas, 233.) Barcelona: Seix Barral. pp. 424. Trans. from G. 1962a by Ma. Rosa Borrás. Contents conform to those of G. 1962a.

1966c "Acercamiento al inconsciente." *El hombre y sus símbolos.* pp. 18–103. Madrid: Aguilar. pp. 320. Trans. from E. 1964a by Luis Escolar Bareño.

1968a *Consideraciones sobre la historia actual.* (Colección Punto Omega, 14.) Madrid: Guadarrama. pp. 162. Trans. from G. 1946a by Luis Alberto Martín Baro.

1969a *Los complejos y el inconsciente.* Madrid: Alianza. pp. 452. Trans. from Fr. 1962a by Jesús López Pacheco.

1970a *Arquetipos e inconsciente colectivo.* Buenos Aires: Paidós. pp. 217. Trans. from G. 1954b,2,3,4,8, by Miguel Murmis.

SWEDISH

1934a *Det omedvetna i normalt och sjukt själsliv.* Stockholm: Natur och Kultur. pp. 139. Trans. from G. 1926a by Gunnar Nordstrand.

1934b "Inledning." Esther Harding: *Vi kvinnor. En psykologisk tolkning.* pp. 7–11. Stockholm: Hökerberg. Trans. from E. 1933b by Signe Hallström.

1936a *Själen och dess problem i den moderna människans liv.* Stockholm: Natur och Kultur. pp. 232. Partial trans. of G. 1931a by Gunnar Nordstrand (omits G. 1931a,5,8, and 13). Contents:
   1. "Författarens förord." Trans. from G. 1931a,1.
   2. "Den moderna psykoterapiens problema." Trans. from G. 1931a,2.
   3. "Den analytiska psykologiens förhållande till det litterära konstverket." Trans. from G. 1931a,3.
   4. "Freud och Jung som motsatser." Trans. from G. 1931a,4.
   5. "Psykologiska typer." Trans. from G. 1931a,6.
   6. "Själens struktur." Trans. from G. 1931a,7.
   7. "Den arkaistiska människan." Trans. from G. 1931a,9.
   8. "Livets höjdpunkt." Trans. from G. 1931a,10.
   9. "Äktenskapet som psykologiskt förhållande." Trans. from G. 1931a,11.
   10. "Världsåskådningen och den analytiska psykologien." Trans. from G. 1931a,12.
   11. "Själens problem i den moderna människans liv." Trans. from G. 1931a,14.

1941a *Psykologiska typer.* Stockholm: Natur och Kultur. pp. 350. Trans. from (?pts. of) G. 1921a by Ivar Alm. Contents:
   Inledning.
   I. Allmän beskrivning av typerna.
   II. Typproblemet i idéhistorian.
   III. Individualitet och kollektivitet.

148

IV. Den förenande symbolen.
Definitioner.
Anmärkningar.
Noter.

1954a *Svar på Job.* Stockholm: Natur och Kultur. pp. 137. Trans. from G. 1952a by Hjalmar Sundén.

1964a *Mitt liv. (Minnen, drömmar, tankar.)* Recorded and ed. by Aniela Jaffé. Stockholm: Natur och Kultur. pp. 304. Trans. from G. 1962a by Ivar Alm. Contents conform to those of G. 1962a, except that G. 1962a, 9–11 have been combined into one chapter, "Drömmar och visioner," and the appendix consists solely of G. 1962a,15,ii.

1965a *Det omedvetna.* Stockholm: Wahlström & Widstrand. pp. 143. Trans. from G. 1943a by Heidi Parland.

1966a "Mötet med det omedvetna." *Människan och hennes symboler.* pp. 18–103. In collaboration with M.-L. von Franz, Joseph L. Henderson, Jolande Jacobi, and Aniela Jaffé. Stockholm: Forum. pp. 320. Trans. from E. 1964a by Karin Stolpe.

1967a *Jaget och det omedvetna.* Stockholm: Wahlström & Widstrand. pp. 149. Trans. from G. 1935a by Heidi Parland.

TURKISH

1954a "Remiz (Symbole)." *Mason Dergisi*, IV:16 (4 Oct.), 803–09. Trans. from E. 1955g by S. T. Türk.

1964a "Psikoloji ve edebiyat." *Psikanaliz acısından edebiyat*. pp. 52–78. Istanbul: Atac Kitabevi. pp. 78. Trans. from Fr. 1955a by Selâhattin Hilâv. Also contains an article by Freud and one by Adler.

1965a *Psikoloji ve din*. Istanbul: Oluş Yayınevi. pp. 128. Trans. from E. 1938a by Ender Gürol.

II

THE COLLECTED WORKS OF C. G. JUNG

DIE GESAMMELTEN WERKE
VON C. G. JUNG

The contents of the two editions are coordinated on facing pages. Paragraph numbers (column at right) are given only for the *Collected Works*; they are the same for the *Gesammelte Werke* except for discrepancies in volumes 6, 8, 11, and 14, which are explained in each volume. Page numbers are given in ( ) following each title. The cross-references indicate, in general, the immediate derivation of each work, with further references as may be useful. Republications (chiefly paperback reprints) derived *from* the texts in the collected volumes are also indicated.

The Collected Works of C. G. Jung. Edited by †Herbert Read, Michael Fordham, and Gerhard Adler; executive editor (from 1967), William McGuire. Translated by †R.F.C. Hull, except as otherwise noted. New York: Pantheon Books for Bollingen Foundation, 1953–1960; Bollingen Foundation (distributed by Pantheon Books, a Division of Random House), 1961–1967. Princeton, New Jersey: Princeton University Press, 1967–1978. (Bollingen Series XX.) London: Routledge & Kegan Paul, 1953–1978. (The New York/Princeton and London edns. are identical except for title-pages and binding. Reprintings vary.)

CW 1   *Psychiatric Studies*. (Collected Works, 1.) 1957: 1st edn. 1970: 2d edn.

    1. "On the Psychology and Pathology of So-Called   1–150
        Occult Phenomena." (3–88) Trans. from G. 1902a.

    2. "On Hysterical Misreading." (89–92) Trans.   151–65
        from G. 1904b.

    3. "Cryptomnesia." (95–106) Trans. from G. 1905a.   166–86

    4. "On Manic Mood Disorder." (109–34) Trans.   187–225
        from G. 1903a.

    5. "A Case of Hysterical Stupor in a Prisoner in   226–300
        Detention." (137–56) Trans. from G. 1902b.

    6. "On Simulated Insanity." (159–87) Trans. from   301–55
        G. 1903b.

    7. "A Medical Opinion on a Case of Simulated   356–429
        Insanity." (188–205) Trans. from G. 1904c.

    8. "A Third and Final Opinion on Two Contra-   430–77
        dictory Psychiatric Diagnoses." (209–18) Trans.
        from G. 1906d.

    9. "On the Psychological Diagnosis of Facts." (219–   478–84
        21) Trans. from G. 1905d.

CW 2   *Experimental Researches*. (Collected Works, 2.) 1973. Trans. by Leopold Stein in collaboration with Diana Riviere.

    1. "The Associations of Normal Subjects." (3–196)   1–498
        By C. G. Jung and Franz Riklin. Trans. from G.
        1906a,1.

Die gesammelten Werke von C. G. Jung. Edited by †Marianne Niehus-Jung, †Lena Hurwitz-Eisner, †Franz Riklin, Lilly Jung-Merker, and Elisabeth Rüf. Zurich: Rascher, 1958–1970. Olten: Walter, 1971–

GW 1 *Psychiatrische Studien.* (Gesammelte Werke, 1.) 1966. TR.—Italian: 1970b.

1. "Zur Psychologie und Pathologie sogenannter okkulter Phäno-mene." (1–98) G. 1902a repub. Repub. as G. 1971c,1.
2. "Über hysterisches Verlesen." (99–102) G. 1904b repub. Repub. as G. 1971c,2.
3. "Kryptomnesie." (103–15) G. 1905a, slightly rev. Repub. as G. 1971c,3.
4. "Über manische Verstimmung." (117–46) G. 1903a repub. Repub. in G. 1971c,4.
5. "Ein Fall von hysterischem Stupor bei einer Untersuchungs-gefangenen." (147–67) G. 1902b repub.
6. "Über Simulation von Geistesstörung." (169–201) G. 1903b repub.
7. "Ärztliches Gutachten über einen Fall von Simulation geistiger Störung." (203–21) G. 1904c repub.
8. "Obergutachten über zwei widersprechende psychiatrische Gut-achten." (223–33) G. 1906d repub., with minor title change.
9. "Zur psychologischen Tatbestandsdiagnostik." (235–37) G. 1905d repub.

GW 2 *Experimentelle Untersuchungen.* (Gesammelte Werke, 2.) 1978? With translations from the English by Sabine Lucas.

1. "Experimentelle Untersuchungen über Assoziationen Gesun-der." (. . . . .) By C. G. Jung and Franz Riklin. G. 1906a,1 repub.

2. "An Analysis of the Associations of an Epileptic."   499–559
(197–220) Trans. from G. 1906a,2.

3. "The Reaction-time Ratio in the Association Ex-   560–638
periment." (221–71) Trans. from G. 1906a,3.

4. "Experimental Observations on the Faculty of   639–59
Memory." (272–87) Trans. from G. 1905c.

5. "Psychoanalysis and Association Experiments."   660–727
(288–317) Trans. from G. 1906a,4.

6. "The Psychological Diagnosis of Evidence." (318–   728–92
52) Trans. from G. 1941d.

7. "Association, Dream, and Hysterical Symptom."   793–862
(353–407) Trans. from G. 1909a,1.

8. "The Psychopathological Significance of the Asso-   863–917
ation Experiment." (408–25) Trans. from G.
1906b.

9. "Disturbances of Reproduction in the Association   918–38
Experiment." (426–38) Trans. from G. 1909a,2.

10. "The Association Method." (439–65) Trans. from   939–98
an unpub. German ms. in part by Leopold Stein,
completed by Jean Rhees and rev. by Diana Riviere. Contents partly derived from It. 1908a. Cf.
CW 2,16.

11. "The Family Constellation." (466–79) Trans. from   999–1014
an unpub. German ms. in part by Leopold Stein,
completed by Jean Rhees and rev. by Diana Riviere. Contents resemble those of Fr. 1907a.

12. "On the Psychophysical Relations of the Associa-   1015–35
tion Experiment." (483–91) E. 1907a repub. with
slight title change.

13. "Psychophysical Investigations with the Galva-   1036–79
nometer and Pneumograph in Normal and Insane
Individuals." (492–553) By Frederick Peterson
and C. G. Jung. E. 1907b repub., slightly rev.

14. "Further Investigations on the Galvanic Phenom-   1080–1311
enon and Respiration in Normal and Insane
Individuals." (554–80) By Charles Ricksher and
C. G. Jung. E. 1908a repub., slightly rev.
Appendix:

15. "Statistical Details of Enlistment." (583–85)   1312–15
Trans. from G. 1906c.

2. "Analyse der Assoziationen eines Epileptikers." (. . . . .) G. 1906a,2 repub.

3. "Über das Verhalten der Reaktionszeit beim Assoziationsexperimente." (. . . . .) G. 1906a,3 repub.

4. "Experimentelle Beobachtungen über das Erinnerungsvermögen." (. . . . .) G. 1905c repub.

5. "Psychoanalyse und Assoziationsexperiment." (. . . . .) G. 1906a,4 repub.

6. "Die psychologische Diagnose des Tatbestandes." (. . . . .) G. 1941d repub.

7. "Assoziation, Traum und hysterisches Symptom." (. . . . .) G. 1909a,1 repub.

8. "Die psychopathologische Bedeutung des Assoziationsexperimentes." (. . . . .) G. 1906b repub.

9. "Über die Reproduktionsstörungen beim Assoziationsexperiment." (. . . . .) G. 1909a,2 repub.

10. "Die Assoziationsmethode." (. . . . .) First pub., from a manuscript.

11. "Die familiäre Konstellation." (. . . . .) First pub., from a manuscript.

12. "Über die psychophysischen Beziehungen des Assoziationsexperimentes." (. . . . .) Trans. from CW 2,12.

13. "Psychophysische Untersuchungen mit dem Galvanometer und Pneumographen bei Normalen und Geisteskranken." By Frederick Peterson and C. G. Jung. (. . . . .) Trans. from CW 2,13.

14. "Weitere Untersuchungen über das galvanische Phänomen und die Respiration bei Normalen und Geisteskranken." By Charles Ricksher and C. G. Jung. (. . . . .) Trans. from CW 2,14.

Anhang:

15. "Statistisches von der Rekrutenaushebung." (. . . . .) G. 1906c repub.

16. "New Aspects of Criminal Psychology." (586–96)   1316–47
Trans. from It. 1908a. Cf. CW 2,10.

17. "The Psychological Methods of Investigation Used   1348
in the Psychiatric Clinic of the University of
Zurich." (597) Trans. from G. 1910r.

18. "On the Doctrine of Complexes." (598–604) E.   1349–56
1913a repub., slightly rev.

19. "On the Psychological Diagnosis of Evidence: The   1357–88
Evidence-Experiment in the Näf Trial." (605–14)
Trans. from G. 1937b.

CW 3   *The Psychogenesis of Mental Disease.* (Collected Works, 3.) 1960.

1. "The Psychology of Dementia Praecox." (1–151)   1–316
Trans. from G. 1907a. Repub. as E. 1974c.

2. "The Content of the Psychoses." (153–78) Trans.   317–87
from G. 1914a.

3. "On Psychological Understanding." (179–93)   388–424
Trans. from G. 1914a ("Supplement").

4. "A Criticism of Bleuler's Theory of Schizophrenic   425–37
Negativism." (197–202) Trans. from G. 1911c.

5. "On the Importance of the Unconscious in Psycho-   438–65
pathology." (203–10) E. 1916a,11 repub.

6. "On the Problem of Psychogenesis in Mental   466–95
Disease." (211–25) E. 1919a repub., slightly rev.

7. "Mental Disease and the Psyche." (226–30) Trans.   496–503
from G. 1928c.

8. "On the Psychogenesis of Schizophrenia." (233–49)   504–541
E. 1939d repub. Prepub. as E. 1959a,8.

9. "Recent Thoughts on Schizophrenia." (250–55)   542–552
Cf. E. 1957h.

10. "Schizophrenia." (256–71) Trans. from G. 1958i.   553–584

11. "Letter to the Second International Congress of
Psychiatry Symposium on Chemical Concepts of
Psychosis, 1957." (272) E. 1958d repub. Written
to Max Rinkel (Apr. 1957). TR.—German: 1973a.

CW 4   *Freud and Psychoanalysis.* (Collected Works, 4.) 1961.

1. "Freud's Theory of Hysteria: A Reply to Aschaf-   1–26
fenburg." (3–9) Trans. from G. 1906g.

16. "Neue Aspekte der Kriminalpsychologie." (. . . . .) Trans. from CW 2,16.

17. "Die an der Psychiatrischen Klinik in Zürich gebräuchlichen psychologischen Untersuchungsmethoden." (. . . . .) G. 1910r repub.

18. "Ein kurzer Überblick über die Komplexlehre." (. . . . .) First pub., from a ms.

19. "Zur psychologischen Tatbestandsdiagnostik: Das Tatbestandsexperiment im Schwurgerichtsprozess Näf." (. . . . .) G. 1937b repub.

GW 3 *Psychogenese der Geisteskrankheiten.* (Gesammelte Werke, 3.) 1968. TR.—Italian: 1971a.

1. "Über die Psychologie der Dementia praecox: Ein Versuch." (1–170) G. 1907a repub.

2. "Der Inhalt der Psychose." (171–215) G. 1914a repub. Repub. as G. 1973d,1. (Including Nachtrag: "Über das psychologische Verständnis pathologische Vergänge.")

3. "Kritik über E. Bleuler: Zur Theorie des schizophrenen Negativismus." (217–224) G. 1911c repub.

4. "Über die Bedeutung des Unbewussten in der Psychopathologie." (225–34) Trans. from E. 1914b by Klaus Thiele-Dohrmann, and slightly rev. Repub. as G. 1973d,3.

5. "Über das Problem der Psychogenese bei Geisteskrankheiten." (235–52) Trans. from E. 1919a by Klaus Thiele-Dohrmann. Repub. as G. 1973d,2.

6. "Geisteskrankheit und Seele." (253–60) G. 1928c repub. with change to the original title of ms. Repub. as G. 1973d,4.

7. "Über die Psychogenese der Schizophrenie." (261–81) Trans. from E. 1939d by Klaus Thiele-Dohrmann.

8. "Neuere Betrachtungen zur Schizophrenie." (283–91) G. 1959f repub.

9. "Die Schizophrenie." (293–312) G. 1958i repub. Repub. as G. 1973d,5.

GW 4 *Freud und die Psychoanalyse.* (Gesammelte Werke, 4.) 1969.

1. "Die Hysterielehre Freuds. Eine Erwiderung auf die Aschaffenburgsche Kritik." (1–10) G. 1906g repub. Repub. as G. 1972e,1.

2. "The Freudian Theory of Hysteria." (10–24)   27–63
Trans. from G. 1908m.

3. "The Analysis of Dreams." (25–34) Trans. from   64–94
Fr. 1909a by Philip Mairet and rev. by R.F.C.
Hull. Repub. as E. 1974a,1.

4. "A Contribution to the Psychology of Rumour."   95–128
(35–47) Trans. from G. 1910q.

5. "On the Significance of Number Dreams." (48–55)   129–53
Trans. from G. 1911e. Repub. as E. 1974a,2.

6. "Morton Prince, *The Mechanism and Interpre-*   154–93
tation of Dreams: A Critical Review." (56–73)
Trans. from G. 1911b.

7. "On the Criticism of Psychoanalysis." (74–77)   194–96
Trans. from G. 1910o.

8. "Concerning Psychoanalysis." (78–81) Trans.   197–202
from G. 1912g.

9. "The Theory of Psychoanalysis." (83–226) Trans.   203–522
from G. 1955b.

10. "General Aspects of Psychoanalysis." (229–42)   523–56
Trans. from the German ms., a version of which
was subsequently pub. as GW 4,10.

11. "Psychoanalysis and Neurosis." (243–51) E.   557–75
1916a,9, trans. slightly rev., with title change.

12. "Some Crucial Points in Psychoanalysis: A Cor-   576–669
respondence between Dr. Jung and Dr. Loÿ."
(252–89) Trans. from G. 1914b.

13, a and b. "Prefaces to *Collected Papers on Analytical*   670–92
Psychology." (290–97) E. 1916a,1 and E. 1917a,1,
trans. slightly rev.

14. "The Significance of the Father in the Destiny of   693–744
the Individual." (301–23) Trans. from G. 1949a,
with the addition of material trans. from the 1st
edn., i.e. G. 1909c.

15. "Introduction to Kranefeldt's *Secret Ways of the*   745–67
Mind." (324–32) Trans. from G. 1930b.

16. "Freud and Jung: Contrasts." (333–40) Trans.   768–84
from G. 1931a,4.

2. "Die Freudsche Hysterietheorie." (11–28) G. 1908m repub. Repub. as G. 1972e,2.

3. "Die Traumanalyse." (29–40) Trans. from Fr. 1909a by Klaus Thiele-Dohrmann. Repub. as G. 1972e,3.

4. "Ein Beitrag zur Psychologie des Gerüchtes." (41–57) G. 1910q repub. Repub. as G. 1972e,4.

5. "Ein Beitrag zur Kenntnis des Zahlentraumes." (59–69) G. 1911e repub. Repub. as G. 1972e,5.

6. "Morton Prince, M.D. *The Mechanism and Interpretation of Dreams.* Eine kritische Besprechung." (71–93) G. 1911b repub. Repub. as G. 1972e,6.

7. "Zur Kritik über Psychoanalyse." (95–100) G. 1910o repub. Repub. as G. 1972e,7.

8. "Zur Psychoanalyse." (101–06) G. 1912g repub. Repub. as G. 1972e,8.

9. "Versuch einer Darstellung der psychoanalytischen Theorie." (107–255) G. 1955b repub. Repub. as G. 1973b,1.

10. "Allgemeine Aspekte der Psychoanalyse." (257–73) Based on the original, unpub. German ms. Repub. as G. 1972e,9. Cf. E. 1913d.

11. "Über Psychoanalyse." (275–86) Trans. from E. 1916a,8 by Klaus Thiele-Dohrmann. Repub. as G. 1972e,10.

12. "Psychotherapeutische Zeitfragen. Ein Briefwechsel zwischen C. G. Jung und R. Loÿ." (287–331) G. 1914b repub. Repub. as G. 1973b,2.

13. "Vorreden zu den *Collected Papers on Analytical Psychology.*" (333–44) (Text of 2d preface based on the original German ms.) Trans. from E. 1916a,1 and E. 1917a,1 by Klaus Thiele-Dohrmann.

14. "Die Bedeutung des Vaters für das Schicksal des Einzelnen." (345–70) G. 1949a repub. Repub. as G. 1971a,1.

15. "Einführung zu W. M. Kranefeldt: *Die Psychoanalyse.*" (371–82) G. 1930b repub.

16. "Der Gegensatz Freud und Jung." (383–93) G. 1931a,4 repub.

CW 5 *Symbols of Transformation. An Analysis of the Prelude to a Case of Schizophrenia.* (Collected Works, 5.) 1956: 1st edn. 1962: Paperback edn. New York: Harper. 2 vols. 1967: 2d edn. 1974: 2d edn., 2d ptg., with addn. of Author's Note to the First American/English Edition (p. xxx), from E. 1916b. With 65 plates and 43 text illus. Trans. from G. 1952e.

†1. Foreword to the Fourth Swiss Edition. (xxiii–xxvi)
2. Foreword to the Third Swiss Edition. (xxvii)
3. Foreword to the Second Swiss Edition. (xxviii–xxix)
4. Symbols of Transformation.
    Part One:

†I. Introduction. (3–6)	1–3
†II. Two Kinds of Thinking (7–33)	4–46
III. The Miller Fantasies: Anamnesis. (34–38)	47–55
IV. The Hymn of Creation. (39–78)	56–114
V. The Song of the Moth. (79–117)	115–75

    Part Two:

I. Introduction. (121–31)	176–89
II. The Concept of Libido. (132–41)	190–203
III. The Transformation of Libido. (142–70)	204–50
IV. The Origin of the Hero. (171–206)	251–99
V. Symbols of the Mother and of Rebirth. (207–73)	300–418
VI. The Battle for Deliverance from the Mother. (274–305)	419–63
VII. The Dual Mother. (306–93)	464–612
VIII. The Sacrifice. (394–440)	613–82
IX. Epilogue. (441–44)	683–85

Appendix: "Some Instances of Subconscious Creative Imagination," by Miss Frank Miller. (447–62)
† Repub. as E. 1959a,1.

CW 6 *Psychological Types.* (Collected Works, 6.) 1971. [No. 4:] A revision by R.F.C. Hull of the trans. by H. G. Baynes (cf. E. 1923a). Trans. from G. 1921a.

1. Foreword to the First Swiss Edition. (xi–xii)
2. Foreword to the Seventh and Eighth Swiss Editions. (xii–xiii)

GW 5 *Symbole der Wandlung. Analyse des Vorspiels zu einer Schizo-phrenie.* (Gesammelte Werke, 5.) 1973. With 123 text illus. G. 1952e repub. with fewer illus. and additional end matter.

1. Vorrede zur vierten Auflage. (11–15) Dated Sept. 1950.
2. Vorrede zur dritten Auflage. (16) Dated Nov. 1937.
3. Vorrede zur zweiten Auflage. (17–18) Dated Nov. 1924.
4. Symbole der Wandlung.
   Erster Teil:
   I. Einleitung. (21–24)
   II. Über die zwei Arten des Denkens. (25–54)
   III. Vorgeschichte. (55–59)
   IV. Der Schöpferhymnus. (60–105)
   V. Das Lied von der Motte. (106–54)
   Zweiter Teil:
   I. Einleitung. (157–69)
   II. Über den Begriff der Libido. (170–81)
   III. Die Wandlung der Libido. (182–215)
   IV. Die Entstehung des Heros. (216–60)
   V. Symbole der Mutter und der Wiedergeburt. (261–351)
   VI. Der Kampf um die Befreiung von der Mutter. (352–92)
   VII. Die Zweifache Mutter. (393–500)
   VIII. Das Opfer. (501–57)
   IX. Schlusswort. (558–61)
   Anhang: Übersetzungen. (565–93)

GW 6 *Psychologische Typen.* (Gesammelte Werke, 6.) 1960: "Neunte, rev. Auflage." 1967: "Zehnte, rev. Auflage." TR.—Italian: 1969a.

1. Vorworte zur 7. und 8. Auflage. (xi–xii)
2. Vorrede. (xv–xvi)

3. Foreword to the Argentine Edition. (xiv–xv)
Trans. from Sp. 1934a.
4. Psychological Types.

Introduction. (3–7)	1–7
I. The Problem of Types in the History of Classical and Medieval Thought. (8–66)	8–100
II. Schiller's Ideas on the Type Problem. (67–135)	101–222
III. The Apollonian and the Dionysian. (136–46)	223–42
IV. The Type Problem in Human Character. (147–65)	243–74
V. The Type Problem in Poetry. (166–372)	275–460
VI. The Type Problem in Psychopathology. (273–88)	461–83
VII. The Type Problem in Aesthetics. (289–99)	484–504
VIII. The Type Problem in Modern Philosophy. (300–21)	505–41
IX. The Type Problem in Biography. (322–29)	542–55
X. General Description of the Types. (330–407) Repub. as E. 1971a,8.	556–671
XI. Definitions. (408–86)	672–844
Epilogue. (487–95)	845–57

Appendix: Four Papers on Psychological Typology.

5. "A Contribution to the Study of Psychological Types (1913)." (499–509) Trans. from the German ms. Cf. GW 6,4. and Fr. 1913a.	858–82
6. "Psychological Types (1923)." (510–23) Trans. from GW 6,5 (2d edn.).	883–914
7. "A Psychological Theory of Types (1931)." (524–41) E. 1933a,4, repub. trans. slightly rev.	915–59
8. "Psychological Typology (1936)." (542–55) Trans. from GW 6,7 (2d edn.)	960–87

3. Psychologische Typen. G. 1921a repub. with addn. of a def. of
   "Selbst" in chap. 11.
   Einleitung. (1–6)
   1. Das Typenproblem in der antiken und mittelalterlichen
      Geistesgeschichte. (7–69)
   2. Über Schillers Ideen zum Typenproblem. (70–143)
   3. Das Apollinische und das Dionysische. (144–55)
   4. Das Typenproblem in der Menschenkenntnis. (156–76)
   5. Das Typenproblem in der Dichtkunst. (177–292)
   6. Das Typenproblem in der Psychopathologie. (293–309)
   7. Das Problem der typischen Einstellungen in der Ästhetik.
      (310–21)
   8. Das Typenproblem in der modernen Philosophie. (322–46)
   9. Das Typenproblem in der Biographik. (347–56)
   10. Allgemeine Beschreibung der Typen. (357–443) Repub. as
       G. 1972d,2.
   11. Definitionen. (444–528) Repub. as G. 1972d,3.
   12. Schlusswort. (529–37)
Anhang:
   4. "Zur Frage der psychologischen Typen." (541–51) Lecture given
      at the Psychoanalytische Kongress, Munich, Sept. 1913. Repub.
      as G. 1972d,1. Cf. Fr. 1913a and E. 1916a,12.
   5. "Psychologische Typen." (552–67) G. 1925c repub. Repub. as
      G. 1972d,4.
   6. "Psychologische Typologie." (568–86) G. 1931a,6 repub.
   7. "Psychologische Typologie." (587–601) G. 1936b repub.

CW 7 *Two Essays on Analytical Psychology.* (Collected Works, 7.) 1953: 1st edn. 1956: Paperback 1st edn. New York: Noonday (Meridian). 1966: 2d edn. (fully reset). 1972: Paperback 2d edn. Princeton U. P. First Edition:

1. "The Psychology of the Unconscious." (3–117)   1–201
   Trans. from G. 1943a, with omission of some
   prefatory matter.
   a) "Preface to the First Edition." (3–4) Dated
      Dec. 1916.
   b) "Preface to the Second Edition." (4–5) Dated
      Oct. 1918.
   c) "from Preface to the Third Edition." (5–6)
      Dated 1925.
   e) "Preface to the Fifth Edition." (6–7) Dated
      Apr. 1942.
2. "The Relations between the Ego and the Uncon-   202–406
   scious." (121–239) Trans. from G. 1935a. Excerpts repub. as E. 1959a,3.
   a) "Preface to the Second Edition." (121–32)
      Dated Oct. 1934.

Appendixes:
3. "New Paths in Psychology." (243–62) A trans. of   407–36
   an incomplete version of G. 1912d. For trans. of
   complete version, see CW 7,3, 2d edn.
4. "The Structure of the Unconscious." (263–92)   437–507
   Trans. from Fr. 1916a by Philip Mairet. For a
   trans. of the orig. German ms., see CW 7,4, 2d edn.

Second Edition:
1. "On the Psychology of the Unconscious." (1–119)   1–201
   Contains the same prefaces as CW 7, 1st edn.,
   although paging differs, with the following
   addition:
   d) "Preface to the Fourth Edition (1936)." (7)
      Trans. from G. 1943a.
Cf. CW 7,3, below.
2. "The Relations between the Ego and the Uncon-   202–406
   scious." (121–241) Trans. from G. 1935a. Repub.
   as E. 1971a,5.

GW 7 *Zwei Schriften über Analytische Psychologie.* (Gesammelte Werke, 7.) 1964.

  1. "Über die Psychologie des Unbewussten." (1–130) G. 1943a repub.
  2. "Die Beziehungen zwischen dem Ich und dem Unbewussten." (131–264) G. 1935a repub.
Anhang:
  3. "Neue Bahnen der Psychologie." (267–91) G. 1912d repub.
  4. "Die Struktur des Unbewussten." (292–337) Given as lecture to the Zürcher Schule für Analytische Psychologie, 1916. Original ms. titled: "Über das Unbewusste und seine Inhalte." Cf. CW 7,4. First pub. in a French trans. Pub., rev. and exp., as G. 1928a. TR.—English: CW 7,4 (2d edn.) // French: 1916a.

Appendixes:

   3. "New Paths in Psychology." (245–68) Trans.   407–41
     from G. 1912d. Cf. CW 7,1, above.

   4. "The Structure of the Unconscious." (269–304)   442–521
     Trans. from the orig. unpub. German ms., for a
     version of which, see GW 7,4. Cf. CW 7,4, 1st edn.

CW 8   *The Structure and Dynamics of the Psyche.* (Collected Works, 8.)
1960: 1st edn. 1969: 2d edn. (no. 18 extensively revised). With 1
plate (frontisp.).

   1. "On Psychic Energy." (3–66) Trans. from G.   1–130
     1948b,2. Repub. as E. 1969b,1.

   2. "The Transcendent Function." (67–91) Trans.   131–93
     largely from G. 1958b. (Prefatory note partially
     rewritten for this publication.) Repub. as E.
     1971a,9.

   3. "A Review of the Complex Theory." (92–104)   194–219
     Trans. from G. 1948b,3.

   4. "The Significance of Constitution and Heredity   220–31
     in Psychology." (107–13) Trans. from G. 1929i.

   5. "Psychological Factors Determining Human Be-   232–62
     haviour." (114–25) E. 1942a repub. with slight
     alterations based on the orig. German typescript
     (cf. GW 8,5) and reversion to the title of E. 1937a.

   6. "Instinct and the Unconscious." (129–38) Trans.   263–82
     from G. 1948b,6. Repub. as E. 1971a,3.

   7. "The Structure of the Psyche." (139–58) Trans.   283–342
     from G. 1931a,7. Repub. as E. 1971a,2.

   8. "On the Nature of the Psyche." (159–234) E.   343–442
     1954b,2, trans. rev., with title change. Prepub.,
     with some omissions, as E. 1959a,2. Repub. as E.
     1969b,2.

   9. "General Aspects of Dream Psychology." (237–80)   443–529
     Trans. from G. 1948b,4. Repub. as E. 1974a,3.

 10. "On the Nature of Dreams." (281–97) Trans. from   530–69
     G. 1948b,5. Repub. as E. 1959a,7 and as E.
     1974a,4.

 11. "The Psychological Foundations of Belief in   570–600
     Spirits." (301–18) Trans. from G. 1948b,7.

GW 8 *Die Dynamik des Unbewussten.* (Gesammelte Werke, 8.) 1967.

1. "Über die Energetik der Seele." (1–73) G. 1948b,2 repub.
2. "Die transzendente Funktion." (75–104) G. 1958b repub. Repub. as G. 1973c,1.
3. "Allgemeines zur Komplextheorie." (105–20) G. 1948b,3 repub.
4. "Die Bedeutung von Konstitution und Vererbung für die Psychologie." (121–29) G. 1929i repub. Repub. as G. 1973c,2.
5. "Psychologische Determinanten des menschlichen Verhaltens." (131–45) Originally delivered in English as a lecture (cf. E. 1937a) based on an unpub. German ms. Repub. as G. 1973c,3.
6. "Instinkt und Unbewusstes." (147–59) G. 1948b,6 repub.
7. "Die Struktur der Seele." (161–83) G. 1931a,7 repub.
8. "Theoretische Überlegungen zum Wesen des Psychischen." (185–267) G. 1954b,8 repub. Repub. as G. 1973c,4.
9. "Allgemeine Gesichtspunkte zur Psychologie des Traumes." (269–318) G. 1948b,4 repub.
10. "Vom Wesen der Träume." (319–38) G. 1948b,5 repub.
11. "Die psychologischen Grundlagen des Geisterglaubens." (339–60) G. 1948b,7 repub.

12. "Spirit and Life." (319–37) Trans. based on E. 1928a,2.   601–48

13. "Basic Postulates of Analytical Psychology." (338–57) E. 1933a,9, trans. slightly rev.   649–88

14. "Analytical Psychology and *Weltanschauung*." (358–81) Trans. from G. 1931a,12. Cf. E. 1928a,4 for earlier version.   689–741

15. "The Real and the Surreal." (382–84) Trans. from G. 1932h.   742–48

16. "The Stages of Life." (387–403) Trans. from G. 1931a,10, and based on E. 1933a,5. Repub. as E. 1971a,1.   749–95

17. "The Soul and Death." (404–15) E. 1959c repub.   796–815

18. "Synchronicity: An Acausal Connecting Principle." (417–519) E. 1955a, trans. slightly rev. Repub. as E. 1973c,1.   816–968

Appendix:

19. "On Synchronicity." (520–31) E. 1957b, trans. slightly rev. Repub. as E. 1971a,14 and E. 1973c,2.   969–97

CW 9,i   *The Archetypes and the Collective Unconscious.* (Collected Works, 9,i.) 1959: 1st edn. 1968: 2d edn. With 79 plates (29 col.).

1. "Archetypes of the Collective Unconscious." (3–41) Trans. from G. 1954b,2. Repub. as E. 1959a,5. Cf. E. 1939a,3.   1–86

2. "The Concept of the Collective Unconscious." (42–53) E. 1936d and E. 1937b, combined, slightly rev. Repub. as E. 1971a,4. TR.—German: GW 9,i,2.   87–110

3. "Concerning the Archetypes." (54–72) Trans. from G. 1954b,3.   111–47

4. "Psychological Aspects of the Mother Archetype." (75–110) Trans. from G. 1954b,4 with parts incorporated from E. 1943a. Repub. as E. 1959a,6 and E. 1970a,1.   148–98

5. "Concerning Rebirth." (113–47) Trans. from G. 1950a,3. Repub. as E. 1970a,2.   199–258

6. "The Psychology of the Child Archetype." (151–81) E. 1949a,1 repub., trans. rev. (Trans. further rev. for 2d edn.) 1st edn. version repub. as E. 1963a,1. 2d edn. version repub. as E. 1969a.   259–305

12. "Geist und Leben." (361–83) G. 1931a,13 repub.
13. "Das Grundproblem der gegenwärtigen Psychologie." (385–406) G. 1934b,2 repub.
14. "Analytische Psychologie und Weltanschauung." (407–34) G. 1931a,12 repub.
15. "Wirklichkeit und Überwirklichkeit." (435–39) G. 1932h repub.
16. "Die Lebenswende." (441–60) G. 1931a,10 repub.
17. "Seele und Tod." (461–74) G. 1934b,10 repub.
18. "Synchronizität als ein Prinzip akausaler Zusammenhänge." (475–577) G. 1952b repub.
19. "Über Synchronizität." (579–91) G. 1952f repub.

GW 9,i *Die Archetypen und das kollektive Unbewusste.* (Gesammelte Werke, 9,i.) 1976.

1. "Über die Archetypen des kollektiven Unbewussten." (11–51) G. 1954b,1 repub.
2. "Der Begriff des kollektiven Unbewussten." (53–66) Trans. from CW 9,i,2 by Elisabeth Rüf.
3. "Über den Archetypus mit besonderer Berücksichtigung des Animabegriffes." (67–87) G. 1954b,3 repub.
4. "Die psychologischen Aspekte des Mutterarchetypus." (89–123) G. 1954b,4 repub.
5. "Über Wiedergeburt." (125–161) G. 1950a,3 repub.
6. "Zur Psychologie des Kindarchetypus." (163–195) G. 1951b,1 repub.

7. "The Psychological Aspects of the Kore." (182–203)   306–83
   E. 1949a,2 repub., trans. rev. further as in no. 6.
8. "The Phenomenology of the Spirit in Fairytales."   384–455
   (207–54) Trans. from G. 1948a,2. Repub. as E.
   1970a,3. Trans. also pub. in slightly dif. form as
   E. 1954b,1.
9. "On the Psychology of the Trickster-Figure."   456–88
   (255–72) E. 1956a, trans. slightly rev. Repub. as E.
   1970a,4.
10. "Conscious, Unconscious, and Individuation."   489–524
    (275–89) E. 1939a,1, rev. in accordance with G.
    1939e (later German version).
11. "A Study in the Process of Individuation."   525–626
    (290–354) Trans. from G. 1950a,4. Repub. as E.
    1972a,2. Cf. E. 1939a,2.
12. "Concerning Mandala Symbolism." (355–84)   627–712
    Trans. from G. 1950a,5. Repub. as E. 1972a,3.
Appendix:
13. "Mandalas." (387–90) Trans. from G. 1955e.   713–18
    Repub. as E. 1972a,1.

CW 9,ii *Aion: Researches into the Phenomenology of the Self.* (Collected Works, 9,ii.) 1959: 1st edn. 1968: 2d edn. With 3 plates. Trans. from G. 1951a.

Foreword. (ix–xi)
†I. The Ego. (3–7)   1–12
†II. The Shadow. (8–10)   13–19
†III. The Syzygy: Anima and Animus. (11–22)   20–42
†IV. The Self. (23–35)   43–67
†V. Christ, a Symbol of the Self. (36–71)   68–126
VI. The Sign of the Fishes. (72–94)   127–49
VII. The Prophecies of Nostradamus. (95–102)   150–61
VIII. The Historical Significance of the Fish.   162–80
   (103–17)
IX. The Ambivalence of the Fish Symbol.   181–92
   (118–25)
X. The Fish in Alchemy. (126–53)   193–238
XI. The Alchemical Interpretation of the Fish.   239–66
   (154–72)

† Chs. I–V prepub. as E. 1958,2, slightly rev. Chs. I–III repub. as E. 1971a,6.

7. "Zum psychologischen Aspekt der Korefigur." (197–220) G. 1951b,2 repub.

8. "Zur Phänomenologie des Geistes im Märchen." (221–269) G. 1948a,2 repub.

9. "Zur Psychologie der Tricksterfigur." (271–290) G. 1954a repub.

10. "Bewusstsein, Unbewusstes und Individuation." (291–307) G. 1939e repub.

11. "Zur Empirie des Individuationsprozesses." (309–372) G. 1950a,4 repub.

12. "Über Mandalasymbolik." (373–407) G. 1950a,5 repub.

13. "Mandalas (Anhang)." (409–414) G. 1955e repub.

GW 9,ii *Aion; Beiträge zur Symbolik des Selbst.* (Gesammelte Werke, 9,ii.) 1976. Jung's contribution to G. 1951a repub. with rearrangement of title.

Vorrede. (9–11) Dated May 1950.
I. Das Ich. (12–16)
II. Der Schatten. (17–19)
III. Die Syzygie: Anima und Animus. (20–31)
IV. Das Selbst. (32–45)
V. Christus, ein Symbol des Selbst. (46–80)
VI. Das Zeichen der Fische. (81–103)
VII. Die Prophezeiung des Nostradamus. (104–111)
VIII. Über die geschichtliche Bedeutung des Fisches. (112–126)
IX. Die Ambivalenz des Fischsymbols. (127–135)
X. Der Fisch in der Alchemie. (136–165)
XI. Die alchemistische Deutung des Fisches. (166–185)

XII. Background to the Psychology of Christian Alchemical Symbolism. (173–83)   267–86

XIII. Gnostic Symbols of the Self. (184–221)   287–346

XIV. The Structure and Dynamics of the Self. (222–65)   347–421

XV. Conclusion. (266–69)   422–29

CW 10   *Civilization in Transition.* (Collected Works, 10.) 1964: 1st edn. 1970: 2d edn. With 8 plates.

1. "The Role of the Unconscious." (3–28) Trans. from G. 1918b.   1–48

2. "Mind and Earth." (29–49) Trans. from G. 1931a,8.   49–103

3. "Archaic Man." (50–73) Trans. from G. 1931a,9.   104–47

4. "The Spiritual Problem of Modern Man." (74–94) Trans. from G. 1931a,14. Repub. as E. 1971a,12.   148–96

5. "The Love Problem of a Student." (97–112) Trans. from an unpub. ms. also pub. as G. 1971a,3.   197–235

6. "Woman in Europe." (113–33) Trans. from G. 1927a.   236–75

7. "The Meaning of Psychology for Modern Man." (134–56) Trans. from G. 1934b,3.   276–332

8. "The State of Psychotherapy Today." (157–73) Trans. from G. 1934k.   333–70

9. "Preface to *Essays on Contemporary Events.*" (177–78) Trans. from G. 1946a,1.

10. "Wotan." (179–93) Trans. from G. 1946a,2.   371–99

11. "After the Catastrophe." (194–217) Trans. from G. 1946a,5.   400–43

12. "The Fight with the Shadow." (218–26) E. 1947a,2, slightly rev.   444–57

13. "Epilogue to *Essays on Contemporary Events.*" (227–43) Trans. from G. 1946a,6.   458–87

14. "The Undiscovered Self (Present and Future)." (245–305) E. 1958b repub., trans. further rev.   488–588

15. "Flying Saucers: A Modern Myth of Things Seen in the Skies." (307–433) E. 1959b repub., trans. slightly rev.   589–824

XII. Allgemeines zur Psychologie der christlich-alchemistischen Symbolik. (186–196)

XIII. Gnostische Symbole des Selbst. (197–237)

XIV. Die Struktur und Dynamik des Selbst. (238–280)

XV. Schlusswort. (281–284)

GW 10 *Zivilisation im Übergang.* (Gesammelte Werke, 10.) 1974.

1. "Über das Unbewusste." (15–42) G. 1918b repub.

2. "Seele und Erde." (43–65) G. 1931a,8 repub.

3. "Der archaische Mensch." (67–90) G. 1931a,9 repub.

4. "Das Seelenproblem des modernen Menschen." (91–113) G. 1931a,14 repub.

5. "Das Liebesproblem des Studenten." (115–33) G. 1971a,3 repub.

6. "Die Frau in Europa." (135–56) G. 1971a,2 repub.

7. "Die Bedeutung der Psychologie für die Gegenwart." (157–180) G. 1934b,3 repub.

8. "Zur gegenwärtigen Lage der Psychotherapie." (181–99) G. 1934k repub.

9. "Vorwort zu *Aufsätze zur Zeitgeschichte.*" (201–02) G. 1946a,1 repub.

10. "Wotan." (203–218) G. 1946a,2 repub.

11. "Nach der Katastrophe." (219–44) G. 1946a,5 repub.

12. "Der Kampf mit dem Schatten." (245–54) Trans. from CW 10,12 by Elisabeth Rüf. Lecture broadcast in English, B.B.C., 3d Programme, 3 Nov. 1946, and 1st pub. as E. 1946e.

13. "Nachwort zu *Aufsätze zur Zeitgeschichte.*" (255–273) G. 1946a,6 repub.

14. "Gegenwart und Zukunft." (275–336) G. 1957i repub.

15. "Ein moderner Mythus: Von Dingen, die am Himmel gesehen werden." (337–473) G. 1958a repub. with the addn. of a trans. of E. 1959b,1 and 9 by Elisabeth Rüf.

16. "A Psychological View of Conscience." (437–55)   825–57
Trans. from G. 1958c.

17. "Good and Evil in Analytical Psychology."   858–86
(456–68) E. 1960e repub., trans. rev.

18. "Introduction to Toni Wolff's *Studies in Jungian*   887–902
Psychology." (469–76) Trans. from G. 1959e.

19. "The Swiss Line in the European Spectrum."   903–24
(479–88) Trans. from G. 1928e.

20. "The Rise of a New World." (489–95) Trans.   925–34
from G. 1930e.

21. "La Révolution Mondiale." (496–501) Trans.   935–45
from G. 1934i.

22. "The Complications of American Psychology."   946–80
(502–14) E. 1930a, stylistically slightly rev., with
title change.

23. "The Dreamlike World of India." (515–24) E.   981–1001
1939b repub.

24. "What India Can Teach Us." (525–30) E. 1939c   1002–13
repub.

Appendixes:

25. "Editorial. *Zentralblatt*, VI (1933)." (533–34)   1014–15
Trans. from G. 1933e.

26. "A Rejoinder to Dr. Bally." (535–44) Trans. from   1016–34
G. 1934f and (last 3 paragraphs, p. 544) G. 1934g.

27. "Circular Letter." (545–46) Trans. from G. 1934j.   1035–38

28. "Editorial. *Zentralblatt*, VIII (1935)." (547–51)   1039–51
Trans. from G. 1935j.

29. "Editorial Note. *Zentralblatt*, VIII (1935)."   1052–54
(552–53) Trans. from G. 1935k.

30. "Presidential Address to the 8th General Medical   1055–59
Congress for Psychotherapy, Bad Nauheim, 1935."
(554–56) Trans. from a German ms. pub. as GW
10,30.

31. "Contribution to a Discussion on Psychotherapy."   1060–63
(557–60) Trans. from G. 1935h.

32. "Presidential Address to the 9th International   1064–68
Medical Congress for Psychotherapy, Copenhagen,
1937." (561–63) Trans. from a German ms. pub.
as GW 10,32. Congress held 2–4 Oct. 1937.

16. "Das Gewissen in psychologischer Sicht." (475–95) G. 1958c repub.

17. "Gut und Böse in der analytischen Psychologie." (497–510) GW 11,19 repub.

18. "Vorrede zu: Toni Wolff, *Studien zu C. G. Jungs Psychologie.*" (511–18) G. 1959e repub.

19. "Die Bedeutung der schweizerischen Linie im Spektrum Europas." (519–30) G. 1928e repub.

20. "Der Aufgang einer neuen Welt." Eine Besprechung von: H. Keyserling *Amerika. Der Aufgang einer neuen Welt.* (531–37) G. 1930e repub.

21. "Ein neues Buch von Keyserling *La Révolution mondiale et la responsibilité de l'esprit.*" (539–45) G. 1934i repub.

22. "Komplikationen der amerikanischen Psychologie." (547–61) Trans. from CW 10,22 by Elisabeth Rüf.

23. "Die träumende Welt Indiens." (563–74) Trans. from E. 1939b by Elisabeth Rüf.

24. "Was Indien uns lehren kann." (575–80) Trans. from E. 1939c by Elisabeth Rüf.

"Verschiedenes."

25. "Geleitwort." (*Zentralblatt* VI, 1933) (581–82) G. 1933e repub.

26. "Zeitgenössisches." (*Neue Zürcher Zeitung* CLV, 1934) (583–93) G. 1934f and G. 1934g repub.

27. "Rundschreiben." (*Zentralblatt* VII, 1934) (595–96) G. 1934j repub.

28. "Geleitwort." (*Zentralblatt* VIII, 1935) (597–602) G. 1935j repub.

29. "Vorbemerkung des Herausgebers." (*Zentralblatt* VIII, 1935) (603–04) G. 1935k repub.

30. "Begrüssungsansprache zum Achten Allgemeinen Ärztlichen Kongress in Bad Nauheim (1935)." (605–07) Presidential address to the Congress, 27–30 Mar. 1935. TR.—English: CW 10,30.

31. "Votum." (*Schweizerische Ärztezeitung* XVI, 1935) (609–12) G. 1935h repub. with sl. title change.

32. "Begrüssungsansprache zum Neunten Internationalen Ärztlichen Kongress für Psychotherapie in Kopenhagen (1937)." (613–15) Presidential address to the Congress, Copenhagen, 2–4 Oct. 1937. TR.—English: CW 10,32.

33. "Presidential Address to the 10th International   1069–73
Medical Congress for Psychotherapy, Oxford,
1938." (564–67) Given in English. Summary pub.
as E. 1938b. TR.—German: GW 10,33.

CW 11 *Psychology and Religion: West and East.* (Collected Works, 11.)
1958: 1st edn. 1969: 2d edn. With 1 plate (frontisp.).

1. "Psychology and Religion." (3–105) E. 1938a,   1–168
combined with a trans. of G. 1940a. Repub. as E.
1959a,11.

2. "A Psychological Approach to the Dogma of the   169–295
Trinity." (107–200) Trans. from G. 1948a,4.

3. "Transformation Symbolism in the Mass."   296–448
(201–96) Trans. from G. 1954b,6. Cf. E. 1955b.

4. "Foreword to White's *God and the Unconscious.*"   449–67
(299–310) E. 1952c, trans. slightly rev.

5. "Foreword to Werblowsky's *Lucifer and*   468–73
Prometheus." (311–15) E. 1952b, trans. slightly
rev.

6. "Brother Klaus." (316–23) Trans. from G. 1933c.   479–87

7. "Psychotherapists or the Clergy." (327–47) Trans.   488–538
from G. 1932a.

8. "Psychoanalysis and the Cure of Souls." (348–54)   539–52
Trans. from G. 1928g.

9. "Answer to Job." (355–470) E. 1954a repub. with   553–758
the addn. of E. 1956c as "Prefatory Note," both
sl. rev. Repub. as E. 1971a,15. Pub. without
"Prefatory Note" as E. 1960a and E. 1965aa.
"Important phrase" restored to "Prefatory Note"
(2d sentence, 4th par.) in the 2d ptg. of the 2d edn.
of this vol. (1973) and repub. in this form as E.
1973a. Cf. E. 1976a, letter to S. Doniger (Nov.
1955), for orig. version of "Prefatory Note."

10. "Psychological Commentary on *The Tibetan*   759–830
Book of the Great Liberation." (509–26) E. 1954e
repub. Pt. 1 (par. 759–87) repub. as E. 1971a,13.

11. "Psychological Commentary on *The Tibetan*   759–830
Book of the Dead." (509–26) E. 1957f repub.
with minor alterations.

33. "Begrüssungsansprache zum Zehnten Internationalen Ärztlichen Kongress für Psychotherapie in Oxford (1938)." (617–20) Presidential address delivered in English to the Congress, Oxford, 29 July–2 Aug. 1938. Trans. from CW 10,33 by Elisabeth Rüf.

GW 11 *Zur Psychologie westlicher und östlicher Religion.* (Gesammelte Werke, 11.) 1963.

1. "Psychologie und Religion." (XVII–117) G. 1940a repub. Repub. as G. 1971d,1.
2. "Versuch einer psychologischen Deutung des Trinitätsdogmas." (119–218) G. 1948a,4 repub. with slight title change.
3. "Das Wandlungssymbol in der Messe." (219–323) G. 1954b,6 repub. Repub. as G. 1971d,4.
4. "Vorwort zu V. White: *Gott und das Unbewusste.*" (325–39) G. 1957h repub.
5. "Vorwort zu Z. Werblowsky: *Lucifer und Prometheus.*" (340–44) The original text of the German ms. first pub. in an English trans. TR.—English: 1952b / CW 11,5.
6. "Bruder Klaus." (345–52) G. 1933c repub.
7. "Über die Beziehung der Psychotherapie zur Seelsorge." (355–76) G. 1932a repub. with slight title change. Repub. as G. 1971d,2.
8. "Psychoanalyse und Seelsorge." (377–83) G. 1928g repub. Repub. as G. 1971d,3.
9. "Antwort auf Hiob." (385–506) G. 1961a repub. "Nachwort" (pp. 505–506) lacks paragraph nos. and is taken from a letter to Simon Doniger (Nov. 1955). For full text of letter, see E. 1976a.
10. "Psychologischer Kommentar zu: *Das tibetische Buch der grossen Befreiung.*" (511–49) G. 1955d repub.
11. "Psychologischer Kommentar zum Bardo Thödol (Das tibetanische Totenbuch)." (550–67) G. 1935f repub.

12. "Yoga and the West." (529–37) Cf. E. 1936c for a   859–76
    dif. trans. on which this one is based.
13. "Foreword to Suzuki's *Introduction to Zen*   877–907
    Buddhism." (538–57) Trans. from G. 1939c.
14. "The Psychology of Eastern Meditation."   908–49
    (558–75) Trans. from G. 1943c.
15. "The Holy Men of India." (576–86) Trans. from   950–63
    G. 1944b. (Brief "Vorwort" omitted.)
16. "Foreword to the *I Ching*." (589–608) E. 1950d,   964–1018
    trans. slightly rev.

12. "Yoga und der Westen." (571–80) The original text of a German ms. first pub. in English. TR.—English: 1936c / CW 11,12.

13. "Geleitwort zu D. T. Suzuki: *Die grosse Befreiung.*" (581–602) G. 1939c repub.

14. "Zur Psychologie östlicher Meditation." (603–21) G. 1948a,5 repub.

15. "Über den indischen Heiligen. Einführung zu H. Zimmer: *Der Weg zum Selbst.*" (622–32) G. 1944b repub.

16. "Vorwort zum *I Ging.*" (633–54) Text of the original German ms. Differs from the English version, E. 1950d. TR.—English: 1950d // Italian: 1950a.

Anhang (not in CW 11):

17. "Antwort an Martin Buber." (657–65) G. 1952j repub. with title change. TR.—English: 1957d / 1973e.

18. "Zu *Psychologie und Religion.*" (665–67) From a letter to a Protestant theologian written in 1940.

19. "Gut und Böse in der analytischen Psychologie." (667–81) G. 1959b repub. Repub. as GW 10,17.

20. "Zum Problem des Christussymbols." (681–85) Trans. by Aniela Jaffé from a letter written in English to Victor White (24 Nov. 1953). Text of orig. letter pub. in E. 1976a.

21. "Zu *Antwort auf Hiob.*" (685–86) From a letter to Hans Schär (16 Nov. 1951). Entire text of letter pub. in G. 1972b and trans. in E. 1976a.

22. "Zu *Antwort auf Hiob.*" (687) From a letter to Dorothée Hoch (28 May 1952). Entire text of letter pub. in G. 1972b and trans. in E. 1976a.

23. "Klappentext zur ersten Auflage von *Antwort auf Hiob.*" (687) Jung's description printed on the dust jacket of the 1st edn., ca. Apr. 1952. TR.—English: CW 18,95.

24. "Aus einem Brief an einen protestantischen Theologen." (688) From a letter to Hans Wegmann (19 Dec. 1943). Entire text pub. in G. 1972a and trans. in E. 1973b.

25. "Brief an *The Listener.* Januar 1960." (689–90) Trans. from E. 1960c by Marianne Niehus-Jung. Repub. in G. 1973a.

26. "Zu *Die Reden Gotamo Buddhos.*" (690–93) G. 1956c repub. with title change. TR.—English: CW 18,101.

CW 12 *Psychology and Alchemy.* (Collected Works, 12.) 1953: 1st edn. 1968: 2d edn. (fully reset). With 270 text illus. Trans. from G. 1952d, except no. 1 in 2d edn.

First Edition:
1. Foreword to the Swiss Edition. (vii)
2. Psychology and Alchemy.
   - I. Introduction to the Religious and Psychological Problems of Alchemy. (1–37)   1–43
     Repub. as E. 1959a,10.
   - II. Individual Dream Symbolism in Relation to Alchemy. (39–213).   44–331
   - III. Religious Ideas in Alchemy. (215–451)   332–554
     Epilogue. (453–63)   555–65

Second Edition:
1. "Prefatory Note to the English Edition." (v)
   Trans. from the unpublished ms.
2. "Foreword to the Swiss Edition." (x)
3. Psychology and Alchemy.
   - I. Introduction to the Religious and Psychological problems of Alchemy. (1–37)   1–43
   - II. Individual Dream Symbolism in Relation to Alchemy. (39–223) Repub. as E. 1971a,11 and E. 1974a,6.   44–331
   - III. Religious Ideas in Alchemy. (225–471)   332–554
     Epilogue. (473–83)   555–65

CW 13 *Alchemical Studies.* (Collected Works, 13.) 1967. With 50 plates (1 col.) and 4 text illus.

1. "Commentary on *The Secret of the Golden Flower.*" (1–56) Trans. from G. 1957b,1 and 3.   1–84
2. "The Vision of Zosimos." (57–108) Trans. from G. 1954b,5.   85–144
3. "Paracelsus as a Spiritual Phenomenon." (109–89) Trans. from G. 1942a,2, with the addition of 2 footnotes derived from posthumous papers.   145–238
4. "The Spirit Mercurius." (191–200) Trans. from G. 1948a,3.   239–303
5. "The Philosophical Tree." (251–349) Trans. from G. 1954b,7.   304–482

GW 12 *Psychologie und Alchemie.* (Gesammelte Werke, 12.) 1972. With 271 text illus. G. 1952d repub.

1. Vorwort. (11) Dated January 1943.
2. Vorwort zur zweiten Auflage. (12) Dated July 1951.
3. [Psychologie und Alchemie.]
   I. Einleitung in die religionspsychologische Problematik der Alchemie. (15–54)
   II. Traumsymbole des Individuationsprozesses. (57–260)
   III. Die Erlösungsvorstellungen in der Alchemie. (263–537)
      Epilog. (539–51)

GW 13 *Studien über alchemistische Vorstellungen.* (Gesammelte Werke, 13.) 1978. With 38 plates and 4 text figures.

1. "Kommentar zu *Das Geheimnis der Goldenen Blüte.*" (11–63) G. 1957b,1 and 3 repub.
2. "Die Visionen des Zosimos." (65–121) G. 1954b,5 repub.
3. "Paracelsus als geistige Erscheinung." (123–209) G. 1942a,2 repub., with the addition of 2 footnotes derived from posthumous papers.
4. "Der Geist Mercurius." (211–269) G. 1948a,3 repub.
5. "Der philosophische Baum." (271–376) G. 1954b,6 repub.

CW 14 *Mysterium Coniunctionis. An Inquiry into the Separation and Synthesis of Psychic Opposites in Alchemy.* (Collected Works, 14.) 1963: 1st edn. 1970: 2d edn. With 10 plates. Trans. from G. 1955a and 1956a.

Foreword. (xiii–xix)

I. The Components of the Coniunctio. (3–41)	1–35
II. The Paradoxa. (42–88)	36–103
III. The Personification of the Opposites. (89–257)	104–348
IV. Rex and Regina. (258–381)	349–543
V. Adam and Eve. (382–456)	544–653
VI. The Conjunction. (457–553)	654–789
Epilogue. (554–56)	790–92

CW 15 *The Spirit in Man, Art, and Literature.* (Collected Works, 15.) 1966. 1971: Paperback edn. Princeton U. P.

1. "Paracelsus." (3–12) Trans. from G. 1934b,5.	1–17
2. "Paracelsus the Physician." (13–30) Trans. from G. 1942a,1.	18–43
3. "Sigmund Freud in His Historical Setting." (33–40) Trans. from G. 1934b,6.	44–59
4. "In Memory of Sigmund Freud." (41–49) Trans. from G. 1939d.	60–73
5. "Richard Wilhelm: In Memoriam." (53–62) Trans. from G. 1957b,2.	74–96
6. "On the Relation of Analytical Psychology to Poetry." (65–83) Trans. from G. 1931a,3. Repub. as E. 1971a,10.	97–132
7. "Psychology and Literature." (84–105) Trans. from G. 1950a,2, with the addition of an introduction trans. from a ms. found posthumously and pub. as the "Vorrede" to GW 15,7.	133–62
8. " 'Ulysses': A Monologue." (109–34) Trans. from G. 1934b,7. Letter to James Joyce (27 Sept. 1932), included in the Appendix, pp. 133–34, is E. 1966d repub. Repub. as E. 1975a.	163–203
9. "Picasso." (135–41) Trans. from G. 1932g.	204–14

GW 14 *Mysterium Coniunctionis. Untersuchung über die Trennung und Zusammensetzung der seelischen Gegensätze in der Alchemie.* Unter Mitarbeit von Marie-Louise von Franz. (Gesammelte Werke, 14.) In two volumes. 1968. Vol. 2 contains 7 plates and 3 text illus. G. 1955a and 1956a reprinted, front matter reset, and with the addn. of a trans. of Greek and Latin texts, bibliography, and an editor's foreword. For contents, see G. 1955a and G. 1956a. Paragraph nos. conform to those of G. 1955a and G. 1956a and vary from CW 14.

Note: Ergänzungsband: *"Aurora Consurgens." Ein dem Thomas von Aquin zugeschriebenes Dokument der alchemistischen Gegensatzproblematik,* von Dr. M.-L. von Franz. (Gesammelte Werke, 14, Ergänzungsband.) Olten: Walter. 1973. Published as a supplemental volume to the Gesammelte Werke.

GW 15 *Über das Phänomen des Geistes in Kunst und Wissenschaft.* (Gesammelte Werke, 15.) 1971.

1. "Paracelsus." (11–20) G. 1934b,5 repub. Cf. G. 1952c.
2. "Paracelsus als Arzt." (21–41) G. 1942a,1 repub.
3. "Sigmund Freud als kulturhistorische Erscheinung." (43–51) G. 1934b,6 repub.
4. "Sigmund Freud." (53–62) G. 1939d repub.
5. "Zum Gedächtnis Richard Wilhelms." (63–73) G. 1957b,2 repub.
6. Über die Beziehungen der analytischen Psychologie zum dichterischen Kunstwerk." (75–96) G. 1931a,3 repub.
7. "Psychologie und Dichtung." (97–120) G. 1950a,2 repub. with the addition of a "Vorrede" pub. here for the first time in the original German, found posthumously. TR. (including "Vorrede")—English: CW 15,7.
8. " 'Ulysses' Ein Monolog." (121–49) G. 1934b,7 repub. "Anhang" (pp. 146–49) includes a trans. by Elisabeth Rüf of a letter written to James Joyce in English (27 Sept. 1932). For text of orig. letter, see CW 15,8 and E. 1973b.
9. "Picasso." (151–57) G. 1934b,8 repub.

CW 16 *The Practice of Psychotherapy. Essays on the Psychology of the Transference and Other Subjects.* (Collected Works, 16.) 1954: 1st edn. 1966: 2d edn. (no. 13 fully reset). With 3 plates and 10 text illus.

1. "Foreword to the Swiss Edition (1958)." Trans. from GW 16,1. (2d edn. only.)

Part One.

2. "Principles of Practical Psychotherapy." (3–20)   1–27
Trans. from G. 1935k.

3. "What is Psychotherapy?" (21–28) Trans. from   28–45
G. 1935g.

4. "Some Aspects of Modern Psychotherapy." (29–35)   46–65
E. 1930b repub. TR.—German: GW 16,4.

5. "The Aims of Psychotherapy." (36–52) Trans.   66–113
from G. 1931a,5.

6. "Problems of Modern Psychotherapy." (53–75)   114–74
Trans. from G. 1931a,2.

7. "Psychotherapy and a Philosophy of Life."   175–91
(76–83) Trans. from G. 1943e.

8. "Medicine and Psychotherapy." (84–93) Trans.   192–211
from G. 1945e.

9. "Psychotherapy Today." (94–110) Trans. from   212–29
G. 1945f.

10. "Fundamental Questions of Psychotherapy."   230–54
(111–25) Trans. from G. 1951d.

Part Two.

11. "The Therapeutic Value of Abreaction." (129–38)   255–93
E. 1928a,11, trans. slightly rev. and with title change.

12. "The Practical Use of Dream-Analysis." (139–61)   294–352
Trans. from G. 1934b,4. Repub. as E. 1974a,5.

13. "The Psychology of the Transference." (163–321)   353–539
1st edn. [(163–323) 2d edn.] Trans. from G.
1946c. (Trans. rev. for 2d edn.) Repub. (2d edn.
version) as E. 1969d. Introduction (1st edn.
version) repub. as E. 1959a,9.

Appendix (2d edn. only):

14. "The Realities of Practical Psychotherapy."   540–64
(327–38) Trans. from an unpub. ms. Lecture given
to II. Tagung für Psychotherapie, Bern, 28 May
1937.

GW 16 *Praxis der Psychotherapie. Beiträge zum Problem der Psychotherapie und zur Psychologie der Übertragung.* (Gesammelte Werke, 16.) 1958. With 3 plates and 11 text illus.

1. "Geleitwort des Autors." (ix–x) Dated Aug. 1957. TR.—English: CW 16,1.

2. "Grundsätzliches zur praktischen Psychotherapie." (1–20) G. 1935l repub. Repub. as G. 1972c,2.

3. "Was ist Psychotherapie?" (21–29) G. 1935g repub. Repub. as G. 1972c,3.

4. "Einige Aspekte der modernen Psychotherapie." (30–37) Trans. from CW 16,4 by the editors. Repub. as G. 1972c,4.

5. "Ziele der Psychotherapie." (38–56) G. 1931a,5 repub.

6. "Die Probleme der modernen Psychotherapie." (57–81) G. 1931a,2 repub.

7. "Psychotherapie und Weltanschauung." (82–89) G. 1946a,4 repub. Repub. as G. 1972c,6.

8. "Medizin und Psychotherapie." (90–99) G. 1945e repub. Repub. as G. 1972c,7.

9. "Die Psychotherapie in der Gegenwart." (100–17) G. 1946a,3 repub. Repub. as G. 1972c,8.

10. "Grundfragen der Psychotherapie." (118–33) G. 1951d repub. Repub. as G. 1972c,1.

11. "Der therapeutische Wert des Abreagierens." (137–47) Trans. from E. 1921a by the editors. Repub. as G. 1972c,5.

12. "Die praktische Verwendbarkeit der Traumanalyse." (148–71) G. 1934b,4 repub.

13. "Die Psychologie der Übertragung." (173–345) G. 1946c repub.

CW 17 *The Development of Personality.* (Collected Works, 17.) 1954.

 1. "Psychic Conflicts in a Child." (1–35) Trans.   1–79
  from G. 1946b,2. Repub. as E. 1969c,1.

 2. "Introduction to Wickes's *Analyse der Kinder-*   80–97
  seele." (37–46) Trans. from G. 1931e. Repub. as
  E. 1966c.

 3. "Child Development and Education." (47–62)   98–126
  E. 1928a,13, Lecture I, slightly rev. Repub. as E.
  1969c,2. TR.—German: GW 17,3.

 4. "Analytical Psychology and Education." (63–132)   127–229
  Trans. from G. 1946b,1. Repub. as E. 1969c,3.

 5. "The Gifted Child." (133–45) Trans. from G.   230–52
  1946b,3. Repub. as E. 1969c,4.

 6. "The Significance of the Unconscious in   253–83
  Individual Education." (149–64) Trans. from a
  German ms. subsequently pub. as G. 1971a,5.

 7. "The Development of Personality." (165–86)   284–323
  Trans. from G. 1934b,9.

 8. "Marriage as a Psychological Relationship."   324–45
  (187–201) Trans. from G. 1931a,11. Repub. as E.
  1959a,12 and as E. 1971a,7.

CW 18 *The Symbolic Life; Miscellaneous Writings.* (Collected Works, 18.)
1975. Trans. by R.F.C. Hull with contributions from others. (Translations are Hull's except as otherwise noted.)

 1. "The Tavistock Lectures." (1–18) E. 1968a   1–415
  repub.

 2. "Symbols and the Interpretation of Dreams."   416–607
  (18–264) Written in English in 1961. English ms.
  here rev. by R.F.C. Hull. Pub., extensively rev.
  and rearranged under the supervision of John
  Freeman in collaboration with Marie-Louise von
  Franz, with title change, as E. 1964a.

 3. "The Symbolic Life." (267–90) E. 1954c repub.,   608–96
  sl. rev.

 4. "On Spiritualistic Phenomena." (293–308)   697–740
  Trans. from G. 1905e.

 5. "Foreword to Jung: *Phenomènes occultes.*"   741–45
  (309–11) Trans. from the German ms. Cf. Fr.
  1939a,1.

GW 17 *Über die Entwicklung der Persönlichkeit.* (Gesammelte Werke, 17.) 1972.

1. "Über Konflikte der kindlichen Seele." (11–47) G. 1946b,2 repub.
2. "Einführung zu Frances G. Wickes *Analyse der Kindesseele.*" (49–58) G. 1931e repub. with title change.
3. "Die Bedeutung der Analytischen Psychologie für die Erziehung." (59–76) G. 1971a,4 repub.
4. "Analytische Psychologie und Erziehung." (77–153) G. 1946b,1 repub.
5. "Der Begabte." (155–68) G. 1946b,3 repub.
6. "Die Bedeutung des Unbewussten für die individuelle Erziehung." (169–87) G. 1971a,5 repub.
7. "Vom Werden der Persönlichkeit." (189–211) G. 1934b,9 repub.
8. "Die Ehe als psychologische Beziehung." (213–27) G. 1931a,11 repub.

GW 18 *Das symbolische Leben.* (Gesammelte Werke, 18.) [Not yet published.]

6. "Psychology and Spiritualism." (312–16) Trans.   746–56
from G. 1948e.

7. "Foreword to Moser: *Spuk: Irrglaube oder*   757–81
Wahrglaube?" (317–20) Jung's Contribution.
(320–26) Trans. from G. 1950e.

8. "Foreword to Jaffé: *Apparitions and Precog-*   782–89
nition." (327–29) E. 1963b repub., trans. sl. rev.

9. "The Present Status of Applied Psychology."   790–93
(333–34) Trans. from G. 1908o by Wolfgang
Sauerländer.

10. "On Dementia Praecox." (335) Trans. from   794
G. 1910s.

11. "Review of Sadger: *Konrad Ferdinand Meyer.*"   795–96
(336–38) Trans. from G. 1909h.

12. "Review of Waldstein: *Das unbewusste Ich.*"   797–99
(339–42) Trans. from G. 1909i.

13. "Crime and the Soul." (343–46) E. 1932c repub.   800–21
with minor rev. in accordance with the German
version, G. 1933a.

14. "The Question of Medical Intervention."   822–25
(347–48) Trans. from G. 1950g.

15. "Foreword to Custance: *Wisdom, Madness and*   826–31
Folly." (349–52) E. 1952a repub., trans. rev.

16. "Foreword to Perry: *The Self in Psychotic*   832–38
Process." (353–56) E. 1953e repub.

17. "Foreword to Schmaltz: *Komplexe Psychologie*   839–40
und körperliches Symptom." (357–58) Trans.
from G. 1955c.

18. "Sigmund Freud: *On Dreams.*" (361–68) Trans.   841–70
from a German ms. found posthumously and
dated 25 January 1901. Prepub. as E. 1973d,1.
Apparently a report given to colleagues at
Burghölzli Mental Hospital.

19. "Review of Hellpach: *Grundlinien einer*   871–83
Psychologie der Hysterie." (369–73) Trans.
from G. 1905b.

20. "Reviews of Psychiatric Literature (1906–1910)."   884–921
(374–87) Trans. from G. 1906e, f, and h; 1907b,c,
and d; 1908e, f, g, h, and k; 1909d–g; and 1910a–j.

21. "The Significance of Freud's Theory for Neurology and Psychiatry." (388–89) Trans. from G. 1908d by Wolfgang Sauerlander.   922

22. "Review of Stekel: *Nervöse Angstzustände und ihre Behandlung*." (390–91) Trans. from G. 1908j by Wolfgang Sauerlander.   923–24

23. "Editorial Preface to the *Jahrbuch* (1909)." (392) Trans. from G. 1909b.   925

24. "Marginal Notes on Wittels: *Die sexuelle Not*." (393–96) Trans. from G. 1910l. Prepub. as E. 1973d,2.   926–31

25. "Review of Wulffen: *Der Sexualverbrecher*." (397) Trans. from G. 1910p.   932–33

26. "Abstracts of the Psychological Works of Swiss Authors." (398–421) Trans. from G. 1910m. List of abstracts made for the *Folia-Neurobiologica* follows. Cf. G. 1908c,i, and l.   934–1025

27. "Review of Hitschmann: *Freuds Neurosenlehre*." (422) Trans. from G. 1911d.   1026

28. "Annual Report by the President of the International Psychoanalytic Association." (423–26) Trans. from G. 1911g by Wolfgang Sauerländer.   1027–33

29. "Two Letters on Psychoanalysis." (427–29) Trans. from G. 1912e and f.   1034–40

30. "On the Psychoanalytic Treatment of Nervous Disorders." (430–32) Trans. from G. 1912h.   1041–54

31. "A Comment on Tausk's Criticism of Nelken." (433–37) Trans. from G. 1913d. Prepub. as E. 1973d,3.   1055–64

32. "Answers to Questions on Freud." (438–40) E. 1968f repub. Written in English and dated 7 Aug. 1953.   1065–76

33. "The Concept of Ambivalence." (443–45) Trans. from G. 1911h by Wolfgang Sauerlander.   1077–81

34. "Contributions to Symbolism." (446) Trans. from G. 1911f by Wolfgang Sauerlander.   1082–83

35. "Adaptation, Individuation, Collectivity." (449–54) Trans. from the unpub. German typescripts found posthumously and dated Oct. 1916. Prepub. as E. 1970c.   1084–1106

36. "Foreword to the Hungarian Edition of *On the Psychology of the Unconscious*." (455–56). Trans. from the German ms. dated Jan. 1944. Cf. Hu. 1948a.   1107–09

37. "Forewords to Jung: *Über psychische Energetik und das Wesen der Träume*." (459–60) Trans. from G. 1948b,1.   1110–12

38. "On Hallucination." (461) Trans. from G. 1933f.   1113–14

39. "Foreword to Schleich: *Die Wunder der Seele*." (462–66) Trans. from G. 1934e.   1115–20

40. "Foreword to Jacobi: *The Psychology of C. G. Jung*." (467–68) E. 1962c repub., trans. rev. Pub. in a dif. trans. as E. 1942c.   1121–23

41. "Foreword to the Spanish Edition." (See no. 40.) (468) Trans. from the German ms. Cf. Sp. 1947a.   1124

42. "Foreword to Harding: *Psychic Energy*." (469–70) E. 1947e repub., trans. sl. rev.   1125–28

43. "Address on the Occasion of the Founding of the C. G. Jung Institute, Zurich, 24 April 1948." (471–76) Trans. from the unpub. German typescript.   1129–41

44. "Depth Psychology." (477–86) Trans. from G. 1951c.   1142–62

45. "Foreword to the First Volume of Studies from the C. G. Jung Institute." (487–88) Trans. from G. 1949e.   1163–64

46. "Foreword to F. Fordham: *Introduction to Jung's Psychology*." (489–90) E. 1953d repub.   1165–67

47. "Foreword to M. Fordham: *New Developments in Analytical Psychology*." (491–93) E. 1957g repub.   1168–73

48. "An Astrological Experiment." (494–501) Trans. from G. 1958f with the exception of par. 1187, which was subsequently added to the German ms., and par. 1188, added to a letter by the translator, dated 23 Apr. 1954.   1174–92

49. "Letters on Synchronicity." (502–09) To Markus Fierz (21 Feb. 1950; 2 Mar. 1950; 20 Oct. 1954; 28 Oct. 1954). ?Trans. from the orig. German letters. To Michael Fordham (1 July 1955). Written in English.   1193–1212

50. "The Future of Parapsychology." (510–11) E. 1963e repub.   1213–22

51. "The Hypothesis of the Collective Unconscious." (515–16) Trans. from G. 1932i.   1223–25

52. "Foreword to Adler: *Entdeckung der Seele.*" (517) Trans. from G. 1934d.   1226–27

53. "Foreword to Harding: *Woman's Mysteries.*" (518–20) E. 1955e repub., trans. rev.   1228–33

54. "Foreword to Neumann: *The Origins and History of Consciousness.*" (521–22) E. 1954f repub.   1234–37

55. "Foreword to Adler: *Studies in Analytical Psychology.*" (523–24) E. 1966e repub.   1238–44

56. "Foreword to Jung: *Gestaltungen des Unbewussten.*" (525–26) Trans. from G. 1950a,1.   1245–47

57. "Foreword to Wickes: *Von der inneren Welt des Menschen.*" (527–28) Trans. from G. 1953b.   1248–49

58. "Foreword to Jung: *Von den Wurzeln des Bewusstseins.*" (529) Trans. from G. 1954b,1.   1250–51

59. "Foreword to van Helsdingen: *Beelden uit het onbewuste.*" (530–31) Trans. from G. 1957f.   1252–55

60. "Foreword to Jacobi: *Complex/Archetype/Symbol.*" (532–33) E. 1959e repub.   1256–58

61. "Foreword to Bertine: *Human Relationships.*" (534–36) E. 1958e repub., trans. sl. rev.   1259–63

62. "Preface to de Laszlo: *Psyche and Symbol.*" (537–42) E. 1958a,1 repub., sl. rev.   1264–75

63. "Foreword to Brunner: *Die Anima als Schicksalsproblem des Mannes.*" (543–47) Trans. from G. 1963a.   1278–83

64. "Report on America." (551) Trans. from G. 1910n.   1284

65. "On the Psychology of the Negro." (552) Trans. from G. 1913c.   1285

66. "A Radio Talk in Munich." (553–57) Trans. from an unpub. German ms. dated 19 Jan. 1930.   1286–91

67. "Forewords to Jung: *Seelenprobleme der Gegenwart.*" (558–60) Trans. from G. 1931a,1 and from the orig. German ms. pub. in trans. as the Foreword to It. 1959c. Dated Dec. 1930, July 1932, and March 1959.   1292–95

68. "Foreword to Aldrich: *The Primitive Mind and Modern Civilization.*" (561–63) E. 1931b repub., trans. sl. rev.   1296–99

69. "Press Communiqué on Visiting the United States (1936)." (564–65) Unpub. typescript written in English and dated Sept. 1936.   1300–04

70. "Psychology and National Problems." (566–81) Unpublished typescript written in English. Lecture given at the Institute of Medical Psychology (Tavistock Clinic), London, 14 Oct. 1936.   1305–42

71. "Return to the Simple Life." (582–88) Trans. from G. 1941e.   1343–56

72. "Epilogue to Jung: *L'Homme à la découverte de son âme.*" (589–90) Trans. from Fr. 1944a,9 by A.S.B. Glover.   1357–59

73. "Marginalia on Contemporary Events." (591–603) Trans. from a German typescript dated 1945, the last 9 pars. of which were pub. as G. 1946g.   1360–83

74. "Answers to *Mishmar* on Hitler." (604–05) Trans. from a letter written 14 Sept. 1945 in German to Eugen Kolb, Swiss representative for the Israeli newspaper, *Al Hamishmar*. Cf. He. 1974a.   1384–87

75. "Techniques of Attitude Change Conducive to World Peace (Memorandum to UNESCO)." (606–13) Unpublished typescript/manuscript written in English in response to a request from UNESCO.   1388–1402

76. "The Effect of Technology on the Human Psyche." (614–15) Trans. from G. 1949g.   1403–07

77. "Foreword to Neumann: *Depth Psychology and a New Ethic.*" (616–22) E. 1969e repub., trans. sl. rev.   1408–20

78. "Foreword to Baynes: *Analytical Psychology and the English Mind.*" (623–24) E. 1950b repub.   1421–27

79. "Rules of Life." (625) Trans. from G. 1954f.   1428–30

80. "On Flying Saucers." (626–31) Trans. from G. 1954e.   1431–44

81. "Statement to the United Press International." (631–32) Trans. from G. 1958h.   1445–46

82. "Letter to Keyhoe." (632–33) E. 1959g repub.   1447–51

83. "Human Nature Does Not Yield Easily to Idealistic Advice." (634–35) E. 1955h repub.   1452–55

84. "On the Hungarian Uprising." (636) Trans. from G. 1956f and G. 1957c, here combined.   1456–57

85. "On Psychodiagnostics." (637) Trans. from G. 1958g.   1458–60

86. "If Christ Walked the Earth Today." (638) E. 1958i repub. with title change.   1461

87. "Foreword to *Hugh Crichton Miller 1877–1959*." (639–41) E. 1961b repub., sl. rev.   1462–65

88. "Why I Am Not a Catholic." (645–47) Trans. by Hildegard Nagel from a letter written in German to H. Irminger (22 Sept. 1944) and never sent.   1466–72

89. "The Definition of Demonism." (648) Trans. from a definition written in July 1945, of which only the first sentence and the references were pub. as G. 1949h.   1473–74

90. "Foreword to Jung: *Symbolik des Geistes*." (649–50) Trans. from G. 1948a,1.   1475–77

91. "Foreword to Quispel: *Tragic Christianity*." (651–53) Trans. from an unpub. German ms.   1478–82

92. "Foreword to Abegg: *Ostasien denkt anders*." (654–55) E. 1955j repub.   1483–85

93. "Foreword to Allenby: *The Origins of Monotheism*." (656–59) Trans. from an unpub. German ms.   1486–96

94. "The Miraculous Fast of Brother Klaus." (660–61) Trans. from G. 1951e. Rev. from a letter to Fritz Blanke (10 Nov. 1948). Cf. E. 1973b for a trans. of entire orig. letter.   1497–98

95. "Concerning 'Answer to Job'." (662) Trans. from GW 11,23 by Ruth Horine. Jung's description, printed on the dust jacket of the orig. edn., ca. 1 April 1952. Cf. G. 1952a.   1498a

96. "Religion and Psychology: A Reply to Martin Buber." (663–70) E. 1973e repub. (German text pub. in GW 11.)   1499–1513

97. "Address at the Presentation of the Jung Codex." 1514–17
(671–72) Given in Zurich, 15 Nov. 1953. Trans.
from a German ms. pub. as G. 1975a,4. (Cf.
no. 135, below.)

98. "Letter to Père Bruno." (673–78) Trans. from 1518–31
Fr. 1956b by A.S.B. Glover and Jane A. Pratt.
Dated 5 Nov. 1953. Cf. letters to Bruno (22 Dec.
1954; 20 Nov. 1956) in E. 1975a.

99. "Letter to Père Lachat." (679–91) Trans. from 1532–57
the French by A.S.B. Glover. Dated 27 March
1954. Cf. letters to Lachat (18 Jan. and 29 June
1955) in E. 1975a.

100. "On Resurrection." (692–96) Written in English 1558–74
in reply to an inquiry and dated 19 Feb. 1954.

101. "On the Discourses of the Buddha." (697–99) 1575–80
Trans. from G. 1956c. (German text pub. as
GW 11,26.)

102. "Foreword to Froboese-Thiele: *Träume—eine* 1581–83
Quelle religiöser Erfahrung?" (700–01) Trans.
from G. 1957e.

103. "Jung and Religious Belief." (702–44) E. 1958c 1584–1690
repub., with minor stylistic rev., addl. footnotes,
and addn. of title. Cf. letter to H. L. Philp (11
June 1957) in E. 1976a.

104. "Foreword to a Catalogue on Alchemy." (747) 1691
E. 1968d repub., sl. rev. and with the addn. of a
title.

105. "Faust and Alchemy." (748–50) Trans. from G. 1692–99
1950b by Hildegard Nagel.

106. "Alchemy and Psychology." (751–53) Written 1700–04
in English for the *Encyclopedia Hebraica*, and
pub. here with minor stylistic rev. TR.—Hebrew:
1950/51a.

107. "Memorial to J. S." (757–58) E. 1955c repub. 1705–10
Spoken in English in memory of Jerome Schloss,
1927.

108. "Foreword to Schmid-Guisan: *Tag und Nacht*." 1711–12
(759–60) Trans. from G. 1931d.

109. "Hans Schmid-Guisan: In Memoriam." (760–61) 1713–15
Trans. from G. 1932d.

110. "On the Tale of the Otter." (762–64) Trans. from G. 1932b. — 1716–22

111. "Is There a Freudian Type of Poetry?" (765–66) Trans. from the unpub. German ms. Cf. Fr. 1932b. — 1723–24

112. "Foreword to Gilbert: *The Curse of the Intellect.*" (767) Written in English for the book, which was never pub., and dated Jan. 1934. — 1725–26

113. "Foreword to Jung: *Wirklichkeit der Seele.*" (768–69) Trans. from G. 1934b,1. — 1727–29

114. "Foreword to Mehlich: *J. H. Fichtes Seelenlehre und ihre Beziehung zur Gegenwart.*" (770–72) Trans. from G. 1935e. — 1730–36

115. "Foreword to von Koenig-Fachsenfeld: *Wandlungen des Traumproblems von der Romantik bis zur Gegenwart.*" (773–75) Trans. from G. 1935d. — 1737–41

116. "Foreword to Gilli: *Der dunkle Bruder.*" (776–78) Trans. from G. 1938d. — 1742–47

117. "Gérard de Nerval." (779) Trans. from G. 1946d. — 1748

118. "Foreword to Fierz-David: *Dream of Poliphilo.*" (780–81) E. 1950c repub., trans. rev. — 1749–52

119. "Foreword to Crottet: *Mondwald.*" (782–83) Trans. from G. 1949c. — 1753–54

120. "Foreword to Jacobi: *Paracelsus: Selected Writings.*" (784–85) E. 1951b repub., sl. rev. — 1755–59

121. "Foreword to Kankeleit: *Das Unbewusste als Keimstätte des Schöpferischen.*" (786) "Jung's Contribution." (786–87) Trans. from G. 1959d. — 1760–68

122. "Foreword to Serrano: *The Visits of the Queen of Sheba.*" (788) E. 1960b repub., somewhat rev. Cf. E. 1966c,1. — 1769

123. "Is There a True Bilingualism?" (789) Trans. from Fr. 1961d by R.F.C. Hull. — 1770–73

124. "Review of Heyer: *Der Organismus der Seele.*" (793–94) Trans. from G. 1933d. — 1774

125. "Review of Heyer: *Praktische Seelenheilkunde.*" (794–96) Trans. from G. 1936d. — 1775–79

126. "On the *Rosarium Philosophorum.*" (797–800) Trans. from G. 1938b. — 1780–89

127. "Preface to an Indian Journal of Psychotherapy."   1790–91
     (801) E. 1956e repub.
128. "On Pictures in Psychiatric Diagnosis." (802)   1792
     Trans. from G. 1959h by Hildegard Nagel.
129. "Foreword to Evans: *The Problem of the*   1793–94
     Nervous Child." (805–06) E. 1920a repub.
130. "Foreword to Harding: *The Way of All*   1795–1802
     Women." (807–10) E. 1933b repub.
131. "Depth Psychology and Self-Knowledge."   1803–17
     (811–19) E. 1969f repub.
132. "Foreword to Spier: *The Hands of Children.*"   1818–21
     (820–21) E. 1944b repub., trans. rev.
133. "Foreword to the Hebrew Edition of Jung: 1822–24
     Psychologie und Erziehung." (822) Trans. from
     an unpub. German ms. Cf. He. 1958a.
     Appendix.
134. "Foreword to *Psychologische Abhandlungen,*   1825
     Volume I.*" (825) Trans. from G. 1914c by
     Lisa Ress.
135. "Address at the Presentation of the Jung   1826–34
     Codex." (826–29) Item no. 97, above, the trans.
     revised and augmented by Lisa Ress, from a
     German ms.

III

SEMINAR NOTES

SEMINAR NOTES

References are added, in square brackets, to the copies in the Kristine Mann Library, Analytical Psychology Club of New York. * = not examined.

1923   *[Human Relationships in Relation to the Process of Individuation.]* Unpub. typescript. 27 + 11 pp. Given at Polzeath, Cornwall, England, July 1923. Unauthorized longhand notes taken for their own use by M. Esther Harding and Kristine Mann. Also known as the "Cornwall Seminar." [KML 1]

1925a   *[Analytical Psychology.]* Notes on the Seminar in Analytical Psychology . . . [Comp. by Cary F. de Angulo and rev. by C. G. Jung.] Arranged by members of the class. Zurich: multigraphed typescript. 227 pp. Figs. Given in Zurich, 23 Mar.–6 July 1925. Indexed. Cf. Sem. 1939 index. Spine title: *Analytical Psychology.* [KML 2]

1925b   *[Dreams and Symbolism.]* Lectures at Swanage. Xeroxed typescript. 101 pp. Given at Swanage, England, July–Aug. 1925. Unauthorized longhand notes taken by M. Esther Harding. Also known as the "Swanage Seminar." [KML 3]

1928–30   *Dream Analysis.* Notes of the Seminars in Analytical Psychology . . . [1930: 1st edn.] Zurich: multigraphed typescript. 6 pts. in 5 vols. *1938: 2d [unalt.] edn. Ed. by Carol S. Baumann. 1958: 3d [unalt.] edn. Zurich: Privately printed [typewriter comp., offset] for the Psychology Club Zurich. 2 vols. Given in Zurich, 7 Nov. 1928–25 June 1930.

Contents of 1st edn. (vols.):

  1:   7 Nov.–12 Dec. 1928. Arranged by Anne Chapin. 68 pp.
  2/3:   23 Jan.–26 June 1929. Comp. and ed. by Charlotte H. Deady. 285 pp.
  4:   9 Oct.–11 Dec. 1929. Comp. and ed. by Mary Foote. 212 pp.
  5:   22 Jan.–26 Mar. 1930. Comp. and ed. by Mary Foote. 190 pp.
  6:   7 May–25 June 1930. Arranged and ed. by Mary Foote. 219 pp. Includes index of dreams in all vols., pp. 218–19.
Indexed in Sem. 1932b index and in Sem. 1939 index.

Contents of 3d edn. (vols.):

1: 7 Nov. 1928–26 June 1929. 215 pp. Notes with this edn. say that the material was comp. and ed. by Mary Foote from the notes of Anne Chapin and Ethel Taylor.

2: 9 Oct. 1929–25 June 1930. 298 pp. Notes with this edn. say that the material was comp. and ed. by Charlotte H. Deady and re-ed. by Carol F. Baumann. [KML 6, S. 3 & 4]

1930–31 *Bericht über das deutsche Seminar . . .* Comp. and ed. by Olga von Koenig-Fachsenfeld. 1931–32, 2d ptg. Stuttgart: Privately printed. 2 vols. Given in Küsnacht/Zurich, 6 Oct. 1930–10 Oct. 1931. Contents (vols.):

1: 6–11 Oct. 1930. 113 pp. Figs + 21 plates. Also contains R. Heyer: "Bericht über C. G. Jungs analytisches Seminar." *Zentralblatt für Psychotherapie . . .* , 4:1, 104–10.

2: 5–10 Oct. 1931. 153 pp. Figs. + 16 plates.

Spine title: *Deutsches Seminar.* ?Also known as *Zur Psychologie der Individuation.* [KML 8,9]

1930–34 [*Interpretation of Visions.*] Notes of the Seminars in Analytical Psychology. Ed. by Mary Foote. Autumn 1930–Winter 1934. Zurich: multigraphed typescript. 11 vols. + 1 of 29 plates. *1939–41: New edn. Given in Zurich, 15 Oct. 1930–21 Mar. 1934. Indexed in Sem. 1932b index and Sem. 1939 index. Spine title: *Visions.* [KML ?]

Excerpts pub. in 10 installments, each titled "The Interpretation of Visions. Excerpts from the Notes of Mary Foote." Selected and ed. by Jane A. Pratt. *Spring 1960–69.* New York: Analytical Psychology Club. Installments:

1. 30 Oct.–5 Nov. 1930. *Spring 1960.* pp. 107–48.
2. 12 Nov.–9 Dec. 1930. *Spring 1961.* pp. 109–51.
3. 13 Jan.–25 Mar. 1931. *Spring 1962.* pp. 107–57.
4. 6 May–24 June 1931. *Spring 1963.* pp. 102–47.
5. 11 Nov.–16 Dec. 1931. *Spring 1964.* pp. 97–138.
6. 16 Dec.–10 Feb. 1932. *Spring 1965.* pp. 100–41.
7. 17 Feb.–9 Mar. 1932. *Spring 1966.* pp. 121–53.
8. 9 Mar.–22 June 1932. *Spring 1967.* pp. 86–147.
9. 1 June 1932–18 Jan. 1933. *Spring 1968.* pp. 53–132.
10. 25 Jan.–21 June 1933. *Spring 1969.* pp. 7–72.

Republ. as *The Visions Seminars.* With parts 11–13 ed. by Patricia Berry. Zurich: Spring Publs., 1976. 2 vols. pp. 534, 28 pls.

1932a With J. W. Hauer: *The Kundalini Yoga.* Notes on the seminar given by J. W. Hauer with Psychological Commentary by C. G. Jung. Comp. by Mary Foote. Autumn 1932. [1st edn.] Zurich: multigraphed typescript. 216 pp. illus. *1940: 2d edn. Given at the Psychologischer Club Zurich, by Hauer 3–8 Oct. and by Jung 12, 19, and 26 Oct. and 2 Nov. 1932. 1st edn. contains the following material of Jung's:

  1. "Psychological Commentary." Lectures I–IV. (131–216) Lectures I–III given in English. Lecture IV given in German, "arranged by [Toni] Wolff for the report of the German seminar, with additional material from Dr. Jung," and trans. by Cary F. Baynes.

Also known as the "Tantra Yoga Seminars." [KML 10]

1st 2 lectures repub., sl. rev., as "Psychological Commentary on Kundalini Yoga. Lectures One and Two." *Spring 1975.* pp. 1–32. Zurich: Analytical Psychology Club of New York.

Also issued in a German version: *Bericht über das Seminar von Prof. Dr. J. W. Hauer.* 3–8 Oktober 1932 im Psychologischer Club Zurich. 1933: Zurich: multigraphed typescript. Contains the following Jung material:

  1. "Erstes–Viertes englische(s) Seminar(e)." (105–48) [?Trans. and] ed. by Linda Fierz and Toni Wolff from the notes of the English seminars, with the exception of the fourth seminar, as noted above under the English version.

  2. "Westliche Parallelen zu den tantrischen Symbolen." (153–58) Condensed version of seminar given during the same period as those above.

1932b [*Index to Dream Analysis and Interpretation of Visions; Notes of the English Seminars,*] Autumn 1928–Spring 1932. Comp. by Carol Sawyer [Baumann]. 1932: Zurich: multigraphed typescript. 36 pp. Includes chronological list of dreams and visions, and list of reference books mentioned. Incorporated in Sem. 1939, index. Paging corresponds to that of the first edns. Spine title: *Index to Dreams and Visions, 1928–32.*

1933 *Bericht über das Berliner Seminar* . . . 1933. [1st edn.]. Berlin: multigraphed typescript. 199 pp. 1950's, 2d ptg. Zurich. 165 pp. Given in Berlin, 26 June–1 July 1933. Contains the following Jung material:

1. "Stenogramm des Seminars . . ." (1–165) Shorthand notes of the seminars.
2. "Stenogramm des Zwiegesprächs von . . . Jung und A. Weizsäcker in der Funkstunde Berlin," 26 June 1933. (166–73) Interview broadcast over Berlin radio on 26 June 1933.

Also known as the "Berliner Seminare" and possibly as "Über Träume." A 2d vol. of seminars given in Berlin in 1934 is said to exist.

1933–41   *Modern Psychology*. Notes on lectures . . . [1934?–42, 1st edn.] Zurich: multigraphed typescript. 6 vols. 1959–60: 2d edn. Zurich: Privately printed [typewriter comp., offset]. 6 vols. in 3. Given at the Eidgenössische Technische Hochschule, Zurich, 20 Oct. 1933–11 July 1941.

Arrangement of contents in the 1st edn. (vols.):

1:   *Modern Psychology*. 20 Oct. 1933–23 Feb. 1934. 77 pp.
2:   *Modern Psychology*. 20 Apr. 1934–12 July 1935. 163 pp. Both these vols. comp. and trans., from shorthand notes, by Elizabeth Welsh and Barbara Hannah.
3:   *Process of Individuation*: [*Eastern Texts*]. 28 Oct. 1938–23 June 1939. 166 pp. Comp. and trans. by Barbara Hannah.
4:   *Process of Individuation: Exercitia Spiritualia of St. Ignatius of Loyola*. 16 June 1939–8 Mar. 1940. 42 pp. Comp. and trans. from the shorthand notes of Riwkah Schärf by Barbara Hannah.
5:   *Process of Individuation: Alchemy I*. 8 Nov. 1940–28 Feb. 1941. pp. 157. Comp. and trans. from the shorthand notes of Riwkah Schärf by Barbara Hannah.
6:   *Process of Individuation: Alchemy II*. 2 May–11 July 1941. pp. 152. Comp. and trans. from the shorthand notes of Riwkah Schärf by Barbara Hannah.

Arrangement of contents in the 2d edn. (vols.):

1/2: *Modern Psychology*.
3/4: *The Process of Individuation*: [*Eastern Texts*]. (11–101) *The Process of Individuation: Exercitia Spiritualia of St. Ignatius of Loyola*. (102–264)
5/6: *The Process of Individuation: Alchemy I*. (11–130) *The Process of Individuation: Alchemy II*. (135–231). Index (235–53). [KML 15, 16]

1934-39 *Psychological Analysis of Nietzsche's Zarathustra.* Notes on Seminars . . . Ed. by Mary Foote. Spring 1934–Winter 1939. 1st edn. Zurich: multigraphed typescript. 10 vols. + index vol. *[n.d.: 2d edn.] Given in Zurich. Vol. 1–3 typed double-spaced; 4–10 single-spaced.* In the 2d edn., spacing is the same in all vols. [KML 17, 18]

Extracts of vol. 7 pub. as follows: [1] "Answer by Dr. Jung to a Question Concerning the Archaic Elements in the Self. Zurich Seminar June 3, 1936." *Bull. APC*, 30:5 (May), 14–19. A version, taken from some student's notes, of Jung's spoken reply given in the course of his seminar, Zurich, 3 June 1936. (The seminar notes above contain a dif. version, Pt. 7, pp. 80–85.) [2] "Comments on a Passage from Nietzsche's Zarathustra (1936)." *Spring 1972.* pp. 149–61. Zurich: Analytical Psychology Club of New York. Excerpted from the seminar notes, Pt. 7, Lecture 2 (13 May 1936), pp. 18–29, and slightly re-edited.

Index vol.: *Index of the Notes on Psychological Analysis of Nietzsche's Zarathustra* . . . Vols. 1–10, 1934–1939 [1st edn.]. Comp. by Mary Briner. 1942, Zurich: multigraphed typescript. 58 pp. [KML 19]

1934 * *[Bericht über das Basler Seminar.]* 1–6 October 1934. No editor named. Basel, 1935: multigraphed typescript, untitled. pp. 89.

1935 *Fundamental Psychological Conceptions.* A Report of Five Lectures . . . Ed. by Mary Barker and Margaret Game for the Analytical Psychology Club, London, 1936. London: multigraphed typescript. 235 pp. Given under the auspices of the Institute of Medical Psychology, London, 30 Sept.–4 Oct. 1935. Pub., sl. rev., with title change, as E. 1968a and CW 18,1. Also known as the "London Lectures" and as the "Tavistock Lectures." [KML 20]

1935-36 *Lectures at the ETH, Zurich, Oct. 1935–July 1936. Comp. by Barbara Hannah, Una Gauntlett Thomas, and Elizabeth Baumann.

1936-37a *Dream Symbols of the Individuation Process.* Ed. from members' notes by Kristine Mann, M. Esther Harding, and Eleanor Bertine, with the help of Sallie Pinckney. New York: multigraphed typescript. 1937–38. 2 vols. Based on shorthand transcripts "as near verbatim as possible." Contents (vols.):

1: Seminar at Bailey Island, Maine. 20–25 Sept. 1936. Also known as the "Bailey Island Seminar."

2: Seminar in New York City, 16–18, 25–26 Oct. 1937. Also known as the "New York Seminar." [KML 22]

1936–37b *Seminar über Kinderträume und ältere Literatur über Traum-Interpretation.* Ed. by Hans H. Baumann. [?1937] Zurich: multigraphed typescript. 115 pp. Given at the Eidgenössische Technische Hochschule, Zurich, Winter Semester 1936–37. Spine title: *Kinderträume. W.S. 1936–37.* [KML 21]

Excerpt trans. and pub. as follows: "A Seminar with C. G. Jung: Comments on A Child's Dream (1936–37)." *Spring 1974.* pp. 200–23. Zurich: Analytical Psychology Club of New York. Trans. by Eugene H. Henley from the seminar above.

1937 * *Bericht über die Berliner Vorträge.* 28–29 September 1937. Ed. by Marianne Stark. Berlin, 1937: multigraphed typescript. pp. 55, with 52 photographs.

1938–39 *Psychologische Interpretation von Kinderträumen und ältere Literatur über Träume.* Ed. by Liliane Frey and Riwkah Schärf from stenographic transcripts. [n.d. 1st edn.] [1950's] 2d edn. Zurich: [Privately printed for the C. G. Jung-Institut] Eidgenössische Technische Hochschule. 217 pp. Given at the ETH, Zurich, 25 Oct. 1938–7 Mar. 1939. Spine title: *Kinderträume, W.S. 1938/39.* A supplementary vol. of students' papers, made up for the 1st edn., has been added to the 2d edn. as an "Anhang." [KML 24, 25] Trans. as follows: *Psychological Interpretation of Children's Dreams.* Notes on Lectures . . . 1938–39. Zurich: multigraphed typescript. 143 pp. Trans. from the German above by Mary Foote, with the help of Cornelia Brunner. Spine title: *Children's Dreams.* [KML 23]

1939 [*Index to Analytical Psychology, Dream Analysis, and Interpretation of Visions*; Notes of the English Seminars, 1925–Winter 1934.] Comp. by Mary Briner. 1939. Zurich: multigraphed typescript. 59 pp. Incorporates Sem. 1932b index. Includes list of dreams and visions, list of reference books mentioned, and word index. Paging corresponds to that of the 1st edns. Spine title: *Index 1925–1934.* [KML 4]

1939–40 *Psychologische Interpretation von Kinderträumen.* Ed. by Liliane
Frey and Aniela Jaffé from the stenographic transcripts of Riwkah
Schärf. Date of 1st edn. not known. 1950's: 2d edn. Zurich: [Privately
printed for the C. G. Jung-Institut] Eidgenössische Technische
Hochschule. 195 pp. Given at the Hochschule, Zurich, Winter
Semester 1939–40. Spine title: *Kinderträume. W.S. 1939/40.* A sup-
plementary vol. of students' papers, made up for the 1st edn., has
been added to the 2d edn. as an "Anhang." [KML 26, 27]

INDEXES

INDEX 1: TITLES

Including the titles of all English and German items and of original works in other languages. Also see Index 2 under names of authors for whose book Jung wrote a preface, etc.

A

Abstracts, *Folia neuro-biologica*: Jung, Métral, Lombard, Claparède, Flournoy, Leroy Lemaître, G. 1908c; Piéron, Revault d'Allones, Hartenberg, Dumas, Dromard, Marie, Janet, Pascal, Vigouroux et Juquelier, G. 1908i; Varendonck, Claparède, Katzaroff, Maeder, Rouma, G. 1908l

"Abstracts of the Psychological Works of Swiss Authors (1910)": CW 18,26

"Adaptation": E. 1970c,1, CW 18,35

"Adaptation, Individuation, Collectivity (1916)": CW 18,35

"Address at the Presentation of the Jung Codex": G. 1975a,4, CW 18,97

"Address Given at the Opening Meeting of the C. G. Jung Institute of Zurich, 24 April 1948": E. 1948b

"Ärztliches Gutachten über einen Fall von Simulation geistiger Störung": G. 1904c, GW 1,7

"After the Catastrophe": E. 1946a, 1947a,6, CW 10,11

"Aims of Psychotherapy, The": E. 1933a,3, CW 16,5

Aion: G. 1951a, GW 9,ii; CW 9,ii; Excerpts: E. 1950a, 1958a,2, 1971a,6

Alchemical Studies: CW 13

"Alchemistic Text Interpreted As If It Were a Dream, An": E. 1947c

"Alchemy and Psychology": CW 18,106

Alchemy and the Occult. A Catalogue . . . , Prefatory Note: E. 1968d, CW 18,104

"Alhemiya upesyhologiya": He. 1950/51a

"Allgemeine Aspekte der Psychoanalyse": G. 1972e,9, GW 4,10

"Allgemeine Beschreibung der Typen": G. 1972d,2, GW 6,3,10

"Allgemeine Gesichtspunkte zur Psychologie des Traumes": G. 1928b,3, 1948b,4, GW 8,9

Allgemeines zur Komplextheorie: G. 1934a, 1948b,3, GW 8,3

"An der psychiatrischen Klinik in Zürich gebräuchlichen psychologischen Untersuchungsmethoden, Die": G. 1910r

"Analyse der Assoziationen eines Epileptikers": G. 1905g, 1906a,2

"Analyse des rêves, L' ": Fr. 1909a

"Analysis of Dreams, The": E. 1974a,1, CW 4,3

"Analysis of the Associations of an Epileptic, An": E. 1918a,2, CW 2,2

Analytical Psychology: E. 1916a

Analytical Psychology: Seminar Notes, 1925a

"Analytical Psychology and Education": E. 1928a,13, 1969c,3, CW 17,4

"Analytical Psychology and Weltanschauung": E. 1928a,4, CW
8,14

Analytical Psychology Club:
E. 1942b, 1949b, 1950a, 1953b

Analytical Psychology Club, Papers
of: E. 1940a, 1948a&d, 1951a

Analytical Psychology; Its Theory
and Practice. The Tavistock
Lectures: E. 1968a

Analytische Psychologie und
Erziehung: G. 1926b, G. 1946b,1,
GW 17,4

"Analytische Psychologie und Weltanschauung": G. 1931a,12,
GW 8,14

"Annual Report by the President
of the International Psychoanalytic Association": CW 18,28

"Answer by Dr. Jung to a Question
Concerning the Archaic Elements
in the Self . . .": Seminar Notes,
1934–39

"Answer to Buber": E. 1957d

Answer to Job: E. 1954a, 1960a,
1965a, 1971a,15, 1973a, CW 11,9

"Answers to Mishmar on Adolf
Hitler": CW 18,74

Answers to questionnaire, "The
Future of Parapsychology":
E. 1963e

Answers to questions on Goethe:
G. 1932c

"Answers to Questions on Freud":
E. 1968f, CW 18,32

"Antrittsvorlesung": G. 1934a

"Antwort an Martin Buber":
GW 11,17

Antwort auf Hiob: G. 1952a,
1961a, GW 11,9; "Klappentext
zur ersten Auflage": GW 11,22

"Approaching the Unconscious":
E. 1964a

"Archaic Man": E. 1933a,7, CW
10,3

"Archaische Mensch, Der": G.
1931a,9, 1931f, GW 10,3

Archetypes and the Collective
Unconscious, The: CW 9,i

"Archetypes of the Collective
Unconscious," E. 1939a,3, 1959a,5,
CW 9,i,1

"Association, Dream, and Hysterical
Symptom": CW 2,7

"Association, Dream, and Hysterical
Symptoms": E. 1918a,5

"Association Method, The": E.
1910a, 1916a,3, 1917a,3, CW 2,10

"Associations d'idées familiales":
Fr. 1907a

"Associations of Normal Subjects,
The": E. 1918a,1, CW 2,1

"Assoziation, Traum und hysterisches Symptom": G. 1906j,
1909a,1

"Astrological Experiment, An
(1958)": CW 18,48

"Astrologisches Experiment, Ein":
G. 1958f

"Aufgang einer neuen Welt, Der":
G. 1930e, GW 10,20

Aufsätze zur Zeitgeschichte: G.
1946a; Vorwort zu: GW 10,9;
Nachwort zu: GW 10,13

"Aus einem Brief an einen
protestantischen Theologen":
GW 11,24

Aux frontières de la connaissance . . . , "Préface": Fr. 1959a

B

"Bailey Island Seminar": Seminar
Notes, 1936–37a

"Banalized beyond Endurance":
E. 1958i

"Basic Postulates of Analytic
Psychology, The": E. 1933a,9,
CW 8,13

Basic Writings of C. G. Jung: E.
1959a

"Bedeutung der Analytischen
Psychologie für die Erziehung,
Die": G. 1971a,4, GW 17,3

"Bedeutung der Psychologie für
die Gegenwart, Die": G. 1934b,3,
GW 10,7

"Bedeutung der schweizerischen

Linie im Spektrum Europas,
Die": G. 1928e, GW 10,19
"Bedeutung des Unbewussten für
die individuelle Erziehung, Die":
G. 1971a,5, GW 17,6
*Bedeutung des Vaters für das
Schicksal des Einzelnen, Die:*
G. 1909c, 1949a, 1971a,1, GW 4,14
"Bedeutung von Konstitution und
Vererbung für die Psychologie,
Die": G. 1929i, 1973c,2, GW 8,4
"Begabte, Der": G. 1946b,3 GW
17,5
"Begriff des kollektiven Unbewuss-
ten, Der": GW 9,i,2
"Begrüssungsansprache zum Achten
Internationalen Ärztlichen
Kongress für Psychotherapie,
Bad Nauheim (1935)": GW
10,30
"Begrüssungsansprache zum
Neunten Internationalen
Ärztlichen Kongress für Psycho-
therapie, Kopenhagen (1937)":
GW 10,32
"Begrüssungsansprache zum
Zehnten Internationalen
Ärztlichen Kongress für Psycho-
therapie, Oxford (1938)": GW
10,33
"Beispiele europäischer Mandalas":
G. 1929b,I,7, 1938a,4
"Beitrag zur Kenntnis des Zahlen-
traumes, Ein": G. 1911e, 1972e,5,
GW 4,5
"Beitrag zur Psychologie des
Gerüchtes, Ein": G. 1910q,
1972e,4, GW 4,4
"Beiträge zur Symbolik": G. 1911f
"Beiträge zur Symbolik des Selbst":
G. 1951a, 1954c,4, GW 9,ii
"Bemerkung zur Tauskschen Kritik
der Nelkenschen Arbeit, Eine":
G. 1913d
"Bericht über Amerika": G. 1910n
Bericht über das Basler Seminar:
Seminar Notes, 1934
Bericht über das Berliner Seminar
. . . : Seminar Notes, 1933

Bericht über das deutsche Seminar
. . . : Seminar Notes, 1930–31
"Bericht über das Vereinsjahr
1910–11": G. 1911g
Bericht über die Berliner Vorträge:
Seminar Notes, 1937
"Berliner Seminare": Seminar
Notes, 1933
Bewusstes und Unbewusstes: G.
1957a
"Bewusstsein, Unbewusstes und
Individuation": G. 1939e
*Beziehung der Psychotherapie zur
Seelsorge, Die:* G. 1932a
*Beziehungen zwischen dem Ich und
dem Unbewussten, Die:* G. 1928a,
1935a, GW 7,2
"Blick in die Verbrecherseele. Das
Doppelleben des Kriminellen
. . .": G. 1933a
"Bologna Enigma, The": E. 1946f
"Brief an *The Listener.* Januar
1960": GW 11,25
"Brief von Prof. C. G. Jung an
den Verfasser": G. 1964a
"Brief zur Frage der Synchronizität,
Ein": G. 1961c
Briefe: I, 1906–45: G. 1972a; II,
1946–55: G. 1972b; III, 1956–61:
G. 1973a
Briefwechsel (with Freud): G. 1974a
"Brother Klaus": E. 1946c, CW 11,6
"Bruder Klaus": G. 1933c, GW 11,6
"Buchanzeige." Review of Hitsch-
mann: G. 1911d
"Buchanzeige." Review of Wulffen:
G. 1910p

C

"C. G. Jung et l'astrologie": Fr.
1954b
"C. G. Jung on Flying Saucers":
E. 1954h
"C. G. Jung on the Question of
Flying Saucers": E. 1955i, 1959i,3
"Case of Hysterical Stupor in a
Prisoner in Detention, A": CW
1,5

"Challenge of the Christian Enigma, The. A Letter . . . to Upton Sinclair": E. 1953g

"Child Development and Education": E. 1969c,2, CW 17,3

Children's Dreams: Seminar Notes, 1938–39

"Christian Legend, The. An Interpretation": E. 1955f

"Circular letter (1934)": CW 10,27

Circular letter: "Sehr geehrte Kollegen . . . (I.12.34)": G. 1934j

Circular letter to *Zentralblatt* subscribers (1 Dec. 1934): E. 1946d,1

Civilization in Transition: CW 10

Collected Papers on Analytical Psychology: E. 1916a, 1917a; Prefaces to: CW 4,13; Vorreden zu den: GW 4,13

"Comment on Tausk's Criticism of Nelken, A": E. 1973d,3, CW 18,31

"Commentary" (*The Secret of the Golden Flower*): E. 1931a,1, 1962b,2

"Commentary on *The Secret of the Golden Flower*": E. 1958a,9, CW 13,1

Commentary on W. Pöldinger: "Zur Bedeutung bildnerischen Gestaltens in der psychiatrischen Diagnostik": G. 1959h

"Comments on a Passage from Nietzsche's *Zarathustra*. (1936)": Seminar Notes, 1934–39

"Communication, A": E. 1955f

"Complications of American Psychology, The": CW 10,22

"Concept of Ambivalence, The": CW 18,33

"Concept of the Collective Unconscious, The": E. 1936 a&d, 1937b, 1971a,4, CW 9,i,2

"Conception of the Unconscious, The": E. 1917a,16

"Concerning 'Answer to Job' ": CW 18,95

"Concerning Mandala Symbolism": E. 1972a,3, CW 9,i,12

"Concerning Psychoanalysis": CW 4, 8

"Concerning Rebirth": E. 1970a,2, CW 9,i,5

"Concerning Synchronicity": E. 1953c

"Concerning the Self": E. 1951a

"Conscious, Unconscious, and Individuation": CW 9,i,10

"Content of the Psychoses, The": G. 1916a,14, 1917a,14, CW 3,2

Contribution entitled "Deutsche Schweiz" . . . : G. 1908o

Contribution on hallucination . . . : G. 1933f

"Contribution to a Discussion on Psychotherapy": CW 10,31

Contribution to discussion of paper by Frank and Bezzola . . . : G. 1907f

Contribution to "Eine Tat-Umfrage . . .": G. 1959g

Contribution to "Rundfrage über ein Referat . . .": G. 1950g

Contribution to symposium: *Aufstand der Freiheit*: G. 1957c

Contribution to symposium: "The Frontiers of Knowledge": G. 1959f; E. 1957h

Contribution to symposium: "Das geistige Europa und die ungarische Revolution": G. 1956f

"Contribution to the Psychology of Rumour, A": E. 1916a,5, 1917a,5, CW 4,4

"Contribution to the Study of Psychological Types, A": E. 1916a,12, 1917a,12, CW 6,5

Contribution to *Trunken von Gedichten* . . . : G. 1953a

Contributions to Analytical Psychology: E. 1928a

"Contributions to Symbolism": CW 18,34

"Cornwall Seminar": Seminar Notes, 1923

"Crime and the Soul": E. 1932c, CW 18,13

"Criticism of Bleuler's 'Theory of Schizophrenic Negativism,' A": E. 1916a,7, 1917a,7, CW 3,4
"Cryptomnesia": CW 1,3

D

"Dämonie": G. 1949h
"De Sulphure": G. 1948c
"Definition of Demonism, The": CW 18,89
"Depth Psychology (1948)": CW 18,44
"Depth Psychology and Self-Knowledge": E. 1969f, CW 18,131
"Deutsche Schweiz," contribution to "Der gegenwärtige Stand . . .": G. 1908o
Deutsches Seminar: Seminar Notes, 1930–31
Development of Personality, The: CW 17
"Development of the Personality, The": E. 1939a,6, CW 17,7
Diagnostische Assoziationsstudien, I. Beitrag: G. 1904a; III. Beitrag: G. 1905g; IV. Beitrag: G. 1905h, 1906i; IX. Beitrag: G. 1907e
Diagnostische Assoziationsstudien: Beiträge zur experimentellen Psychopathologie: Vol. I: G. 1906a; Summary, Fr. 1908a; Vol. II: G. 1909a
"Dichter, Der": G. 1950a,2
"Difference between Eastern and Western Thinking, The": E. 1971a,13
"Different Aspects of Rebirth, The": E. 1944a
Dissertation: G. 1902a
"Disturbances of Reproduction in the Association Experiment": CW 2,9
"Dr. Hans Schmid-Guisan": G. 1932d
"Dr. Jung on Unconventional Aerial Objects": E. 1958f
"Dr. Jung Sets the Record Straight": E. 1958g

"Dr. Jung's Contribution to the Voice of America Symposium . . .": E. 1957h
Dream Analysis: Seminar Notes, 1928–30
"Dream Analysis in Its Practical Application": E. 1933a,1
"Dream Symbols of the Individuation Process": E. 1959d; Seminar Notes, 1936–37a
"Dream Symbols of the Process of Individuation": E. 1939a,4
"Dreamlike World of India, The": E. 1939b, CW 10,23
Dreams: E. 1974a
Dreams and Symbolism: Seminar Notes, 1925b
"Drei Fragen an Prof. C. G. Jung": G. 1958g
Dynamik des Unbewussten, Die: GW 8

E

"Editorial. *Zentralblatt*, VI (1933)": CW 10,25
"Editorial. *Zentralblatt*, VIII (1935)": CW 10,28
"Editorial Note. *Zentralblatt*, VIII (1935)": CW 10,29
Editorial note to the series: *Psychologische Abhandlungen*: G. 1914c
"Editorial Preface to the *Jahrbuch*": CW 18,23
"Effect of Technology on the Human Psyche, The": CW 18,76
"Ehe als psychologische Beziehung, Die": G. 1925b, 1931a,11, GW 17,8
Einführung in das Wesen der Mythologie: G. 1941c, 1951b
"Einführung zu Frances G. Wickes 'Analyse der Kindesseele' ": GW 17,2
"Einführung zu W. M. Kranefeldt: 'Die Psychoanalyse' ": G. 1930b, GW 4,15

"Einige Aspekte der modernen
Psychotherapie": G. 1972c,4,
GW 16,4
"Einige Bemerkungen zu den
Visionen des Zosimos": G. 1938c
"Einleitung in die religionspsycho-
logische Problematik der
Alchemie": G. 1944a,2,
1957a,2, GW 12,3,I
Einzelne in der Gesellschaft, Der:
G. 1971a
"Entlarvung der viktorianischen
Epoche. Freud kulturhistorisch
gesehen": G. 1932f
"Entschleierung der Seele, Die":
G. 1931g
"Epilogue to 'Essays on Contempo-
rary Events' ": E. 1947a,7, CW
10,13
"Epilogue to Jung: L'Homme à la
découverte de son âme": CW
18,72; Fr. 1944a,9, 1962a,9
"Erdbedingtheit der Psyche, Die":
G. 1927a
Erinnerungen, Träume, Gedanken:
G. 1962a
"Erklärung der Redaktion":
G. 1913b
"Erlösungsvorstellungen in der
Alchemie, Die": G. 1937a,
1944a,4, GW 12,3,III
Essays on a Science of Mythology
. . . : E. 1949a, 1963a, 1969a
Essays on Contemporary Events:
E. 1947a; "Preface": E. 1947a,1,
CW 10,9
"Europäischer Kommentar." Das
Geheimnis der goldenen Blüte:
G. 1938a,3, 1957b,3
"Examples of European Mandalas":
E. 1931a,2, CW 13,1, pp. 56ff.
"Excerpts from Selected Letters":
E. 1971b
Excerpts of letters to Illing (26
Jan. & 10 Feb. 1955): G. 1956d
"Experiences Concerning the
Psychic Life of the Child": E.
1910a,3

"Experimental Observations on the
Faculty of Memory": CW 2,4
Experimental Researches: CW 2
"Experimentelle Beobachtungen
über das Erinnerungsvermögen":
G. 1905c
"Experimentelle Untersuchungen
über Assoziationen Gesunder":
G. 1904a, 1906a,1

F

"Face to Face" (22 Oct. 1959):
E. 1960c
"Fall von C. G. Jung": G. 1950e
"Fall von hysterischem Stupor bei
einer Untersuchungsgefangenen,
Ein": G. 1902b, GW 1,5
"Familial Constellations": E.
1910a,2
"Family Constellation, The": CW
2,11
"Fastenwunder des Bruder Klaus,
Das": G. 1951e
"Faust and Alchemy": CW 18,105
"Faust und die Alchemie": G. 1950b
"Fight with the Shadow, The":
E. 1946e, CW 10,12
"Flying Saucers: A Modern Myth
of Things Seen in the Skies":
CW 10,15
Flying Saucers. A Modern Myth
of Things Seen in the Skies:
E. 1959b
"Foreword to a Catalogue on
Alchemy": CW 18,104
"Foreword to Abegg: Ostasien
denkt anders": CW 18,92
"Foreword to Adler: Entdeckung
der Seele": CW 18,52
"Foreword to Adler: Studies in
Analytical Psychology": CW
18,55
"Foreword to Aldrich: The Primi-
tive Mind and Modern
Civilization": CW 18,68
"Foreword to Allenby: The Origins
of Monotheism": CW 18,93

"Foreword to Baynes: *Analytical Psychology and the English Mind*": CW 18,78

"Foreword to Bertine: *Human Relationships*": CW 18,61

"Foreword to Brunner: *Die Anima als Schicksalsproblem des Mannes*": CW 18,63

"Foreword to Crottet: *Mondwald*": CW 18, 119

"Foreword to Custance: *Wisdom, Madness and Folly*": CW 18,15

"Foreword to Evans: *The Problem of the Nervous Child*": CW 18,129

"Foreword to Fierz-David: *Dream of Poliphilo*": CW 18,118

"Foreword to F. Fordham: *Introduction to Jung's Psychology*": CW 18,46

"Foreword to M. Fordham: *New Developments in Analytical Psychology*": CW 18,47

"Foreword to Froboese-Thiele: *Träume—eine Quelle religiöser Erfahrung?*": CW 18,102

"Foreword to Gilbert: *The Curse of the Intellect*": CW 18,112

"Foreword to Gilli: *Der dunkle Bruder*": CW 18,116

"Foreword to Harding: *Psychic Energy*": CW 18,42

"Foreword to Harding: *The Way of All Women*": CW 18,130

"Foreword to Harding: *Woman's Mysteries*": CW 18,53

"Foreword to *Hugh Crichton-Miller 1877–1959*": CW 18,87

"Foreword to Jacobi: *Complex/Archetype/Symbol*": CW 18,60

"Foreword to Jacobi: *Paracelsus: Selected Writings*": CW 18,120

"Foreword to Jacobi: *The Psychology of C. G. Jung*": CW 18,40

"Foreword to Jaffé: *Apparitions and Precognition*": CW 18,8

"Foreword to Jung: *Gestaltung des Unbewussten*": CW 18,56

"Foreword to Jung: *Phénomènes occultes*": CW 18,5

"Foreword to Jung: *Symbolik des Geistes*": CW 18,90

"Foreword to Jung: *Von den Wurzeln des Bewusstseins*": CW 18,58

"Foreword to Jung: *Wirklichkeit der Seele*": CW 18,113

"Foreword to Kankeleit: *Das Unbewusste als Keimstätte des Schöpferischen*": CW 18,121

"Foreword to Koenig-Fachsenfeld: *Wandlungen des Traumproblems ...*": CW 18,115

"Foreword to Mehlich: *J. H. Fichtes Seelenlehre und ihre Beziehung zur Gegenwart*": CW 18,114

"Foreword to Moser: *Spuk*": CW 18,7

"Foreword to Neumann: *Depth Psychology and a New Ethic*": CW 18,77

"Foreword to Neumann: *The Origins and History of Consciousness*": CW 18,54

"Foreword to Perry: *The Self in Psychotic Process*": CW 18,16

"Foreword to Quispel: *Tragic Christianity*": CW 18,91

"Foreword to Schleich: *Die Wunder der Seele*": CW 18,39

"Foreword to Schmaltz: *Komplexe Psychologie und körperliches Symptom*": CW 18,17

"Foreword to Schmid-Guisan: *Tag und Nacht*": CW 18,108

"Foreword to Serrano: *The Visits of the Queen of Sheba*": CW 18,122

"Foreword to Spier: *The Hands of Children*": CW 18,132

"Foreword to Studies from the C. G. Jung Institute, Zurich": E. 1967d

"Foreword to Suzuki's *Introduction to Zen Buddhism*": CW 11,13

"Foreword to *Symbols of Trans-
formation*": E. 1954d
"Foreword to the First Volume of
Studies from the C. G. Jung
Institute. (1948)": CW 18,45
"Foreword to the Hebrew edition
of Jung: *Psychology and Educa-
tion*": CW 18,133
"Foreword to the Hungarian
Edition of Jung: *On the Psychol-
ogy of the Unconscious*": CW
18,36
"Foreword to the *I Ching*": E.
1958a,6, CW 11,16
"Foreword to the Spanish Edition"
[of Jacobi: *The Psychology of
C. G. Jung*]: CW 18,41
"Foreword to van Helsdingen:
Beelden uit het onbewuste":
CW 18,59
"Foreword to Werblowsky's
Lucifer and Prometheus": CW
11,5
"Foreword to White's *God and
the Unconscious*": CW 11,4
"Foreword to Wickes: *Von der
inneren Welt des Menschen*
(1953)": CW 18,57
Foreword to K. A. Ziegler:
"Alchemie II": E. 1946b, 1968d,
CW 18,104
"Forewords to Jung: *Seelen-
probleme der Gegenwart* (1930,
1932, 1959)": CW 18,67
"Forewords to Jung: *Über psych-
ische Energetik und das Wesen
der Träume* (1928, 1947)":
CW 18,37
*Four Archetypes: Mother, Rebirth,
Spirit, Trickster*: E. 1970a
Frau in Europa, Die: G. 1927b,
1929a, 1971a,2, GW 10,6
"Freud and Jung: Contrasts":
E. 1933a,6, CW 4,16
Freud and Psychoanalysis: CW 4
Freud/Jung Letters, The: E. 1974b
Freud und die Psychoanalyse: GW 4
"Freudian Theory of Hysteria,

The": CW 4,2
"Freud's Theory of Hysteria: A
Reply to Aschaffenburg": CW 4,1
"Freudsche Hysterietheorie, Die":
G. 1908m, 1972e,2, GW 4,2
*Fundamental Psychological Con-
ceptions: A Report of Five
Lectures*: E. 1968a; Seminar
Notes, 1935
"Fundamental Questions of Psycho-
therapy": CW 16,10
"Further Investigations on the
Galvanic Phenomenon and Res-
piration in Normal and Insane
Individuals": E. 1908a, CW 2,14
"Future of Parapsychology, The":
E. 1963e, CW 18,50

G

"Gegensatz Freud und Jung, Der":
G. 1929f, 1931a,4, GW 4,16
"Gegenwart und Zukunft": G.
1957i, GW 10,14
"Gegenwärtige Stand der an-
gewandten Psychologie in den
einzelnen Kulturländern,"
Contribution . . . : G. 1908o
*Geheimnis der Goldenen Blüte,
Das. Ein chinesisches Lebens-
buch*: G. 1929b, 1938a, 1957b
"Geheimrat Sommer zum 70.
Geburtstag": G. 1934l
"Geist der Psychologie, Der":
G. 1947a
"Geist Mercurius, Der": G. 1943b,
1948a,3
"Geist und Leben": G. 1926c,
1931a,13, GW 8,12
"Geisteskrankheit und Seele":
G. 1928c, 1973d,4, GW 3,6
"Geleitbrief." *Mensch als Persön-
lichkeit und Problem, Der*:
G. 1963b
"Geleitwort." *Praxis der Psycho-
therapie*: GW 16,1
"Geleitwort." (*Zentralblatt VI*,
1933): GW 10,25

"Geleitwort." (*Zentralblatt* VIII, 1935): G. 1935j, GW 10,28
"Geleitwort des Herausgebers": G. 1933e, GW 10,25
"Geleitwort zu den 'Studien aus dem C. G. Jung-Institut Zürich' ": G. 1949e
"General Aspects of Dream Psychology": E. 1974a,3, CW 8,9
"General Aspects of Psychoanalysis": CW 4,10
"General Aspects of the Psychology of the Dream": E. 1956b
"Gérard de Nerval": G. 1946d; CW 18,117
"Gespräch mit C. G. Jung. Über Tiefenpsychologie und Selbsterkenntnis": G. 1943f
Gestaltungen des Unbewussten: G. 1950a; Foreword to: CW 18,56
"Gewissen, Das." Lecture series, C. G. Jung Institute, Zurich: G. 1958c
"Gewissen in psychologischer Sicht, Das": G. 1958c, GW 10,16
"Gifted Child, The": E. 1969c,4, CW 17,5
"God, the Devil, and the Human Soul": E. 1958b
Göttliche Kind in mythologischer und psychologischer Beleuchtung, Das: G. 1941a
Göttliche Mädchen, Das: G. 1941b
Göttliche Schelm, Der: G. 1954a
"Good and Evil in Analytical Psychology": E. 1960e, CW 10,17
"Grundfragen der Psychotherapie": G. 1951d, 1972c,1, GW 16,10
"Grundproblem der gegenwärtigen Psychologie, Das": G. 1934b,2, GW 8,13
"Grundsätzliches zur praktischen Psychotherapie": G. 1935l, 1972c,2, GW 16,2
"Gut und Böse in der analytischen Psychologie": G. 1959b, GW 10,17, GW 11,19

H

Habilitationsschrift: G. 1905h
"Hans Schmid-Guisan: In Memoriam": CW 18,109
"Heilbare Geisteskranke? Organisches oder funktionelles Leiden?": G. 1928c
"Heinrich Zimmer": G. 1962a,15,viii
"Holy Men of India, The": CW 11,15
"Hors des lieux communs": Fr. 1958d
Hugh Crichton-Miller, 1877–1959, A Personal Memoir . . ., "Foreword": E. 1961b, CW 18,87
"Human Behaviour": E. 1942a
"Human Nature Does Not Yield Easily to Idealistic Advice": E. 1955h, CW 18,83
Human Relationships in Relation . . .: Seminar Notes, 1923
"Hypothese des kollektiven Unbewussten, Die": G. 1932i
"Hypothesis of the Collective Unconscious (1932)": CW 18,51
"Hysterielehre Freuds, Die . . .": G. 1906g, 1972e,1, GW 4,1

I

I Ching, The, or Book of Changes, "Foreword": E. 1950d, 1958a,6, CW 11,16
I Ging: "Vorwort zum": GW 11,16
Ich und das Unbewusste, Das: G. 1928a
"Idea of Redemption in Alchemy The": E. 1939a,5
"If Christ Walked the Earth Today": E. 1958i, CW 18,86
"In Memory of Richard Wilhelm": E. 1931a,3, 1962b,3
"In Memory of Sigmund Freud": CW 15,4
"In Old Age": E. 1971b,10
Index of the Notes on . . . Zarathustra: Seminar Notes, 1934-39

Index to Analytical Psychology . . . :
Seminar Notes, 1939
*Index to Dream Analysis and
Interpretation of Visions* . . . :
Seminar Notes, 1932b
*Index to Dreams and Visions,
1928–32*: Seminar Notes, 1932b
Index 1925–1934: Seminar Notes,
1939
"Individual and Mass Psychology":
E. 1947a,2, 1947f
"Individual Dream Symbolism in
Relation to Alchemy": E. 1971a,
11, 1974a,6, CW 12,2, Pt. II
"Individuation and Collectivity":
E. 1970c,2
Inhalt der Psychose, Der: G. 1908a,
1914a, 1973d,1, GW 3,2
"Instinct and the Unconscious":
E. 1919b, 1928a,10, 1971a,3,
CW 8,6
"Instinkt und Unbewusstes": G.
1928b,4, 1948b,6, GW 8,6
Integration of the Personality, The:
E. 1939a
*Interpretation of Nature and the
Psyche, The*: E. 1955a
Interpretation of Visions, The:
Seminar Notes, 1930–34
"Interview with C. G. Jung, An":
E. 1943b
*Introduction to a Science of
Mythology*: E. 1949a
"Introduction to the Religious and
Psychological Problems of
Alchemy": E. 1959a,10, CW
12,2,I (1st edn.), 3,I (2nd edn.)
"Introduction to Toni Wolff's
Studies in Jungian Psychology":
CW 10,18
"Introductions by C. G. Jung":
E. 1950e
"Is There a Freudian Type of
Poetry?": CW 18,111
"Is There a True Bilingualism?":
CW 18,123

J

"Jung and Religious Belief":
CW 18,103
"Jung on Freud": E. 1962a, 1&6
"Jung on Life after Death":
E. 1962a,12
"Jung on the UFO . . .": E. 1959i
"Jungian Method of Dream
Analysis": E. 1947d
"Jung's Commentary to *Brother
Klaus*": E. 1946c
"Jung's View of Christianity":
E. 1962a,13

K

"Kampf mit dem Schatten, Der":
GW 10,12
Kinderträume. W.S. 1936–37:
Seminar Notes, 1936–37b
Kinderträume. W.S. 1938/39:
Seminar Notes, 1938–39
Kinderträume. W.S. 1939/40:
Seminar Notes, 1939–40
"Klappentext zur ersten Auflage
von *Antwort auf Hiob*": GW
11,23
"Komplexe und Krankheitsursachen
bei Dementia praecox": G. 1908b
Kranefeldt, W. M.: *Psychoanalyse*,
"Einführung": G. 1930b, GW
4,15; *Secret Ways of the Mind*,
"Introduction": E. 1932a, CW
4,15
"Kritik über E. Bleuler: 'Zur
Theorie des schizophrenen
Negativismus' ": G. 1911c, GW
3,3
"Kryptomnesie": G. 1905a, 1971c,3,
GW 1,3
Kundalini Yoga, The: Seminar
Notes, 1932a

L

"Leben die Bücher noch?": G.
1952h
"Lebenswende, Die": G. 1931a,10,
GW 8,16

Lectures at the ETH: Seminar
Notes, 1935–36
"Letter from Dr. Jung": E. 1913c
"Letter of Professor C. G. Jung to
the Author": E. 1968c
"Letter on Parapsychology and
Synchronicity, A . . .": E. 1961a
"Letter to Keyhoe": CW 18,82
"Letter to Miss Pinckney": E. 1948c
"Letter to Père Lachat": CW 18,99
"Letter to the editor (Jan. 1960)":
E. 1960c
Letter to the editors on the effect
of technology on the psyche:
G. 1949g
"Letter to the Second International
Congress for Psychiatry . . . 1957":
CW 3,11
Letters. 1: 1906–1950: E. 1973b;
Excerpts: E. 1971b,1–4,8
Letters. 2: 1951–1961: E. 1976a;
Excerpts: E. 1971b,5–7,9–10
"Letters on Synchronicity": CW
18,49
"Letters to a Friend: Part I":
E. 1972c; Part II: E. 1972d
"Letter to Père Bruno": CW 18,98
Lexikon der Pädagogik: G. 1951c
"Liebesproblem des Studenten,
Das": G. 1971a,3, GW 10,5
"London Lectures": Seminar Notes,
1935
"Love Problem of the Student,
The": E. 1928a,7, CW 10,5

M

"Mach immer alles gut und richtig":
G. 1954f
Man and the Future. An inter-
national symposium. Copen-
hagen: Dan. 1957a
Mandala Symbolism: E. 1972a
"Mandalas": G. 1955e, GW 9,i,13;
E. 1955g, 1972a,1, CW 9,i,13
"Marginal Note on F. Wittels:
Die sexuelle Not (1910)": E.
1973d,2, CW 18,24

"Marginalia on Contemporary
Events": CW 18,73
"Marriage as a Psychological
Relationship": E. 1926a, 1928a,6,
1959a,12, 1971a,7, CW 17,8
"Mass and the Individuation
Process, The": E. 1955l
"Meaning of Individuation, The":
E. 1939a,1
"Meaning of Psychology for Modern
Man, The": CW 10,7
"Medical Opinion on a Case of
Simulated Insanity, A": CW 1,7
"Medicine and Psychotherapy":
CW 16,8
"Medizin und Psychotherapie":
G. 1945e, 1972c,7, GW 16,8
Mehlich, R.: J. H. Fichtes
Seelenlehre . . . , "Vorwort":
G. 1935e; Foreword to: E. 1950e,
CW 18,114
Meier, C. A., Antike Inkubation
und moderne Psychotherapie,
"Geleitwort zu den 'Studien aus
dem C. G. Jung-Institut Zürich' ":
G. 1949e
"Memorial to J. S.": E. 1955c,
CW 18,107
Memories, Dreams, Reflections:
E. 1962a, 1966a
Mensch und Seele . . . : G. 1971b
Mensch und seine Symbole, Der:
G. 1968a
"Mental Disease and the Psyche":
CW 3,7
"Message of the Honorary
President": E. 1958d
"Mind and Earth": CW 10,2
"Mind and the Earth": E. 1928a,3
"Mind of East and West, The":
E. 1955j
"Mind of Man Reaches Out, The":
E. 1957c
"Miraculous Fast of Brother Klaus,
The": CW 18,94
Modern Man in Search of a Soul:
E. 1933a

Modern Psychology: Seminar Notes, 1933–41; cf. Fr. 1907a

"Moderner Mythus, Ein . . .": GW 10,15

Moderner Mythus, Ein . . .: G. 1958a

"Morton Prince, M.D.: *The Mechanism and Interpretation of Dreams . . .*": G. 1911b, 1972e,6, GW 4,6; CW 4,6

Moser, Fanny, *Spuk*, "Foreword to": CW 18,7; "Vorrede" and contribution: G. 1950e

Mysterium Coniunctionis . . .: G. 1955a, 1956a, GW 14, vols. 1 & 2; CW 14

N

"Nach der Katastrophe": G. 1945c, 1946a,5, GW 10,11

"Nachtrag, Ein": G. 1934g

"Nachwort." (*Aufsätze zur Zeitgeschichte*): G. 1946a,6

"Nachwort." Koestler, Arthur, *Von Heiligen und Automaten*: G. 1961b

" 'National Character' and Behavior in Traffic. A Letter from Dr. Jung": E. 1959j

" 'Nationalcharakter' und Verkehrsverhalten": G. 1958j

Naturerklärung und Psyche: G. 1952b

"Neue Bahnen der Psychologie": G. 1912d, GW 7,3

"Neuere Betrachtungen zur Schizophrenie": G. 1959f, GW 3,8

"Neues Buch von Keyserling, Ein": G. 1934i, GW 10,21

Neumann, Erich, *Depth Psychology and a New Ethic*, "Foreword": E. 1969e, CW 18,77; *Origins and History of Consciousness*, "Foreword": E. 1954f, CW 18,54; *Ursprungsgeschichte des Bewusstseins*, "Vorwort": G. 1949f

"New Aspects of Criminal Psychology": CW 2,16

"New Paths in Psychology": E. 1916a,15, CW 7,3

"New Thoughts on Schizophrenia": E. 1959f

"New York Seminar": Seminar Notes, 1936–37a

"1937 Letter from C. G. Jung, A": E. 1968g

"Nuove redute della psicologia criminale, Le": It. 1908a

O

"Obergutachten über zwei (sich) widersprechende psychiatrische Gutachten": G. 1906d, GW 1,8

"On Dementia Praecox": CW 18,10

"On Disturbances in Reproduction in Association Experiments": E. 1918a,6

"On Einstein and Synchronicity": E. 1971b,5

"On Flying Saucers": CW 18,80

"On Hallucination": CW 18,38

"On Hysterical Misreading": CW 1,2

"On Manic Mood Disorder": CW 1,4

"On Mescalin": E. 1971b,6

"On Pictures in Psychiatric Diagnosis": CW 18,128

"On Psychic Energy": E. 1969b,1, CW 8,1

"On Psychical Energy": E. 1928a,1

"On Psychoanalysis": E. 1916a,9, 1917a,9

"On Psychodiagnostics": CW 18,85

"On Psychological Understanding": E. 1915c, CW 3,3

"On Psychophysical Relations of the Associative Experiment": E. 1907a

"On Resurrection": CW 18,100

"On Simulated Insanity": CW 1,6

"On Some Crucial Points in Psychoanalysis": E. 1916a,10, 1917a,10

"On Spiritualistic Phenomena": CW 18,4

"On Suicide": E. 1971b,9
"On Synchronicity": E. 1957b,
1971a,14, 1973c,2, CW 8,19
"On the Criticism of Psycho-
analysis": CW 4,7
"On the Discourses of the Buddha":
CW 18,101
"On the Doctrine of Complexes":
E. 1913a, CW 2,18
"On the Hungarian Uprising":
CW 18,84
"On the Importance of the Uncon-
scious in Psychopathology":
E. 1914b, 1916a,11, 1917a,11,
CW 3,5
"On the Nature of Dreams":
E. 1948a, 1959a,7, 1974a,4,
CW 8,10
"On the Nature of the Psyche":
E. 1969b,2, CW 8,8;
Excerpts: E. 1959a,2
On the Nature of the Psyche:
E. 1969b
"On the Problem of Psychogenesis
in Mental Diseases": E. 1919a,
CW 3,6
"On the Psychoanalytic Treatment
of Nervous Disorders": CW 18,30
"On the Psychogenesis of Schizo-
phrenia": E. 1939d, 1959a,8,
CW 3,8
"On the Psychological Diagnosis of
Evidence": CW 2,19
"On the Psychological Diagnosis of
Facts": CW 1,9
"On the Psychology and Pathology
of So-Called Occult Phenomena":
E. 1916a,2, 1917a,2, CW 1,1
On the Psychology of Eastern
Meditation: E. 1947b, 1949b
"On the Psychology of the Negro":
CW 18,65
"On the Psychology of the Spirit":
E. 1948d
"On the Psychology of the Trick-
ster": E. 1955d
"On the Psychology of the Trick-
ster Figure": E. 1956a, 1970a,4,
CW 9,i,9

"On the Psychology of the Uncon-
scious": CW 7,1 (2nd edn.)
On the Psychology of the Uncon-
scious, Foreword to the Hun-
garian edn. of: CW 18,36
"On the Psychophysical Relations
of the Association Experiment":
CW 2,12
"On the Relation of Analytical
Psychology to Poetic Art":
E. 1923b, 1928a,8
"On the Relation of Analytical
Psychology to Poetry": E.
1971a,10, CW 15,6
"On the Rosarium Philosophorum":
CW 18,126
"On the Shadow and Protestant-
ism": E. 1971b,7
"On the Significance of Number-
Dreams": E. 1916a,6, 1917a,6,
1974a,2, CW 4,5
"On the Tale of the Otter":
CW 18,110

P

Paracelsica. Zwei Vorlesungen . . . :
G. 1942a
"Paracelsus": G. 1929g, 1934b,5,
GW 15,1
Paracelsus: G. 1952c
Paracelsus: Selected Writings,
"Foreword to the English
Edition": E. 1951b; Foreword to:
CW 18,120
"Paracelsus als Arzt": G. 1941f,
1942a,1, GW 15,2
"Paracelsus als geistige Erschein-
ung": G. 1942a,2
"Paracelsus as a Spiritual
Phenomenon": CW 13,3
"Paracelsus the Physician": CW 15,2
"Parapsychologie hat uns mit
unerhörten Möglichkeiten
bekanntgemacht, Die": G. 1956b
Perry, John Weir: The Self in
Psychotic Process . . . , "Fore-
word": E. 1953e, CW 18,16

Phenomènes occultes, Foreword to: CW 18,5

"Phenomenology of the Spirit in Fairy Tales, The": E. 1954b,1, 1958a,3, 1970a,3, CW 9,i,8

"Philosophical Tree, The": CW 13,5

"Philosophische Baum, Der": G. 1945g, 1954b,7

"Picasso": G. 1932g, 1934b,8, GW 15,9; E. 1940a, E. 1953i, CW 15,9

"Plight of Woman in Europe, The": E. 1930d

Portable Jung, The: E. 1971a

"Practical Use of Dream-Analysis, The": E. 1974a,5, CW 16,12

Practice of Psychotherapy, The . . .: CW 16

"Praktische Verwendbarkeit der Traumanalyse, Die": G. 1931c, 1934b,4, GW 16,12

Praxis der Psychotherapie. Beiträge zum Problem der Psychotherapie und zur Psychologie der Übertragung: GW 16

"Preface," *Psychotherapy* (Calcutta): E. 1956e, CW 18,127

"Preface by C. G. Jung": E. 1954g

"Preface by C. G. Jung. *Ostasien Denkt Anders . . .*": E. 1953f

"Preface by Dr. Jung": E. 1960d

"Preface to an Indian Journal of Psychotherapy": CW 18, 127

"Preface to de Laszlo: *Psyche and Symbol*": CW 18,62

"Preface to 'Essays on Contemporary Events' ": CW 10,9

"Prefaces to *Collected Papers on Analytical Psychology*": CW 4,13

"Present State of Applied Psychology, The": CW 18,9

"Presidential Address . . . 1935": CW 10,30

"Presidential Address . . . 1937": CW 10,32

"Presidential Address . . . 1938": E. 1938b, CW 10,33

"Press Communiqué on Visiting the United States": CW 18,69

"Principles of Practical Psychotherapy": CW 16,2

"Probleme der modernen Psychotherapie, Die": G. 1929d, 1931a,2, GW 16,6

Probleme der Psychotherapie: G. 1972c

"Problems of Modern Psychotherapy": E. 1931d, 1933a,2, CW 16,6

Process of Individuation: Alchemy I: Seminar Notes, 1933–41

Process of Individuation: Alchemy II: Seminar Notes, 1933–41

Process of Individuation: [Eastern Texts]: Seminar Notes, 1933–41

Process of Individuation: Exercitia Spiritualia . . .: Seminar Notes, 1933–41

Psyche and Symbol. A Selection from the Writings of C. G. Jung: E. 1958a; "Preface": E. 1958a,1, CW 18,62

Psychiatric Studies: CW 1

Psychiatrie und Okkultismus: G. 1971c

Psychiatrische Studien: GW 1

"Psychic Conflicts in a Child": E. 1969c,1, CW 17,1

"Psychoanalyse": G. 1912e

"Psychoanalyse und Assoziationsexperiment": G. 1906a,4, 1906i

"Psychoanalyse und Seelsorge": G. 1928g, 1971d,3, GW 11,8

"Psycho-analysis": E. 1913d, 1915d

"Psychoanalysis": E. 1915d, 1916a,8, 1917a,8

"Psycho-Analysis and Association Experiments": E. 1918a,4

"Psychoanalysis and Association Experiments": CW 2,5

"Psychoanalysis and Neurosis": CW 4,11

"Psychoanalysis and the Cure of Souls": CW 11,8

Psychogenese der Geisteskrankheiten: GW 3

Psychogenesis of Mental Disease, The: CW 3

Psychological Analysis of Nietzsche's Zarathustra. Notes on the Seminar: Seminar Notes, 1934–39

"Psychological Approach to the Dogma of the Trinity, A": CW 11,2

"Psychological Aspects of the Kore, The": E. 1949a,2, 1963a,2, 1969a, CW 9,i,7

"Psychological Aspects of the Mother Archetype, The": E. 1943a, 1959a,6, 1970a,1, CW 9,i,4

"Psychological Commentary." *The Kundalini Yoga*: Seminar Notes, 1932a

"Psychological Commentary." *The Tibetan Book of the Great Liberation*: E. 1954e, CW 11,10

"Psychological Commentary on 'The Tibetan Book of the Dead,' ": E. 1957f, 1958a,8, CW 11,11

"Psychological Diagnosis of Evidence, The": CW 2,6

"Psychological Factors Determining Human Behavior": E. 1937a, CW 8,5

"Psychological Foundations of Belief in Spirits, The": E. 1920b, 1928a,9, CW 8,11

Psychological Interpretation of Children's Dreams . . . : Seminar Notes, 1938–39

"Psychological Methods of Investigation . . . , The": CW 2,17

Psychological Reflections . . . : E. 1953a, 1970b

" 'Psychological Reflections' on Youth and Age": E. 1972e

"Psychological Theory of Types, A": E. 1933a,4, CW 6,7

"Psychological Types": E. 1925b, 1928a,12, CW 6,6

Psychological Types, or, The Psychology of Individuation: E. 1923a, CW 6; Excerpts: E. 1959a,4, 1971a,8

"Psychological View of Conscience, A": CW 10,16

Psychologie der Übertragung, Die: G. 1946c, GW 16,13

Psychologie der unbewussten Prozesse, Die. Ein Überblick . . . : G. 1917a, 1918a

Psychologie und Alchemie: G. 1944a, 1952d, GW 12

"Psychologie und Dichtung": G. 1930a, 1950a,2, 1954c,2, GW 15,7

Psychologie und Erziehung: G. 1946b; Foreword to the Hebrew edn. of: He. 1958a; CW 18,133

"Psychologie und Religion": G. 1971d,1, GW 11,1

Psychologie und Religion . . . : G. 1940a, 1971d

"Psychologie und Spiritismus": G. 1948e

Psychologische Abhandlungen: 1: G. 1914c; 3: G. 1931a; 4: G. 1934b; 5: G. 1944a; 6: G. 1948a; 7: G. 1950a; 8: G. 1951a; 9: G. 1954b; 10: G. 1955a; 11: G. 1956a

Psychologische Abhandlungen. Editorial note to the series: G. 1914c

Psychologische Betrachtungen: G. 1945a

"Psychologische Determinanten des menschlichen Verhaltens": G. 1973c,3, GW 8,5

"Psychologische Diagnose des Tatbestandes, Die": G. 1905f, 1906k

Psychologische Diagnose des Tatbestandes, Die: G. 1941d

Psychologische Interpretation von Kinderträumen . . . : Seminar Notes, 1938–39

"Psychologische Typen": G. 1925c, 1972d,4, GW 6,5

Psychologische Typen: G. 1921a, GW 6

"Psychologische Typologie" (1931): G. 1931a,6, GW 6,6

"Psychologische Typologie" (1936): G. 1936b, GW 6,7

"Psychologischen Aspekte des
Mutterarchetypus, Die": G.
1939b, 1954b,4, GW 9,i,4
"Psychologischen Grundlagen des
Geisterglaubens, Die": G.
1928b,5, 1948b,7, GW 8,11
"Psychologischer Kommentar zum
Bardo Thödol": G. 1935f,2,
GW 11,11
"Psychologischer Kommentar." *Das
tibetische Buch der grossen
Befreiung*: G. 1955d
"Psychologischer Kommentar zu:
*Das tibetische Buch der grossen
Befreiung*": GW 11,10
Psychology and Alchemy: CW 12
Psychology and Education: E. 1969c
"Psychology and Literature":
E. 1933a,8, CW 15,7
"Psychology and National Prob-
lems": CW 18,70
"Psychology and Poetry": E. 1930c
"Psychology and Religion":
E. 1959a,11, CW 11,1
Psychology and Religion: E. 1938a
*Psychology and Religion: West and
East*: CW 11
"Psychology and Spiritualism":
CW 18,6
"Psychology, East and West":
E. 1955k
"Psychology of Dementia Praecox,
The": CW 3,1
*Psychology of Dementia Praecox,
The*: E. 1909a, 1936b, 1974c
"Psychology of Dreams, The":
E. 1916a,13, 1917a,13
"Psychology of Eastern Meditation,
The": CW 11,14
"Psychology of the Child Archetype,
The": E. 1949a,1, 1958a,4,
1963a,1, CW 9,i,6
"Psychology of the Transference,
The": CW 16,13; Excerpts:
E. 1959a,9
*Psychology of the Transference,
The*: E. 1969d
"Psychology of the Unconscious,
The": CW 7,1 (1st edn.)
Psychology of the Unconscious,

*The. A Study of the Transforma-
tion Symbolisms of the Libido
...*: E. 1916b
"Psychology of the Unconscious
Processes, The": E. 1917a,15
"Psychopathological Significance of
the Association Experiment,
The": CW 2,8
"Psychopathologische Bedeutung
des Assoziationsexperimentes,
Die": G. 1906b
"Psycho-physical Investigations with
the Galvanometer and Pneumo-
graph in Normal and Insane
Individuals": E. 1907b, CW 2,13
"Psychotherapeutische Zeitfragen.
Ein Briefwechsel...": G. 1973b,2,
GW 4,12
*Psychotherapeutische Zeitfragen.
Ein Briefwechsel...*: G. 1914b
"Psychotherapie in der Gegenwart,
Die": G. 1945f, 1946a,3, 1972c,8,
GW 16,9
"Psychotherapie und Welt-
anschauung": G. 1943e, 1946a,4,
1954c,3, 1972c,6, GW 16,7
"Psychotherapists or the Clergy":
E. 1933a,11, 1956d, CW 11,7
"Psychotherapy and a Philosophy
of Life": E. 1947a,5, CW 16,7
"Psychotherapy Today": E. 1942b,
1947a,4, CW 16,9

Q

"Question of Medical Intervention,
The": CW 18,14
"Question of the Therapeutic Value
of Abreaction, The": E. 1921a,
1928a,11

R

"Radio Talk in Munich, A (1930)":
CW 18,66
"Rätsel von Bologna, Das":
G. 1945b
"Randbemerkungen zu dem Buch
von [Fr.] Wittels: *Die sexuelle
Not*": G. 1910l

"Randglossen zur Zeitgeschichte":
  G. 1946g
"Reaction-Time in Association
  Experiments, The": E. 1918a,3
"Reaction-time Ratio in the
  Association Experiment, The":
  CW 2,3
"Real and the Surreal, The":
  CW 8,15
"Realities of Practical Psycho-
  therapy, The": CW 16,14
"Recent Thoughts on Schizo-
  phrenia": CW 3,9
"Recollections of . . . the U. S.":
  E. 1971b,4
Reden Gotamo Buddhos, Die:
  Statement in publisher's brochure
  (on): G. 1956c, GW 11,26
"Referate über psychologische
  Arbeiten schweizerischer
  Autoren (bis Ende 1909)":
  G. 1910m
"Rejoinder to Dr. Bally":
  G. 1934f; CW 10,26
"Relation of the Ego to the
  Unconscious, The": E. 1928b,2
"Relations between the Ego and
  the Unconscious, The": E.
  1971a,5, CW 7,2; Excerpts:
  E. 1959a,3
"Released to United Press from
  Dr. Jung": E. 1958h
"Religion and Psychology: A Reply
  to Martin Buber": E. 1973e, CW
  18,96
"Religion und Psychologie":
  G. 1952j
"Réponse à la question du
  bilinguisme": Fr. 1961d
"Report on America (1910)":
  CW 18,64
"Return to the Simple Life":
  E. 1945b, CW 18,71
Review of Bechterew: G. 1910d
Review of Becker: G. 1910h
Review of Bleuler: *Affektivität* . . . :
  G. 1906f
Review of Bleuler: *Zur Theorie des
  schizophrenen Negativismus*:
  G. 1911c

Review of Bruns: G. 1906e
Review of Bumke: G. 1909f
Review of Cramer: G. 1910i
Review of Dost: G. 1910c
Review of Dubois: G. 1908f
Review of Ehrenfels: *Grund-
  begriffe der Ethik*: G. 1909g
Review of Ehrenfels: *Sexualethik*:
  G. 1910a
Review of Eschle: G. 1908e
Review of Forel: G. 1910j
Review of Freud: *Zur Psychopatho-
  logie* . . . : G. 1908k
Review of Hellpach: *Grundlinien
  einer Psychologie der Hysterie*:
  G. 1905b; CW 18,19
Review of Heyer: *Der Organismus
  der Seele*: G. 1933d; CW 18,124
Review of Heyer: *Praktische
  Seelenheilkunde*: G. 1936d;
  CW 18,125
Review of Hitschmann: *Freuds
  Neurosenlehre*: G. 1911d, CW
  18,27
Review of Keyserling: *Amerika* . . . :
  G. 1930e
Review of Kleist: G. 1909d
Review of Knapp: G. 1907c
Review of Loewenfeld: G. 1909e
Review of Lomer: G. 1908g
Review of Meyer: G. 1908h
Review of Moll: G. 1907b
Review of Näcke: G. 1910g
Review of Pilcz: G. 1910b
Review of Prince: G. 1911b
Review of Reibmayer: G. 1910f
Review of Reichardt: G. 1907d
Review of Sadger: *Konrad
  Ferdinand Meyer*: G. 1909h;
  CW 18,11
Review of Stekel: *Nervöse
  Angstzustände*: G. 1908j; CW
  18,22
"Review of the Complex Theory,
  A": CW 8,3
Review of Urstein: G. 1910e
Review of Waldstein: *Das
  unbewusste Ich*: G. 1909i; CW
  18,12
Review of Wernicke: G. 1906h

Review of Wulffen: *Der Sexual-
verbrecher*: G. 1910p; CW 18,25
"Reviews of Psychiatric Literature
(1906–10)": CW 18,20
"Révolution Mondiale, La":
CW 10,21
"Richard Wilhelm": G. 1930c,
1931b, 1962a,15,vii
"Richard Wilhelm: In Memoriam":
CW 15,5
"Rise of a New World, The":
CW 10, 20
"Role of the Unconscious, The":
CW 10,1
"Rückkehr zum einfachen Leben":
G. 1941e
"Rules of Life": CW 18,79
"Rundschreiben" (*Zentralblatt* VII,
1934): GW 10,27

S

"Schatten, Animus und Anima":
G. 1948f
"Schizophrenia": CW 3,10
"Schizophrenie, Die": G. 1958i,
1973d,5, GW 3,9
Schweizer Lexikon: G. 1949h
Secret of the Golden Flower, The:
E. 1931a, 1962b
"Seele und Erde": G. 1931a,8,
GW 10,2
"Seele und Tod:" G. 1934b,10&h,
GW 8,17
"Seelenproblem des modernen
Menschen, Das": G. 1928f,
1929e, 1931a,14, GW 10,4
Seelenprobleme der Gegenwart:
G. 1931a; Forewords to: CW
18,67
"Seelischen Probleme der
menschlichen Altersstufen, Die":
G. 1930d
Seminar über Kinderträume . . . :
Seminar Notes, 1936–37b
"A Seminar with C. G. Jung . . .":
Seminar Notes, 1936–37b
VII Sermones ad Mortuos . . . :
G. 1916a; E. 1925a, 1967b

"VII Sermones ad Mortuos":
G. 1962a,15,x; E. 1966a,19
"Shadow, Animus and Anima":
E. 1950a
"Sigmund Freud": G. 1939d, GW
15,4
"Sigmund Freud als kultur-
historische Erscheinung":
G. 1932f, 1934b,6, GW 15,3
*Sigmund Freud/C. G. Jung:
Briefwechsel*, G. 1974a
"Sigmund Freud in His Historical
Setting": E. 1932b, CW 15,3
"Sigmund Freud: *On Dreams*":
E. 1973d,1, CW 18,18
"Significance of Constitution and
Heredity in Psychology, The":
CW 8,4
"Significance of Freud's Theory for
Neurology and Psychiatry, The":
CW 18,21
"Significance of the Father in the
Destiny of the Individual, The":
E. 1916a,4, 1917a,4, CW 4,14
"Significance of the Unconscious in
Individual Education, The":
E. 1928a,14, CW 17,6
"Some Aspects of Modern Psycho-
therapy": E. 1930b, CW 16,3
"Some Crucial Points in Psycho-
analysis: A Correspondence . . .":
CW 4,12
"Soul and Death, The": E. 1945a,
1959c, CW 8,17
"Spirit and Life": E. 1928a,2,
CW 8,12
*Spirit and Nature. Papers from the
Eranos Yearbooks, 1*: E. 1954b
*Spirit in Man, Art, and Literature,
The*: CW 15
"Spirit Mercurius, The": CW 13,4
Spirit Mercury, The: E. 1953b
"Spirit of Psychology, The":
E. 1954b,2, 1957e
"Spiritual Problem of Modern Man,
The": E. 1931c, 1933a,10,
1971a,12, CW 10,4
"Stages of Life, The": E. 1933a,5,
1971a,1, CW 8,16

"State of Psychotherapy Today, The": CW 10,8

Statement in publisher's brochure (on) . . . *Die Reden Gotamo Buddhos*: G. 1956c

Statement on UFO's to UPI (13 Aug. 1958): E. 1959i,1

"Statement to United Press International": E. 1958j, CW 18,81

"Statistical Details of Enlistment": CW 2,15

"Statistisches von der Rekrutenaushebung": G. 1906c

"Stenogramm des Zwiegesprächs von . . . Jung . . .": Seminar Notes, 1933

"Stimme des Innern, Die": G. 1934b,9

Structure and Dynamics of the Psyche, The: CW 8

"Structure of the Psyche, The": E. 1971a,2, CW 8,7

"Structure of the Unconscious, The": CW 7,4

"Struktur der Seele, Die": G. 1928d, 1931a,7, GW 8,7

"Struktur des Unbewussten, Die": GW 7,4

Studien aus dem C. G. Jung-Institut Zürich: 1: G. 1949e; 4: G. 1952b; 7: G. 1958c; 14: G. 1963a.

Studien aus dem C. G. Jung-Institut Zürich, "Geleitwort zu den . . .": G. 1949e

Studies from the C. G. Jung Institute, Zurich, Foreword to: E. 1967d, CW 18,45

Studies in Word-Association . . . : E. 1918a

"Study in the Process of Individuation, A": E. 1939a,2, 1972a,2, CW 9,i,11

"Swanage Seminar": Seminar Notes, 1925b

"Swiss Line in the European Spectrum, The": CW 10,19

"Swiss National Character, The": E. 1959k

Symbole der Wandlung: G. 1952e, GW 5

"Symbolic Life, The": E. 1961d, CW 18,3

Symbolic Life, The: E. 1954c

Symbolik des Geistes: G. 1948a; Foreword to: CW 18, 90

"Symbols and the Interpretation of Dreams": CW 18,2

Symbols of Transformation: CW 5; Excerpts: E. 1959a,1; Foreword to: E. 1954d

"Synchronicity: An Acausal Connecting Principle": E. 1955a, 1973c,1, CW 8,18

Synchronicity: An Acausal Connecting Principle: E. 1973c

"Synchronizität als ein Prinzip akausaler Zusammenhänge": G. 1952b, GW 8,18

T

"Tantra Yoga Seminars": Seminar Notes, 1932a

Tavistock Lectures, Die: G. 1969a

Tavistock Lectures, The: E. 1968a

"Tavistock Lectures, The": CW 18,1; Seminar Notes, 1935

"Techniques of Attitude Change Conducive to World Peace (Memorandum to UNESCO) (1948)": CW 18,75

Terry Lectures, The; Yale University: E. 1938a

"Théodore Flournoy": G. 1962a, 15,vi

"Theoretische Überlegungen zum Wesen des Psychischen": G. 1954b,8, 1954c,5, 1973c,4, GW 8,8

"Theory of Psychoanalysis, The": E 1913b, 1914a, 1915b, CW 4,9

Theory of Psychoanalysis, The: E. 1915a

"Therapeutic Value of Abreaction, The": CW 16,11

"Therapeutische Wert des Abre-
agierens, Der": G. 1972c,5,
GW 16,11
"Third and Final Opinion on Two
Contradictory Psychiatric
Diagnoses, A": CW 1,8
"Three Early Papers": E. 1973d
Tibetanische Totenbuch, Das,
"Einführung": G. 1935f
"Tiefenpsychologie": G. 1951c
"To a Colleague on Suicide":
E. 1971b,8
". . . to a little daughter": E. 1971b,1
"to a solicitous colleague": E.
1971b,2
". . . to Freud": E. 1971b,3
"Träumende Welt Indiens, Die":
GW 10,23
"Transcendent Function, The":
E. 1971a,9, CW 8,2
Transcendent Function, The:
E. 1957a
"Transformation Symbolism in the
Mass": E. 1955b, 1958a,5, CW
11,3
"Transzendente Funktion, Die":
G. 1958b, 1973c,1, GW 8,2
"Traumanalyse, Die": G. 1972e,3,
GW 4,3
"Traumsymbole des Individuations-
prozesses": G. 1936a, 1944a,3,
GW 12,3,II
"Tschang Scheng Schu. Die Kunst
das menschliche Leben . . .":
G. 1929h
"Two Chapters from *The Inter-
pretation of Nature and the
Psyche*": E. 1958a,7
*Two Essays on Analytical Psychol-
ogy*: E. 1928b, CW 7
"Two Letters on Psychoanalysis
. . .": CW 18,29
Two letters to the author. Gerster,
Georg: G. 1954e
"Two Posthumous Papers. 1916":
E. 1970c
Typologie: G. 1972d

U

*Über das Phänomen des Geistes in
Kunst und Wissenschaft*: GW 15
"Über das Problem der Psycho-
genese bei Geisteskrankheiten":
G. 1973d,2, GW 3,5
"Über das Rosarium Philoso-
phorum": G. 1938b
"Über das Selbst": G. 1949b
"Über das Unbewusste": G. 1918b,
GW 10,1
"Über das Unbewusste und seine
Inhalte": GW 7,4
"Über das Verhalten der Reaktions-
zeit beim Assoziationsexperi-
mente": G. 1905h, 1906a,3
"Über den Archetypus, mit
besonderer Berücksichtigung
. . .": G. 1936e, 1954b,3, GW 9,i,3
"Über den indischen Heiligen":
G. 1944b, GW 11,15
"Über die Archetypen des kollek-
tiven Unbewussten": G. 1935b,
1954b,2, 1957a,1, GW 9,i,1
"Über die Bedeutung der Lehre
Freuds für Neurologie und
Psychiatrie": G. 1908d
"Über die Bedeutung der Un-
bewussten in der Psychopatho-
logie": G. 1973d,3, GW 3,4
"Über die Beziehung der ana-
lytischen Psychologie zum
dichterischen Kunstwerk":
G. 1922a, 1931a,3, GW 15,6
"Über die Beziehung der Psycho-
therapie zur Seelsorge": G.
1971d,2, GW 11,7
"Über die Energetik der Seele":
G. 1928b,2, 1948b,2, GW 8,1
Über die Energetik der Seele:
G. 1928b
*Über die Entwicklung der Persön-
lichkeit*: GW 17
"Über die psychoanalytische
Behandlung nervöser Leiden":
G. 1912h
"Über die Psychogenese der Schizo-
phrenie": GW 3,7

Über die Psychologie der Dementia praecox: Ein Versuch: G. 1907a, GW 3,1
Über die Psychologie des Unbewussten: G. 1943a, GW 7,1; Foreword to the Hungarian Edn. of: CW 18,36
"Über die Reproduktionsstörungen beim Assoziationsexperiment": G. 1907e, 1909a,2
Über Grundlagen der analytischen Psychologie: G. 1969a
"Über hysterisches Verlesen . . .": G. 1904b, 1971c,2, GW 1,2
"Über Komplextheorie": G. 1934a
Über Konflikte der kindlichen Seele: G. 1910k, 1916b, 1939a, 1946b,2, GW 17,1
"Über Mandalasymbolik": G. 1950a,5, GW 9,i,12
"Über manische Verstimmung": G. 1903a, 1971c,4, GW 1,4
Über psychische Energetik und das Wesen der Träume: G. 1948b
"Über Psychoanalyse": G. 1972e,10, GW 4,11
"Über Psychoanalyse beim Kinde": G. 1912b
"Über Psychologie": G. 1933b
"Über Psychotherapie und Wunderheilungen": G. 1959a
"Über Simulation von Geistesstörung": G. 1903b, GW 1,6
"Über spiritistische Erscheinungen": G. 1905e
"Über Synchronizität": G. 1952f, GW 8,19
". . . Über Tiefenpsychologie und Selbsterkenntnis": G. 1943f, 1947c
"Über Träume": Seminar Notes, 1933
"Über Wiedergeburt": G. 1950a,3, GW 9,i,5
"UFO": E. 1959g
"Ulysses: A Monologue": E. 1953h, CW 15,8
"Ulysses, A Monologue": E. 1949c
"Ulysses . . .": G. 1932e, 1934b,7, GW 15,8

Unbewusste im normalen und kranken Seelenleben, Das . . . Ein Überblick . . .: G. 1926a
"Unconscious in the Normal and Pathological Mind, The": E. 1928b,1
Undiscovered Self, The: E. 1958b
"Undiscovered Self (Present and Future), The": CW 10,14

V

"Verschiedenen Aspekte der Wiedergeburt, Die": G. 1940b
Versuch einer Darstellung der psychoanalytischen Theorie. Neun Vorlesungen . . .: G. 1913a, 1955b, 1973b, 1973b,1, GW 4,9
"Versuch einer psychologischen Deutung des Trinitätsdogmas": GW 11,2
"Versuch zu einer psychologischen Deutung des Trinitätsdogmas": G. 1948a,4
"Visionary Rumour, A": E. 1959h
"Visionen des Zosimos, Die": G. 1954b,5
Visions: Seminar Notes, 1930–34
"Visions of Zosimos, The": CW 13,2
"Vom Werden der Persönlichkeit": G. 1934b,9, GW 17,7
"Vom Wesen der Träume": G. 1945d, 1948b,5, 1952i, 1954c,1, GW 8,10
Von den Wurzeln des Bewusstseins: G. 1954b; Foreword to: CW 18,58
"Von der Psychologie des Sterbens": G. 1935i
"Vorbemerkung der Redaktion": G. 1909b
"Vorbemerkung des Herausgebers." (*Zentralblatt* VII, 1935): G. 1935k, GW 10,29
"Vorrede." F. Froboese-Thiele, *Träume—eine Quelle religiöser Erfahrung?*: G. 1957e
"Vorrede" and contribution to F. Moser, *Spuk*: G. 1950e

"Vorrede zu: Toni Wolff: *Studien zu C. G. Jungs Psychologie*": GW 10,18

"Vorreden zu den *Collected Papers on Analytical Psychology*": GW 4,13

"Vorwort." E. Neumann, *Ursprungsgeschichte des Bewusstseins*: G. 1949f

"Vorwort zu D. T. Suzuki: *Die grosse Befreiung*": GW 11,13

"Vorwort zu V. White: *Gott und das Unbewusste*": GW 11,4

"Vorwort zu Z. Werblowsky: *Lucifer und Prometheus*": GW 11,5

"Vorwort zum I Ging": GW 11,16

"Votum. (*Schweizerische Ärztezeitung* XVI, 1935)": GW 10,81

"Votum. Zum Thema: Schule und Begabung": G. 1943d

"Votum C. G. Jung": G. 1935h

W

"Wandlungen und Symbole der Libido. Beiträge zur Entwicklungsgeschichte des Denkens": pt. I: G. 1911a; pt. II: 1912c

Wandlungen und Symbole der Libido. Beiträge zur Entwicklungsgeschichte des Denkens: G. 1912a, 1925a

"Wandlungssymbol in der Messe, Das": G. 1942c, 1954b,6, 1971d,4, GW 11,3

"Was Indien uns lehren kann": GW 10,24

"Was ist Psychotherapie?": G. 1935g, 1972c,3, GW 16,3

Welt der Psyche: G. 1954c

"Westliche Parallelen zu den tantrischen Symbolen": Seminar Notes, 1932a

"What India Can Teach Us": E. 1939c, CW 10,24

"What Is Psychotherapy?": CW 16,3

"Why and How I Wrote My *Answer to Job*": E. 1956c

"Why I Am Not a Catholic": CW 18,88

Wirklichkeit der Seele: G. 1934b; Foreword to: CW 18,113

"Wirklichkeit und Überwirklichkeit": G. 1932h, GW 8,15

"Wo leben die Teufel? . . .": G 1950f

"Woman in Europe": E. 1928a,5, 1928c, CW 10,6

"Wotan": G. 1936c, 1946a,2, GW 10,10; E. 1937c, 1947a,3, CW 10,10

"Wotan und der Rattenfänger . . .": G. 1956e

Y

"Yoga and the West": E. 1936c, CW 11,12

"Yoga und der Westen": GW 11,12

"Yoga, Zen, and Koestler": E. 1961c

"Your Negroid and Indian Behavior": E. 1930a

Z

"Zeichen am Himmel . . .": G. 1958h

"Zeitgenössisches. (*Neue Zürcher Zeitung*, CLV, 1934)": G. 1934f; CW 10,26

"Ziele der Psychotherapie": G. 1929c, 1931a,5, GW 16,5

Zivilisation im Übergang: GW 10

"Zu *Antwort auf Hiob*" (1951): GW 11,21

"Zu *Antwort auf Hiob*" (1952): GW 11,22

"Zu *Die Reden Gotamo Buddhos*": GW 11,26

"Zu *Psychologie und Religion*": GW 11,18

"Zu unserer Umfrage 'Leben die Bücher noch?' ": G. 1952h

"Zugang zum Unbewussten": G. 1968a

"Zum Gedächtnis Richard Wilhelms": G. 1938a,2, 1957b,2, GW 15,5

"Zum Problem des Christus-
symbols": GW 11,20
"Zum psychologischen Aspekt der
Korefigur": G. 1941b, 1941c,2,
1951b,2, GW 9,i,7
Zum Wesen des Psychischen:
G. 1973c
"Zur Empirie des Individuations-
prozesses": G. 1934c, 1950a,4,
GW 9,i,11
"Zur Frage der psychologischen
Typen": G. 1972d,1, GW 6,4
"Zur gegenwärtigen Lage der
Psychotherapie": G. 1934k,
GW 10,8
"Zur Kritik über Psychoanalyse":
G. 1910o, 1972e,7, GW 4,7
"Zur Phänomenologie des Geistes
im Märchen": G. 1948a,2,
1957a,3, GW 9,i,8
"Zur Psychoanalyse." (17 Jan.):
G. 1912f
"Zur Psychoanalyse." (15 Feb.):
G. 1912g, 1972e,8, GW 4,8
Zur Psychoanalyse: G. 1972e
*Zur Psychogenese der Geisteskrank-
heiten*: G. 1973d
"Zur Psychologie der Schelmen-
figur": G. 1954a
"Zur Psychologie der Trickster-
figur": GW 9,i,9
"Zur Psychologie der Trinitätsidee":
G. 1942b

"Zur Psychologie des Geistes":
G. 1946e
Zur Psychologie des Individuation:
Seminar Notes, 1930–31
"Zur Psychologie des Kind-
Archetypus": G. 1941a, 1941c,1,
1951b,1, GW 9,i,6
"Zur Psychologie des Negers":
G. 1913c
"Zur Psychologie östlicher Medita-
tion": G. 1943c, 1948a,5, 1957a,4,
GW 11,14
*Zur Psychologie und Pathologie
sogenannter occulter Phänomene*:
G. 1902a
"Zur Psychologie und Pathologie
sogenannter okkulter
Phänomene": G. 1971c,1, GW 1,1
*Zur Psychologie westlicher und
östlicher Religion*: GW 11
"Zur psychologischen Tatbestands-
diagnostik": G. 1905d, GW 1,9
"Zur psychologischen Tatbestands-
diagnostik. Das Tatbestands-
experiment im Schwurgerichts-
prozess Näf": G. 1937b
"Zur Tatbestandsdiagnostik":
G. 1908n
"Zur Umerziehung des deutschen
Volkes": G. 1946g
*Zwei Schriften über analytische
Psychologie*: GW 7

INDEX 2: PERSONAL NAMES

Names of editors, compilers, co-authors, authors for whose books Jung wrote reviews or forewords, persons eulogized, translators, and recipients of letters published elsewhere than in the *Letters* or *Briefe* (which are separate from the CW)—in the German and English entries.

A

Abegg, Lily: G. 1950d; E. 1953f;
  CW 18,92
Adler, Alfred: G. 1934d
Adler, Gerhard: G. 1934d, 1952g;
  E. 1966e, 1973b, 1976a, CW 18,52,
  CW 18,55; Fr. 1957a; CW ed.
Aldrich, Charles Roberts: E.
  1928a,13, 1931b, CW 18,68
Allenby, Amy I.: CW 18,93
Anshen, Ruth Nanda: E. 1942a
Aschaffenburg, Gustav: G. 1906g,
  GW 4,1; CW 4,1

B

Bach, Georg R.: G. 1956d
Bailey, Paul C.: E. 1968c
Bally, Gustav: G. 1934f; CW 10,26
Barbault, André: G. 1972b; E.
  1970d, 1976a; Fr. 1952b
Barker, Mary: E. 1968a, Seminar
  Notes, 1935
Bash, K. W.: E. 1942c
Baumann, Carol: E. 1947b, 1947c,
  Seminar Notes, 1928–30, 1932b
Baumann, Elizabeth: Seminar
  Notes, 1935–36
Baumann, Hans H.: Seminar
  Notes, 1936–37b
Baynes, Cary F.: E. 1928a&b,
  1931a&d, 1932b, 1933a&b,
  1936c, 1943a, 1950d, 1953a,
  1962b, Seminar Notes, 1932a
Baynes, H. G.: E. 1920b, 1923a,
  1923b, 1924a&b, 1928a&b,
  1950b, 1953a, CW 6, CW 18,78

Bechterew, W. von: G. 1910d;
  CW 18,20
Becker, Th.: G. 1910h; CW 18,20
Bender, Hans: G. 1958f, 1961c,
  1973a; E. 1976a
Bertine, Eleanor: G. 1957d, 1972b;
  E. 1958e, 1971b,8, 1973b, CW
  18,61, Seminar Notes, 1936–37a;
  It. 1961a
Betschart, Ildefons: G. 1963b
Bezzola, Dumeng: G. 1907f
Binswanger, Hilde: G. 1969a
Bitter, Wilhelm: G. 1959a&b, 1973a;
  E. 1976a
Blanke, Fritz: G. 1951e, 1972b;
  E. 1973b, CW 18,94
Bleuler, Eugen: G. 1906f, 1908b,
  1911c&h, GW 3,3; E. 1916a,7,
  CW 3,4, CW 18,34
Boss, Medard: G. 1950g
Bovet, Theodor: G. 1972b; E.
  1971b,7, 1976a
Brill, A. A.: E. 1909a, 1910a, 1936b
Briner, Mary: E. 1947a,4&5,
  Seminar Notes, 1934–39, 1939
Brody, Daniel: G. 1958b
Bruder Klaus, *see* Niklaus von Flüe
Brunner, Cornelia: G. 1963a;
  CW 18,63, Seminar Notes,
  1938–39
Bruno de Jésus-Marie, Père:
  CW 18,98; Fr. 1956b
Bruns, L.: G. 1906e; CW 18,20
Buber, Martin: G. 1952j, GW 11,17;
  E. 1957d, 1973e, CW 18,96
Bumke, Oswald: G. 1909f; CW
  18,20

Burnett, Hugh: G. 1973a; E. 1960c, 1976a
Burnett, Whit: E. 1957e

C

Campbell, C. MacFie: E. 1925b
Campbell, Joseph: E. 1971a
Carioba, Henny: E. 1958h
Chapin, Anne: Seminar Notes, 1928–30
Claparède, Edouard: G. 1908c,4, 1908l,2
Clark, Robert A.: E. 1956b, 1957d
Coomaraswamy, Ananda K.: E. 1947b
Cornell, A. D.: G. 1961c; E. 1961a, 1976a
Cox, David: E. 1958c, CW 18,103
Cramer, A.: G. 1910i; CW 18,20
Crichton-Miller, Hugh: E. 1961b, CW 18,87
Crottet, Robert: G. 1949c; CW 18,119
Cully, Kendig: G. 1972a; E. 1968g, 1973b
Custance, John: G. 1954d; E. 1952a, CW 18,15

D

Deady, Charlotte H.: Seminar Notes, 1928–30
de Angulo, Cary F.: Seminar Notes, 1925a
de Angulo, Ximena: E. 1943a, 1944a
Degen, Hans: G. 1959f
de Laszlo, Violet Staub: E. 1958a, 1959a, CW 18,62
Dell, W. Stanley: E. 1933a, 1939a, 1949c, 1953a
Denber, Herman C. B.: E. 1958d
Doniger, Simon: G. 1972b, GW 11,9; E. 1956c, 1976a, CW 11,9
Dost, Max: G. 1910c; CW 18,20
Dromard, G.: G. 1908i,5
Dubois, P.: G. 1908f; CW 18,20
Duerr, Therese: E. 1926a

Dumas, G.: G. 1908i,4
Dunn, Alice H.: E. 1953c

E

Eaton, Ralph M.: E. 1932a
Ebon, Martin: E. 1963e
Eder, Edith: E. 1913b, 1914a, 1915b, 1916a
Eder, M. D.: E. 1913b, 1914a, 1915b, 1916a, 1918a
Ehrenfels, Christian von: G. 1909g, 1910a; CW 18,20
Einstein, Albert: E. 1971b,5
Eissler, Kurt R.: G. 1973a, 1974a; E. 1974b, 1976a
Ellmann, Richard: E. 1959l
Ermatinger, Emil: G. 1930a
Eschle, Franz: G. 1908e; CW 18,20
Evans, Elida: E. 1920a, CW 18,129
Evans, Richard I.: G. 1967c; E. 1964b
Evans-Wentz, W. Y.: G. 1935f, 1955d; E. 1954e, 1957f

F

Feifel, Herman: E. 1959c
Fichte, J. H.: G. 1935e
Fierz, Markus: CW 18,49,i
Fierz-David, Linda: G. 1947b; E. 1950c, CW 18,118, Seminar Notes, 1932a
Flesch-Brunningen, Hans: G. 1961b
Flinker, Martin: G. 1957j, 1973a; E. 1976a; Fr. 1961d
Flournoy, Théodore: G. 1908c,5, 1962a,15,vi
Foote, Mary: E. 1974e, 1976a, Seminar Notes, 1928–30, 1930–34, 1932a, 1934–39, 1938–39
Fordham, Frieda: G. 1959c; E. 1053d, CW 18,46; CW ed.
Fordham, Michael: E. 1957g, CW 18,47&49,ii
Forel, August: G. 1910j, 1968b, 1972a; E. 1973b, CW 18,20
Frank, Ludwig: G. 1907f
Franz, Marie-Louise von: G. 1951a, 1955a, 1968a, GW 14; E. 1964a

243

Freeman, John: G. 1968a; E. 1964a
Frei, Gebhard: G. 1957h, 1972b;
    E. 1952c, 1973b; Port. 1964a;
    Sp. 1955b
Freud, Sigmund: G. 1906g,
    1908d,k&m, 1932f, 1934d, 1939d,
    1962a,15,ii, 1972a, 1974a, GW 4;
    E. 1932b, 1933a,6, 1962a,15,
    1968f, 1971b,3, 1973b&d,1,
    1974b&d, CW 4, CW 18,32;
    Du. 1963a,1; It. 1974a
Frey, Liliane: Seminar Notes,
    1938–39, 1939–40
Frey-Wehrlin, C. T.: E. 1965a
Froboese-Thiele, Felicia: G. 1940a,
    1957e, CW 18,102

G

Galliker, A.: G. 1952h, 1972b;
    E. 1976a, Seminar Notes, 1935
Game, Margaret: E. 1968a
Gerster, Georg: G. 1953a, 1954e
Gilbert, J. Allen: CW 18,112
Gilli, Gertrud: G. 1938d; CW
    18,116
Glover, A.S.B.: CW 18,72,98,&99
Göring, M. H.: G. 1934l
Goethe, Johann Wolfgang von:
    G. 1932c.
Graecen, Patricia: G. 1972b;
    E. 1957j, 1959,l,2, 1976a
Gray, Horace: E. 1946c
Grindea, Miron: E. 1959k
Grove, Victor: E. 1944b
Guterman, Norbert: E. 1951b

H

Hahn, R.: G. 1904b
Hanhart, Ernst: G. 1967b; E. 1976a
Hannah, Barbara: E. 1937c, 1947a,3,
    1958e, Seminar Notes, 1933–41,
    1935–36
Harding, M. Esther: G. 1935c,
    1948d, 1949d; E. 1933b, 1947e,
    1955e, CW 18,42,53,&130,
    Seminar Notes, 1923, 1925b,
    1936–37a; Du. 1938a; Fr. 1953d
Harms, Ernest: G. 1946h; E. 1946d

Hartenberg, P.: G. 1908i,3
Hauer, J. W.: Seminar Notes, 1932a
Hecht, Dora: E. 1916a,13&15,
    1917a,15
Hellpach, Willy: G. 1905b; CW
    18,19
Helsdingen, René J. van: G. 1957f;
    CW 18,59
Henley, Eugene H.: E. 1945a&b,
    Seminar Notes, 1936–37b
Herbrich, Elisabeth: G. 1963b,
    1973a; E. 1976a
Hesse, Hermann: E. 1963c, 1966b
Heyer, Gustav Richard: G. 1933d,
    1936d; CW 18,124&125
Heyer-Grote, Lucy: G. 1967c
Hinkle, Beatrice: E. 1916b
Hitschmann, Eduard: G. 1911d;
    CW 18,27
Hoch, Dorothee: G. 1972b, GW
    11,22; E. 1976a
Hoffman, Michael L.: E. 1968f
Horine, Ruth: CW 18,95
Hottinger, Mary: E. 1950c
Hubbard, A. M.: G. 1972b;
    E. 1971b,6, 1976a
Hull, R.F.C.: E. 1925a, 1949a,
    1952b, 1953a, 1954a,b,d&f,
    1955a&b, 1956a, 1957b&f, 1958b,
    1959b,d&e, 1960e, 1963b, 1966e,
    1968a, 1969e&f, 1970b&c, 1971a,
    1973b,d&e, 1974b, 1976a,
    CW 1, CW 3–18
Hurwitz-Eisner, Lena: GW ed.
Hutchins, Patricia, see Graecen,
    Patricia

I

Illing, Hans A.: G. 1955f, 1956d,
    1972b; E. 1957i, 1976a
Irminger, H.: E. 1973b, CW 18,88
Iyer, K. Bharatha: E. 1947b

J

Jacobi, Jolande: G. 1940c, 1943f,
    1945a, 1947c, 1952e, 1957g,
    1971b; E. 1942c, 1943b, 1951b,

1953a, 1959e, 1962c, 1969f, 1970b,
CW 18,40,41,60,120; Du. 1949a;
Fr. 1961e, 1965a; It. 1949c;
Sp. 1947a
Jaffé, Aniela: G. 1950a, 1954c,
1957a, 1958e, 1962a, 1972a&b,
1973a, GW 11,20; E. 1962a,
1963b, 1966a, 1967a, CW 18,8,
Seminar Notes, 1939–40
Janet, Pierre: G. 1908i,7
Jarosy, Ivo: E. 1953i
Jolas, Eugene: E. 1930c
Jones, Ernest: G. 1972b, 1974a;
E. 1914b, 1974b, 1976a
Joyce, James: G. 1972a, GW 15,8;
E. 1959l, 1966d, 1973b, CW 15,8
Jung, Emma: G. 1934b, 1962a,15,
i&iii; E. 1962a,16&17, 1975a
Jung, Marianne, see Niehus-Jung,
Marianne
Jung-Merker, Lilly: GW ed.
Juquelier, P.: G. 1908i,9

K

Kankeleit, Otto: G. 1959d; CW
18,121
Katzaroff, Dimitre: G. 1908l,3
Kennedy, William H.: E. 1950a
Kerényi, Karl: G. 1941a,b,&c,
1951b, 1954a; E. 1949a, 1956a,
1963a, 1969a; Fr. 1953b, 1958a;
It. 1948b, 1965a, 1972a
Keyhoe, Donald: E. 1958g, 1959i,2,
CW 18,82
Keyserling, Hermann, Graf:
G. 1925b, 1927a, 1928e, 1930e,
1934i; E. 1926a, 1959k, 1975a
Kirkham, Ethel D.: E. 1948a, 1954g
Kirsch, Hildegard: E. 1972d
Kirsch, James: G. 1946h, 1972a&b,
1973a; E. 1946d,2, 1972c&d,
1973b, 1975a, 1976a
Kitchin, Derek: E. 1954c
Klaus, Bruder, see Niklaus von der
Flüe
Kleist, Karl: G. 1909d; CW 18,20
Knapp, Albert: G. 1907c; CW 18,20
Koenig-Fachsenfeld, Olga von:
G. 1935d; CW 18,115, Seminar

Notes, 1930–31
Koestler, Arthur: G. 1961b, 1973a;
E. 1961c
Kolb, Eugen: CW 18,74; He. 1974a
Kranefeldt, W. M.: G. 1930b, 1934b,
GW 4,15; E. 1932a, CW 4,15
Krich, A. M.: E. 1928a, 14

L

Lachat, Père William: G. 1972b;
E. 1976a, CW 18,99
Lasky, Melvin J.: G. 1956e, 1961b,
1973a; E. 1961c, 1963f, 1976a
Lemaitre, Aug.: G. 1908c,7
Leonard, M.: G. 1973a; E. 1960c,
1976a
Leroy, E.-Bernard: G. 1908c,6
Loewenfeld, L.: G. 1909e; CW 18,20
Lombard, Emile: G. 1908c,3
Lomer, Georg: G. 1908g; CW 18,20
London, Louis S.: G. 1972a;
E. 1937aa, 1973b
Long, Constance E.: E. 1916a, 1917a
Lorenz, Theodor: E. 1944a
Loÿ, R.: G. 1914b, 1973b,2, GW
4,12; CW 4,12

M

McGuire, William: E. 1974b&d,
CW ed.
MacPhail, Ian: E. 1968d
Maeder, Alphonse: G. 1908l,4
Maier, Emanuel: G. 1972b;
E. 1963c, 1973b
Mairet, Philip: CW 4,3
Manheim, Ralph: E. 1962c, 1967d,
1974b
Mann, Kristine: Seminar Notes,
1923, 1936–37a
Marie, A.: G. 1908i,6
Marmorstein, Miss: E. 1946f
Mehlich, Rose: G. 1935e; E. 1950e,
CW 18,114
Meier, C. A.: G. 1949e, 1959e;
E. 1965a, 1967d
Meier, J.: G. 1959c
Mellon, Mary: E. 1968d
Mellon, Paul: E. 1968d

Métral, M.: G. 1908c,2
Meyer, E.: G. 1908h; CW 18,20
Meyer, Konrad F.: G. 1909h;
  CW 18,11
Michelson, Johann: G. 1912e
Miller, Frank: CW 5
Moll, Albert: G. 1907b; CW 18,20
Moltzer, Mary: E. 1913b, 1914a,
  1915b, 1916a
Moser, Fanny: G. 1950e; CW 18,7
Mountford, Gwen: E. 1959k

N

Näcke, P.: G. 1910g; CW 18,20
Nagel, Hildegard: E. 1942b, 1947e,
  1948b&d, 1950e, 1951a, 1953b&f,
  1954h, 1955d, 1959j, 1961a,
  CW 18,88,105,&128
Nelken, Jan: G. 1913d; E. 1973d,3,
  CW 18,31
Nelson, Benjamin: E. 1963c
Nerval, Gérard de: G. 1946d;
  CW 18,117
Neumann, Erich: G. 1949f,
  1962a,15,v, 1967a, 1973a; E.
  1954f, 1969e, 1976a, CW 18,54
  &77
Neumann, Karl Eugen: G. 1956c
Niehus, Walter: G. 1958a
Niehus-Jung, Marianne: G. 1955d,
  1972a, GW 11,25; GW ed.;
  E. 1971b,1, 1973b
Niklaus von Flüe: G. 1933c,
  GW 11,6; E. 1946c, CW 11,6

O

Oeri, Albert: G. 1945b
Oertley, Alda F.: E. 1940a

P

Pascal, Constanza: G. 1908i,8
Pauli, Wolfgang: G. 1952b;
  E. 1955a; Sp. 1961a
Payne, Virginia: G. 1972b;
  E. 1971b,4, 1973b

Perry, John Weir: E. 1953e,
  CW 18,16
Peterson, Frederick: E. 1907b,
  CW 2,13
Phelan, Gladys: E. 1953b
Philp, Howard L.: G. 1973a;
  E. 1958c, 1976a, CW 18,103
Picasso, Pablo: G. 1932g, 1934b,8,
  GW 15,9; E. 1940a, 1953i,
  CW 15,9
Piéron, H.: G. 1908i,1
Pilcz, Alexander: G. 1910b;
  CW 18,20
Pinckney, Sallie M.: G. 1972b;
  E. 1948c, 1973b, Seminar Notes,
  1936–37a
Pöldinger, Walter: G. 1959h,
  CW 18,128
Pope, A. R.: E. 1957a
Pratt, Jane A.: E. 1973b, 1976a,
  CW 18,98, Seminar Notes,
  1930–34
Prince, Morton: G. 1911b, GW 4,6;
  E. 1925b, CW 4,6

Q

Quispel, Gilles: G. 1975a; CW 18,91

R

Radin, Paul: G. 1954a; E. 1956a;
  Fr. 1958a; It. 1965a
Ramakrishna, Sri: E. 1936c
Rank, Otto: G. 1910n, 1911f
Reibmayer, Albert: G. 1910f;
  CW 18,20
Reichardt, M.: G. 1907d; CW 18,20
Reinecke, Elisabeth: E. 1968c
Ress, Lisa: CW 18,134&135
Revault d'Allones, G.: G. 1908i,2
Rhees, Jean, CW 2,10&11
Ricksher, Charles: E. 1908a,
  CW 2,14
Riklin, Franz: G. 1904a, 1906a,1
  1911h; GW ed.; E. 1918a,1
Rinkel, Max: G. 1973a; E. 1958d,
  CW 3,11
Riviere, Diana: CW 2

Rolfe, Constance: E. 1949d
Rosenthal, Hugo: G. 1934b
Rouma, Georges: G. 1908l,5
Rudin, Joseph: G. 1964a, 1973a;
  E. 1968c, 1976a
Rüf, Elisabeth: GW 10,12,15,22,
  &33, GW 15,8; GW ed.
Rychlak, Joseph F.: G. 1973a;
  E. 1968b, 1976a
Rychner, Max: G. 1932c, 1972a;
  E. 1973b

S

Sadger, Isidor: G. 1909h; CW 18,11
Sandwich, Earl of: G. 1973a;
  E. 1971b,10, 1976a
Sauerlander, Wolfgang: G. 1974a;
  CW 18,9,21,22,28,33&34
Schär, Hans: G. 1972b, GW 11,21;
  E. 1976a
Schärf, Riwkah: G. 1948a; Seminar
  Notes, 1933–41, 1938–39, 1939–40
Schleich, Carl Ludwig: G. 1934e;
  CW 18,39
Schloss, Jerome: E. 1955c, CW
  18,107
Schmaltz Gustav: G. 1955e;
  CW 18,17
Schmid-Guisan, Hans: G. 1931d,
  1932d; CW 18,108&109
Schmitz, Oskar A. H.: G. 1932b;
  E. 1975a
Schnapper, M. B.: E. 1957c
Seelig, Carl: G. 1972b; E. 1971b,5,
  1975a
Senn, Gustav: G. 1945g
Serrano, Miguel: G. 1973a; E.
  1960b, 1966b, 1976a; Sp. 1965a
Shipley, Thorne: E. 1928b,1
Sinclair, Upton: G. 1972b;
  E. 1953g, 1955f, 1976a
Smith, Carleton: E. 1958b
Sommer, Robert: G. 1934l
Speyr, von: G. 1911h
Spiegelberg, Frederic: E. 1972b
Spier, Julius: E. 1944b, CW 18,132
Stein, Leopold: CW 2

Steiner, Gustav: G. 1964b, 1973a;
  E. 1962a, 1976a
Stekel, Wilhelm: G. 1908j; CW
  18,22
Suzuki, Daisetz T.: G. 1939c, GW
  11,13; E. 1949d, CW 11,13

T

Tausk, Victor: G. 1913d; E. 1973d,3,
  CW 18,31
Taylor, Ethel: Seminar Notes,
  1928–30
Thayer, Ellen: E. 1953f, 1954h
Thiele-Dohrmann, Klaus: G. 1968a,
  GW 3,5&7, GW 4,3,11,&13
Thomas, Una Gauntlett: Seminar
  Notes, 1935–36
Thornton, Edward: G. 1973a;
  E. 1965a, 1967f, 1976a
Tischendorf, F. von: G. 1958j,
  1973a; E. 1959j, 1976a
Trinick, John: G. 1973a; E. 1967e,
  1976a

U

Urstein, M.: G. 1910e; CW 18,20

V

Varendonck, J.: G. 1908l,1
Verzar, J.: E. 1953a
Vigouroux, A: G. 1908i,9

W

W., E. [Elizabeth Welsh]: E. 1955g;
  see also Welsh, Elizabeth
Waldstein, Louis: G. 1909i;
  CW 18,12
Wallace, Edith: E. 1960d
Walser, Hans W.: G. 1968b
Wegmann, Hans: G. 1972a, GW
  11,24; E. 1973a
Welsh, Elizabeth: E. 1946a,
  1947a,1&7, 1953a, 1955g&l,
  Seminar Notes, 1933–41

Werblowsky, R. J. Zwi: G. 1962a,
15,iv, 1972b, GW 11,5; E. 1952b,
1976a, CW 11,5
Wernicke, Carl: G. 1906h;
CW 18,20
White, Stuart E.: G. 1948e
White, Victor: G. 1957h, 1972b,
GW 11,4&20; E. 1952c, 1976a,
CW 11,4; Port. 1964a; Sp. 1955b
Whitmont, Edward: E. 1955e
Wickes, Frances G.: G. 1931e,
1953b, 1972a, GW 17,2; E. 1927a,
1966c, 1971b,2, 1973b, CW
17,2, CW 18,57
Wilhelm, Richard: G. 1929b&h,
1930c, 1931b, 1938a, 1957b,
1962a,15,vii; E. 1931a, 1950d,
1962a,18, 1962b; Du. 1963a,3;
It. 1936a
Wilhelm, Salome: E. 1962b

Wilson, William G.: G. 1973a;
E. 1963d, 1968e, 1976a
Winston, Clara: E. 1962a
Winston, Richard: E. 1962a
Wittels, Fritz: G. 1910l; E. 1973d,2
Wolff, Toni: G. 1940a, 1959e,
GW 10,18, GW 11,1; E. 1938a,
CW 10,18, Seminar Notes, 1932a
Woods, Ralph L.: E. 1947d
Wulffen, Erich: G. 1910p; CW
18,25

Z

Zacharias, Gerhard P.: G. 1954c
Ziegler, K. A.: G. 1946f; E. 1946b
Zimmer, Heinrich: G. 1944b, 1962a,
15,viii, GW 11,15
Zosimos: G. 1938c, 1954b,5;
CW 13,2

INDEX 3:

CONGRESSES, ORGANIZATIONS, SOCIETIES, ETC.

Cited in the German and English sections only.

A

Abernethian Society, London:
E. 1936d
Ärztlicher Verein, ?Munich:
G. 1929d
Allgemeine ärztliche Gesellschaft
für Psychotherapie: G. 1931c,
1935g; *see also* International
Medical Congress for Psycho-
therapy
Allgemeiner ärztlicher Kongress
für Psychotherapie, *see* Inter-
national Medical Congress for
Psychotherapy
Alsatian Pastoral Conference, *see*
Elsässische Pastoral konferenz
Analytical Psychology Club,
London: E. 1968a
Analytical Psychology Club of
New York: E. 1936a, 1940c,
1948a+d, 1949c, 1951a
Aristotelian Society, London:
E. 1919b
"Arzt und Seelsorger," *see* Stutt-
garter Gemeinschaft . . .
Australasian Medical Congress,
9th Session, Sydney, Sept. 1911:
E. 1913a

B

B.B.C., *see* British Broadcasting
Corporation
Basel School Council, *see* Basler
staatliche Schulsynode

Basler staatliche Schulsynode:
G. 1943d
Bericht über den . . . allgemeinen
ärztlichen Kongress . . . , *see*
Allgemeiner ärztlicher
Kongress . . .
Bernoullianum, Basel: G. 1905e
British Broadcasting Corporation,
London: E. 1946e, 1960c
British Medical Association.
Section of Neurology & Psycho-
logical Medicine, 82nd annual
meeting, Aberdeen, 29–31 July
1914: E. 1914b
British Psychological Association,
London, 12 July 1919: E. 1919b

C

C. G. Jung Institute, Zurich:
G. 1958c; E. 1948b
Clark University, Worcester, Mass.:
E. 1910a
Conference for Psychology, *see*
Tagung für Psychologie
Congrès des Unions Intellectuels,
see Verband für Intellektuelle
Zusammenarbeit
Congrès international de
Pédagogie, *see* International
Congress of Education
Congress for Psychotherapy, *see*
Tagung für Psychotherapie

D

Dresden, 1931: G. 1933b

249

E

E.T.H., *see* Eidgenössische
Technische Hochschule
Eidgenössische Technische
Hochschule, Zurich: G. 1932i,
1934a; Seminar Notes, 1933–41,
1936–37b, 1938–39, 1939–40
Elsässische Pastoralkonferenz,
Strassburg, May 1932: G. 1932a
Eranos Tagung, Ascona: 1939,
G. 1940b; 1940, G. 1942b; 1941,
G. 1942c; 1942, G. 1943b; 1945,
G. 1946e; 1946, G. 1947a; 1948,
G. 1949b; 1951, G. 1952f

F

Federal Polytechnic Institute, *see*
Eidgenössische Technische
Hochschule
Fordham University, New York:
G. 1913a; E. 1913b

G

General Medical Congress for
Psychotherapy, *see* International
Medical Congress for Psycho-
therapy
Gesellschaft der Aerzte des Kantons
Zürich: G. 1908d
Gesellschaft für deutsche Sprache
und Literatur, Zurich: G. 1922a
Gesellschaft für freie Philosophie,
Darmstadt: G. 1927a
Guild of Pastoral Psychology,
London, seminar talk, 5 Apr.
1939: E. 1954c

H

Harvard University, Cambridge,
Mass. Tercentenary Conference
of Arts and Sciences, Sept. 1936:
E. 1937a
Hottinger Lesezirkel, Zurich:
G. 1931f

I

Institute of Medical Psychology,
London: E. 1968a
International Congress for
Psychiatry, *see* Internationaler
Kongress für Psychiatrie
International Congress of Educa-
tion / Congrès international de
Pédagogie: I, Brussels, Aug. 1911,
G. 1912b; Territet/Montreux,
1923, G. 1925c; London, May
1924, E. 1928a, 13, II–IV
Heidelberg, 1925, E. 1928a,14
International Congress of Peda-
gogy, *see* International Congress
of Education
International Congress of
Psychiatry and Neurology,
Amsterdam, Sept. 1907: G. 1908m
International General Medical
Society for Psychotherapy, Swiss
section, *see* Allgemeine ärztliche
Gesellschaft für Psychotherapy
International Medical Congress,
17th, London, 1913: E. 1916a,9
International Medical Congress
for Psychotherapy / Allgemeiner
ärztlicher Kongress für Psycho-
therapie: III, Baden-Baden,
20–22 April 1928, G. 1928c;
IV, Bad Nauheim, 12 April
1929, G. 1929c; VI, Dresden, 31
April 1931, G. 1931c; VII, Bad
Nauheim, 10–13 May 1934; VIII,
Bad Nauheim, 27–30 Mar. 1935,
CW 10,30; IX, Copenhagen,
2–4 Oct. 1937, CW 10,32; X,
Oxford, 29 July–2 Aug. 1938, E.
1938b; *see also* Allgemeine
ärztliche Gesellschaft für Psychotherapie
International Psychoanalytic
Association, *see* Internationale
psychoanalytische Vereinigung
Internationale psychoanalytische
Vereinigung: 3. Kongress,
Weimar, 21–22 Sept. 1911, G.
1911f+g; Zurich Branch Society,

Zurich, 22 Nov. 1912, G. 1913c;
Congress, Munich, 7–8 Sept. 1913,
Fr. 1913a
Internationaler Kongress für
Psychiatrie, II, Zurich, 1–7 Sept.
1957: G. 1958i; E. 1958d

K

Karlsruhe, 1927: G. 1931a,12
Kulturbund, Vienna: G. 1931g,
1934b,9

L

Literarische Gesellschaft, Augsburg:
G. 1926c
Literarischer Club, Zurich: G.
1929g

M

Medical-Pharmaceutical Society,
see Medizinisch-pharmaceutischer
Bezirksverein
Medizinische Gesellschaft, Zurich:
G. 1935l
Medizinisch-pharmaceutischer
Bezirksverein, Bern: G. 1912h
Mind Association, London: E.
1919b

N

Naturforschende Gesellschaft:
G. 1945g; Zurich, 1 Feb. 1932,
G. 1932i; Basel, 7 Sept. 1941,
G. 1941f
New York Academy of Medicine,
8 Oct. 1912: E. 1916a,9

P

Philosophische Gesellschaft, Zurich:
G. 1931a,12
Private psychoanalytische Verein-
igung: I, Salzburg, 27 April 1908,
G. 1910s; II, Nürnberg, 30–31
March 1910, G. 1910n

Psychoanalytic Congress, see
Internationale psychoanalytische
Vereinigung
Psychologischer Club Zürich:
G. 1922a, 1932a, 1938b, 1941f,
1942b+c, 1943c, 1946d, 1949b,
1950b, 1952f
Psycho-medical Society, London:
E. 1913d, 1915c
Psychotherapeutische Gesellschaft,
Munich: G. 1929d

R

Royal Society of Medicine, Section
of Psychiatry: Annual Meeting,
London, 11 July 1919, E. 1919a;
Meeting, London, 4 April 1939,
E. 1939d.

S

Schweizerische Akademie der
medizinischen Wissenschaft:
G. 1945e
Schweizerische Gesellschaft der
Freunde ostasiatischer Kultur:
G. 1943c
Schweizerische Gesellschaft für
praktische Psychologie: G. 1948f
Schweizerische Gesellschaft für
Psychiatrie: 84. Versammlung,
Prangins, 7–8 Oct. 1933, G. 1933f;
Kommission für Psychotherapie,
4th annual meeting, Zurich, 19
July 1941, G. 1945f
Schweizerische Gesellschaft zur
Geschichte der Medizin und der
Naturwissenschaften: G. 1941f
Schweizerische Paracelsus Gesell-
schaft. Einsiedeln: G. 1942a,2,
1948c
Society for German Language
and Literature, see Gesellschaft
für deutsche Sprache . . .
Society for Nature Research, see
Naturforschende Gesellschaft . . .
Society for Psychical Research,
London: E. 1920b

Society of Public Health, Congress, Zurich, 1929: E. 1930b
Stuttgarter Gemeinschaft "Arzt und Seelsorger": 7. Kongress, 1958, G. 1959a; 8. Kongress, 1959, Fall, Zurich, 1959b
Südwestdeutsche Irrenärzte: 37. Versammlung, Tübingen, 3–4 Nov. 1906, G. 1907f
Swiss Academy of Medical Science, see Schweizerische Gesellschaft für Psychiatrie, Kommission für Psychotherapie
Swiss Psychiatrists, Winter Meeting, see Verein schweizer Irrenärzte
Swiss Society for the History of Medicine and the Natural Sciences, see Schweizerische Gesellschaft zur Geschichte der Medizin . . .

T

Tagung für Psychologie, Zurich, 26 Sept. 1942: G. 1943e
Tagung für Psychotherapie, II, Bern, 28 May 1937: CW 16,14

U

United States Information Agency: E. 1957h
Universität Zürich: G. 1902a, 1905h, 1906b&k, 1971a,3
Universitätsklinik, Zürich, see Universität Zürich
University of Zurich, see Universität Zürich

V

Verband für intellektuelle Zusammenarbeit, Tagung, Prague, Oct. 1928: G. 1928f
Verein schweizer Irrenärzte: Winter Meeting, Bern, 27 Nov. 1910, G. 1911h; Zurich, 1928, G. 1931a,6

W

Wanderversammlung der Südwestdeutschen Psychiater und Neurologen, 66., Badenweiler, 1950: G. 1950g

Y

Yale University, New Haven, Conn.: E. 1938a

Z

Zurich Cantonal Medical Society, see Gesellschaft der Aerzte des Kantons Zürich
Zurich Medical Society, see Medizinische Gesellschaft, Zurich
Zurich Psychoanalytic Society, see Internationale psychoanalytische Vereinigung. Zurich Branch Society
Zurich, Rathaus: G. 1908a, 1933b
Zurich School of Analytical Psychology: Fr. 1916a
Zurich Town Hall, see Zurich, Rathaus

INDEX 4: PERIODICALS

ABBREVIATIONS USED IN THE BIBLIOGRAPHY

Aus d. Jhrsb. = Aus dem Jahresbericht.
Basl. Nach. = Basler Nachrichten.
Bull. APC = Analytical Psychology Club of New York. Bulletin.
CorrespBl. schweizer Ärzte = Correspondenzblatt für schweizer Ärzte.
Eran. Jb. = Eranos-Jahrbuch.
Europ. Rev. = Europäische Revue.
J. abnorm. Psychol. = Journal of Abnormal Psychology.
J. Psychol. Neurol. = Journal für Psychologie und Neurologie.
Jb. psychoanal. psychopath. Forsch. = Jahrbuch für psychoanalytische und
    psychopathologische Forschungen.
Neue Schw. R. = Neue schweizer Rundschau.
Neue Zür. Z. = Neue Zürcher Zeitung.
New Repub. = New Republic.
Psychoanal. Rev. = Psychoanalytic Review.
Schweiz. Z. Strafrecht. = Schweizerische Zeitschrift für Strafrecht.
Revta Occid. = Revista de Occidente.
Z. angew. Psychol. = Zeitschrift für angewandte Psychologie und psycho-
    logische Sammelforschung.
Zbl. Nervenhk. = Zentralblatt für Nervenheilkunde und Psychiatrie.
Zbl. Psychoanal. = Zentralblatt für Psychoanalyse.
Zbl. Psychotherap. = Zentralblatt für Psychotherapie und ihre Grenz-
    gebiete.

A

AA Grapevine; International
    Monthly Journal of Alcoholics
    Anonymous (New York):
    E. 1963d, 1968e
A.P.R.O. Bulletin (Alamogordo,
    N.M.), Organ of the Aerial
    Phenomena Research Organiza-
    tion: E. 1958f&j
Actas Ciba (Buenos Aires): Sp.
    1946a; (Lisbon): Port. 1948a;
    (Rio de Janeiro): Port. 1947a;
    see also Ciba Zeitschrift and
    Revue Ciba
Action et Pensée (Geneva):
    Fr. 1944b

Adam; International Journal
    (Bucharest; London): E. 1959k
Al Hamishmar (Tel Aviv): He.
    1974a
Allgemeine Neueste Nachrichten
    (Munich): G. 1929e
Allgemeine Zeitschrift für Psychia-
    trie und psychisch-gerichtliche
    Medizin (Berlin): G. 1903a
Ambix (London): E. 1946f
American Journal of Psychology
    (Ithaca, N.Y.): E. 1910a
Analytical Psychology Club of
    New York, Bulletin (New York):
    E. 1945b, 1948b+c, 1950e, 1953f,
    1954g+h, 1956c, 1957h, 1958h,
    1959g+j, 1960d, 1963d+f

Annalen der Philosophischen
Gesellschaften . . . , See Philo-
sophische Gesellschaften . . .
Année psychologique (Paris):
Fr. 1908a, 1909a
Archiv für die gesamte Psychologie
(Leipzig): G. 1904b
Archiv für Kriminalanthropologie
und Kriminalistik (Leipzig):
G. 1906b
Archiv für Kriminologie (Leipzig):
G. 1937b
Archives de psychologie (Geneva):
Fr. 1907a, 1913a, 1916a
Arts, Lettres, Spectacles, Musique
(Paris): Fr. 1960b, 1962b
Asia (New York): E. 1939b+c
Astrologie moderne, L' (Paris):
Fr. 1954b
Atenea (Santiago, Chile): Sp. 1933b
Atlantic Monthly, The (Boston):
E. 1958b, 1962a,1,6,12,13
Aus dem Jahresbericht (Zurich),
Annual pub. of the Psychol-
ogischer Club Zurich: G. 1938b,
1946d, 1950b
Australasian Medical Congress.
Transactions. (Sydney): E. 1913a

B

Badener Tagblatt (Baden,
Switzerland): G. 1958h
Basler Nachrichten (Basel): G.
1905e, 1909h+i, 1932d, 1934i,
1939d, 1946g
Basler Stadtbuch; Jahrbuch für
Kultur und Geschichte, ed. by
Fritz Grieber, Valentin Lötscher,
Adolf Portmann. (Basel): G.
1964b
Berliner Tageblatt (Berlin): G.
1928c, 1934h
Black Mountain Review
(Bañalbufar, Mallorca): E. 1955l
Brain; A Journal of Neurology
(London): E. 1907b
British Journal of Medical
Psychology (London): E. 1923b

British Journal of Psychology
(London): E. 1919b, 1921a
British Medical Journal (London):
E. 1914b
Bulletin der schweizerischen
Akademie . . . , See Schweizerische
Akademie . . .

C

Centralblatt, see listings under
Zentralblatt
Character and Personality; An
International Quarterly of
Psychodiagnostics and Allied
Studies (Durham, North Caro-
lina): E. 1932b
Charakter (Berlin): G. 1932f
Chimera (N.Y.; Princeton, N.J.):
E. 1947f
Chinesisch-deutscher Almanach
(Frankfurt am Main): G. 1930a
Ciba, see Actas Ciba and Revue
Ciba
Ciba-Tijdschrift (Basel): Du. 1947b
Ciba Zeitschrift (Basel): G. 1945d;
(Baden): G. 1952i
Correspondenzblatt für schweizer
Ärzte (Basel): G. 1906c,e,f,+h,
1907b,c,+d, 1908d–h,+k,
1909d–g, 1910a–j, 1911h, 1912h
Cosmopolitan (New York): E. 1958i
C.S.I. of New York (New York)
(Civilian Saucer Intelligence):
E. 1959i

D

Darshana (Moradabad, India):
E. 1961d
Dialectica (Neuchâtel): G. 1951d
Du; schweizerische Monatsschrift
(Zurich): G. 1941e, 1943f, 1955e;
E. 1955g

E

Encéphale, L'; Journal de Psychiatrie (Paris): Fr. 1913b, 1952c

Encounter (London): E. 1961c
Eranos-Jahrbuch, ed. by Olga
　Froebe-Kapteyn (Zurich): G.
　1934c, 1935b, 1936a, 1937a, 1938c,
　1939b, 1940b, 1942b+c, 1943b,
　1946e, 1947a, 1949b, 1952f
Espresso, L' (Rome): It. 1961c
Ethik (Sexual- und Gesellschafts-
　Ethik) (Halle): G. 1928g
Europäische Revue (Berlin): G.
　1927b, 1928d+f, 1929h, 1931f+g,
　1932e, 1933d, 1934h

F

Flinker Almanac (Paris): G. 1957j;
　Fr. 1961d
Flying Saucer Review (London):
　E. 1955i
Folia neuro-biologica (Leipzig):
　G. 1908c,i,+l
Form und Sinn (Augsburg): G.
　1926c
Forum (New York): E. 1930a

G

Geneeskundige Courant (Amster-
　dam): Du. 1908a
Guild of Pastoral Psychology,
　Lectures (London): E. 1954c

H

Hamburger akademische Rund-
　schau (Hamburg): G. 1947c
Horisont (Oslo): Nor. 1956a
Horizon (London): E. 1943b
Human Relations (London; Ann
　Arbor, Mich.): E. 1957i

I

International Congress for Psychia-
　try (Proceedings) (Zurich): G.
　1958i
International Journal of Group
　Psychotherapy (New York),

Organ of the American Group
　Psychotherapy Association: E.
　1957i
International Journal of Para-
　psychology (New York): E. 1963e
Internationale Zeitschrift für
　ärztliche Psychoanalyse (Leip-
　zig): G. 1913c+d
Inward Light (Washington, D.C.):
　E. 1955j

J

Jahrbuch für psychoanalytische
　und psychopathologische
　Forschungen (Leipzig): G.
　1909b+c, 1910k–p, 1911a–d,
　1912c, 1913a+b
Journal des poètes, Le (Brussels):
　Fr. 1932b
Journal für Psychologie und
　Neurologie (Leipzig): G. 1902b,
　1903b, 1904a, 1905g+h, 1906i+j,
　1907e
Journal of Abnormal Psychology
　(Boston): E. 1907a, 1908a, 1915c
Journal of Analytical Psychology
　(London): E. 1959h, 1960e
Journal of Mental Science
　(London): E. 1938b, 1939d
Journal of Nervous and Mental
　Disease (New York; Richmond;
　London): E. 1946c
Journal of Religion and Health
　(New York), Organ of the
　Academy of Religion and Mental
　Health: E. 1968f
Journal of State Medicine
　(London): E. 1930b
Jungkaufmann, Der; Schweizer
　Monatschrift für die kauf-
　männische Jugend (Zurich):
　G. 1952h
Jura libre, Le (Delémont, Switz.):
　Fr. 1958d
Juristisch-psychiatrische Grenz-
　fragen (Halle): G. 1906k

K

Katalog der Autographen-Auktion
(Marburg): G. 1967b
Kölnische Zeitung (Cologne):
G. 1929f, 1932c
Kultur, Die (Munich): G. 1956f

L

Lancet, The (London): E. 1914b
Lesezirkel, Der (Zurich): G. 1929g
Lettere ed arti (Venice): It. 1946a
Listener, The (London): E. 1946e,
1960c

M

Mason Dergisi (Istanbul): Turk.
1954a
Medizinische Klinik (Berlin):
G. 1908j
Medizinische Welt (Berlin):
G. 1929i
Merkur (Stuttgart): G. 1952j
Mitteilungen der Schweizerischen
Gesellschaft . . . , see Schweizer-
ische Gesellschaft . . . Mittei-
lungen
Monat, Der (Frankfurt am Main):
G. 1956e
Monatsschrift für Kriminal-
psychologie und Strafrechts-
reform (Heidelberg): G. 1906d
Monatsschrift für Psychiatrie und
Neurologie (Basel): G. 1908m
Münchner medizinische Wochen-
schrift (Munich): G. 1906g
Münchner neueste Nachrichten
(Munich): G. 1935i

N

Naši Razgledi (Ljubljana):
Sl. 1961a
Naturforschende Gesellschaft in
Zürich, Vierteljahrschrift
(Zurich): G. 1932i
Naturforschende Gesellschaft.

Verhandlungen (Basel): G.
1945g
Nederlandsch Tijdschrift voor
Geneeskunde (Amsterdam):
Du. 1914a
Neue Schweizer Rundschau (Zurich)
(published as Wissen und Leben,
1907–18): G. 1928e, 1933b+c,
1936c, 1945c, 1948e
Neue Wissenschaft; Zeitschrift für
Parapsychologie (Obereng-
stringen / Zurich): G. 1951e
Neue Zürcher Zeitung (Zurich):
G. 1912e+f, 1930c–e, 1932g,
1934f+g
Neues Wiener Journal (Vienna):
G. 1933a
New Adelphi (London): E. 1928c
New Republic, The (New York):
E. 1953g, 1955f+h
Nimbus (London): E. 1953h+i
Nova Acta Paracelsica (Basel),
Yearbook of the Schweizerische
Paracelsus Gesellschaft
Einsiedeln: G. 1948c

P

Pastoral Psychology (Great Neck,
N.Y.): E. 1956c+d
Perspektiv (Copenhagen): Dan.
1957a
Philosophische Gesellschaften
Innerschweiz und Ostschweiz,
Annalen: G. 1957h
Prabuddha Bharata (Calcutta):
E. 1931c, 1936c
Proceedings of the International
Congress . . . , see International
Congress . . .
Proceedings of the Royal Society
. . . , see Royal Society . . .
Proceedings of the Society . . . , see
Society . . .
Psyche (Heidelberg): G. 1950g
Psychiatric Quarterly (Utica, N.Y.):
G. 1946h; E. 1946d
Psychiatrisch-Neurologische
Wochenschrift (Halle): G. 1911h

Psychoanalytic Review (New
York): E. 1913b+c, 1914a,
1915b+d, 1963g
Psychological Perspectives (Los
Angeles) Organ of the Analytical
Psychology Club: E. 1972c+d
Psychology Today (Del Mar, Cal.):
E. 1974b
Psycho-Medical Society, Trans-
actions (Cockermouth, England):
E. 1913d
Psychotherapy (Calcutta): E. 1956e

Q

Querschnitt (Berlin): G. 1932h

R

Raschers Jahrbuch für schweizer
Art und Kunst (Zurich): G.
1912d
Revista de Occidente (Madrid):
Sp. 1925a, 1931a, 1932a, 1933a,
1934b, 1936b
Revue Ciba (Basel): Fr. 1945a;
see also Actas Ciba and Ciba
Zeitschrift
Revue d'Allemagne et des pays
de langue allemande (Paris):
Fr. 1933a
Rivista di psicologia applicata
(Florence): It. 1908a
Royal Society of Medicine, Proceed-
ings (London): E. 1919a

S

St. Bartholomew's Hospital Journal
(London): E. 1936d, 1937d
Saturday Review of Literature, The
(New York): E. 1937c
Schweizer Archiv für Neurologie
und Psychiatrie (Zurich): G.
1933f, 1958i
Schweizer Bücherverzeichnis
(Zurich): G. 1950c
Schweizer Erziehungs-Rundschau
(Zurich): G. 1943d

Schweizer Monatshefte (Zurich):
G. 1957i
Schweizerische Ärztezeitung für
Standesfragen (Bern): G.
1935h+i
Schweizerische Akademie der
medizinischen Wissenschaften.
Bulletin (Basel): G. 1945e
Schweizerische Gesellschaft der
Freunde ostasiatischer Kultur.
Mitteilungen (St. Gallen):
G. 1943c
Schweizerische Medizinische
Wochenschrift (Basel): G. 1941f;
E. 1931d
Schweizerische Paracelsus Gesell-
schaft, Yearbook, see Nova Acta
Paracelsica
Schweizerische Zeitschrift für
Psychologie und ihre Anwendung
(Bern): G. 1943e, 1945f
Schweizerische Zeitschrift für
Strafrecht (Bern): G. 1904c,
1905f, 1906i
Schweizerisches medizinisches
Jahrbuch (Basel): G. 1929d
Schweizerland (Zurich): G. 1918b
Society for Psychical Research,
Proceedings (London): E. 1920b
Spring (through 1969, New York;
1970–, Zurich), Annual of the
Analytical Psychology Club of
New York, New York. E. 1942b,
1943a, 1944a, 1945a, 1946a,
1947c, 1948a, 1949c, 1950a, 1951a,
1953c, 1954d, 1955c+d, 1956b,
1957d, 1961a, 1968f, 1969f, 1970c,
1971b, 1973d+e, 1974e
Süddeutsche Monatshefte
(Munich): G. 1936b
Sunday Referee (London): E. 1932c
Synthèses: Revue européenne
(Brussels): Fr. 1955b

T

Table Ronde, La (Paris): Fr.
1957b, 1958c

Tagesanzeiger für Stadt und Kanton Zürich (Zurich): G. 1967b

Tat, Die (Zurich): G. 1959g

Therapie des Monats, Die (Mannheim): G. 1959h

Tomorrow (New York): E. 1955k

Transactions of the Australasian ..., see Australasian Medical Congress ...

Transactions of the Psycho-Medical ..., see Psycho-Medical Society ...

transition (Paris): E. 1930c

Tribune de Genève (Geneva): Fr. 1948a,4

U

UFO Investigator; Facts about Flying Saucers (Washington, D.C.), Organ of the National Investigations Committee on Aerial Phenomena: E. 1958g

Universitas (Stuttgart): G. 1958c, 1959f; E. 1959f

University; A Princeton Magazine (Princeton, N.J.): E. 1972e

V

Verhandlungen der Naturforschenden ..., see Naturforschende Gesellschaft ...

Vierteljahrschrift der Naturforschenden ..., see Naturforschende Gesellschaft ...

Vindrosen (Copenhagen): Dan. 1964a

Volksrecht (Zurich): G. 1905e

Vossische Zeitung (Berlin): G. 1932f

W

Welt, Die (Hamburg): G. 1950f

Weltwoche, Die (Zurich): G. 1954e+f

Wiener Zeitschrift für Nervenheilkunde ... und deren Grenzgebiete (Vienna): G. 1948f

Wissen und Leben (Zurich) (replaces Neue Schweizer Rundschau, 1907–18): G. 1912g

Z

Zeitschrift für angewandte Psychologie und psychologische Sammelforschung (Leipzig): G. 1908n+o, 1910r

Zeitschrift für Menschenkunde; Blätter für Charakterologie und angewandte Psychologie (Munich): G. 1925b

Zeitschrift für Parapsychologie und Grenzgebiete der Psychologie (Bern): G. 1958f, 1961b

Zeitschrift für psychosomatische Medizin (Göttingen): G. 1956d

Zentralblatt für Nervenheilkunde und Psychiatrie (Leipzig): G. 1905b–d, 1907f, 1908b

Zentralblatt für Psychoanalyse und Psychotherapie (Wiesbaden): G. 1910a+s, 1911e–h

Zentralblatt für Psychotherapie und ihre Grenzgebiete einschliesslich der medizinischen Psychologie und psychischen Hygiene (Leipzig): G. 1910n, 1933e, 1934a,j–l, 1935j–l, 1936d+e, 1939e

Zentralblatt für Verkehrs-Medizin, Verkehrs-Psychologie und angrenzende Gebiete (Alfeld/Leine and Bad Godesberg): G. 1958j

Zukunft, Die (Berlin): G. 1905a

Zürcher Student (Zurich), Organ of the student body, University of Zurich: G. 1949g, 1958g

ADDENDA

ITALIAN

These entries were received from a correspondent in Italy too late for inclusion in the Italian section. They have not been integrated into the cross-references in the German and English sections, and some attributions to sources are tentative.

1949d "Introduzione." Charles Robert Aldrich: *Mente primitiva e civiltà moderna.* pp. 13, 16. Turin: Einaudi. Trans. from E. 1931b by Tullio Tentori.

1962b "Sulla sincronicità." *Il Verri*, VII:3 (Aug.), 3–14. Trans. from G. 1952f by C. R.

1962c "L'uomo arcaico." *Magia e civiltà.* pp. 124–51. Ed. by Ernesto de Martino. Milan: Garzanti. Trans. from G. 1931a,9 by ?

1970c "Prefazione." D. T. Suzuki: *Introduzione al Buddismo Zen.* pp. 15–33. Rome: Ubaldini. Trans. from E. 1949d by Grazia Marchianò.

1970d *Psicologia della schizofrenia.* Rome: Newton Compton Italiana. pp. 219. Trans. from G. 1907a by Celso Balducci.

1971b *La malattia mentale.* Rome: Newton Compton Italiana. pp. 235. Trans. by Celso Balducci. Contents:
   1. "Simulazione dell'alienazione mentale." (31–72) Trans. from G. 1903b. Pub. in a dif. trans. as It. 1974b,3.
   2. "Parere medico su un caso di simulazione di malattia mentale." (73–98) Trans. from G. 1904c. Pub. in a dif. trans. as It. 1974b,5.
   3. "Il contenuto delle psicosi." (99–132) Trans. from G. 1908a.
   4. "Critica alla teoria del negativismo schizofrenico secondo Bleuler." (133–42) Trans. from G. 1911c.
   5. "Attualità in tema di psicoterapia. Carteggio con il dottor C. G. Jung, a cura di R. Loÿ." (143–96) Trans. from G. 1914b.

6. "Il problema della psicogenesi della malattia mentale." (197–218) Trans. from GW 3,6.

7. "Importanza terapeutica dell'abreazione." (219–35) Trans. from GW 16,11.

1971c *Inconscio, occultismo e magia*. Rome: Newton Compton Italiana. pp. 251. Trans. by Celso Balducci. Contents:

1. "Psicologia e patologia dei cosidetti fenomeni occulti." (39–140) Trans. from G. 1902a. Pub. in a dif. trans. as It. 1974b,1.

2. "Importanza dell'inconscio in psicopatologia." (141–50) Trans. from GW 3,5.

3. "La struttura dell'inconscio." (151–84) Trans. from GW 7,4.

4. "L'inconscio." (185–216) Trans. from G. 1918b.

5. "Istinto ed inconscio." (217–28) Trans. from G. 1928b,4.

6. "I fondamenti psicologici della credenza negli spiriti." (229–51) Trans. from G. 1928b,5.

1971d *La psicoanalisi e Freud*. Rome: Newton Compton Italiana. pp. 225. Trans. by Liliana Grosso. Pub. in a dif. trans. with addns. as It. 1973a. Contents:

1. "La teoria di Freud sull'isteria: una riposta ad Aschaffenburg." (33–44) Trans. from GW 4,1.

2. "La teoria freudiana dell'isteria." (45–66) Trans. from GW 4,2.

3. "L'analisi dei sogni." (67–80) Trans. from GW 4,3.

4. "Un contributo alla psicologia del pettegolezzo." (81–100) Trans. from GW 4,4.

5. "Sull'importanza dei sogni dei numeri." (101–12) Trans. from GW 4,5.

6. "Morton Prince: 'il meccanismo e l'interpretazione dei sogni' —una revisione critica." (113–38) Trans. from GW 4,6.

7. "Sulla critica alla psicoanalisi." (139–46) Trans. from GW 4,7.

8. "Riguardo alla psicoanalisi." (147–52) Trans. from GW 4,8.

9. "Aspetti generali della psicoanalisi." (153–72) Trans. from GW 4,10.

10. "Psicoanalisi e nevrosi." (173–86) Trans. from GW 4,11.

11. "Prefazione alla 'Raccolta di scritti sulla psicologia analitica.'" (187–98) Trans. from GW 4,13.

12. "L'importanza del padre nel destino dell'individuo." (199–225) Trans. from GW 4,14.

1972c *La dimensione psichica.* Turin: Boringhieri. pp. 345. Trans. by
?Luigi Aurigemma. Contents:
1. "Psicoterapia e concezione del mondo." (37–45) Trans. from
   G. 1943e.
2. "L'essenza dei sogni." (46–66) Trans. from G. 1948b,5.
3. "Psicologia e poesia." (67–89) Trans. from G. 1950a,2.
4. "La funzione trascendente." (90–119) Trans. from G. 1958b.
5. "Gli archetipi dell'inconscio collettivo." (120–161) Trans.
   from G. 1954b,2.
6. "La struttura della psiche (da 'Aion')." (162–97) Trans. from
   G. 1951a,I–IV.
7. "Wotan." (198–213) Trans. from G. 1936c.
8. "La schizofrenia." (214–32) Trans. from G. 1958i.
9. "Riflessioni teoriche sull'essenza della psiche." (233–318)
   Trans. from G. 1954b,8.
10. "La coscienza dal punto di vista psicologico." (319–40) Trans.
    from G. 1958c.

1972d *Psicologia e psichiatria.* Rome: Newton Compton Italiana. pp. 247.
Trans. by Celso Balducci. Contents:
1. "Caso di stupore isterico in una detenuta sottoposta ad istrut-
   toria." (19–46) Trans. from GW 1,5. Pub. in a dif. trans. as
   It. 1974b,2.
2. "Squilibrio affettivo maniacale." (47–84) Trans. from GW
   1,4.
3. "Paralessia isterica." (85–92) Trans. from GW 1,2. Pub. in a
   dif. trans. as It. 1974b,4.
4. "Criptomnesia." (93–110) Trans. from GW 1,3. Pub. in a dif.
   trans. as It. 1974b,6.
5. "Diagnostica psicologica dei fatti." (111–116) Trans. from
   GW 1,9.
6. "Terza e definitiva perizia su due diagnosi psichiatriche contraddittorie." (117–32) Trans. from GW 1,8. Pub in a dif.
   trans. as It. 1974b,7.
7. "Conflitti psichici in una bambina." (133–74) Trans. from
   GW 17,1.
8. "Contributo allo studio dei tipi psicologici." (175–90) Trans.
   from GW 6,4.
9. "La comprensione psicologica dei problemi patologici." (191–
   212) Trans. from GW 3,2, Nachtrag.

10. "Nuove vie della psicologia." (213–47) Trans. from GW 7,3.

1973b "Introduzione." M. Esther Harding: *I misteri della donna.* pp. 7–9. Rome: Astrolabio. Trans. from E. 1955e by Aldo Giuliani.

1974b *Psicologia e patologia dei cosiddetti fenomeni occulti e altri scritti.* Turin: Boringhieri. pp. 223. Trans. by Guido Bistolfi. Contents:
1. "Psicologia e patologia dei cosiddetti fenomeni occulti." (3–98) Trans. from G. 1902a. Pub. in a dif. trans. as It. 1971c,1.
2. "Caso di stupore isterico in una detenuta in carcere preventivo." (99–122) Trans. from G. 1902b. Pub. in a dif. trans. as It. 1972d,1.
3. "Simulazione di malattia mentale." (123–54) Trans. from G. 1903b. Pub. in a dif. trans. as It. 1971b,1.
4. "Paralessia isterica." (155–58) Trans. from G. 1904b. Pub. in a dif. trans. as It. 1972d,3.
5. "Perizia medica su un caso di simulazione di malattia mentale." (159–78) Trans. from G. 1904c. Pub. in a dif. trans. as It. 1971b,2.
6. "Criptomnesia." (179–91) Trans. from G. 1905a. Pub. in a dif. trans. as It. 1972d,4.
7. "Superperizia su due perizie psichiatriche contraddittorie." (192–202) Trans. from G. 1906d. Pub. in a dif. trans. as It. 1972d,6.

1975a *Psicologia analitica. Le conferenze alla Clinica Tavistock 1935.* Milan: Mondadori. pp. 184. Trans. from G. 1969a by Sergio Chiappori.

1975b "Commento psicologico." *Il libro tibetano della Grande Liberazione.* pp. 39–40. Ed. by W. Y. Evans-Wentz. Rome: Newton Compton. Trans. from E. 1954e by Carla Cipollini and Sabatino Piovani.

1975c *Psicologia, linguaggio e associazione verbale.* Rome: Newton Compton. pp. 399. Trans. by Marina Beer. Contents:
1. "Le associazione dei soggetti normali." (11–189) Trans. from GW 2,1.
2. "Analisi delle associazioni di un epilettico." (190–210) Trans. from GW 2,2.

3. "Il coefficiente del tempo di reazione nell-esperimento di associazione." (211–56) Trans. from GW 2,3.

4. "Osservazioni sperimentali sulla facoltà della memoria." (257–71) Trans. from GW 2,4.

5. "Psicoanalisi ed esperimenti di associazione." (272–99) Trans. from GW 2,5.

6. "Associazione, sogni e sintomo isterico." (300–47) Trans. from GW 2,7.

7. "L'importanza dell' esperimento di associazione per la psicopatologia." (348–63) Trans. from GW 2,8.

8. "Disturbi della riproduzione negli esperimenti di associazione." (364–75) Trans. from GW 2,9.

9. "Il metodo dell'associazione." (376–99) Trans. from GW 2,10.

1975d   *La libido. Simboli e trasformazioni.* Rome: Newton Compton. pp. 389. Trans. from G. 1912a by Girolamo Mancuso. Cf. It. 1965b and 1970a.

THE COLLECTED WORKS OF

C. G. JUNG

THE PUBLICATION of the first complete edition, in English, of the works of C. G. Jung was undertaken by Routledge and Kegan Paul, Ltd., in England and by Bollingen Foundation in the United States. The American edition is number XX in Bollingen Series, which since 1967 has been published by Princeton University Press. The edition contains revised versions of works previously published, such as *Psychology of the Unconscious*, which is now entitled *Symbols of Transformation*; works originally written in English, such as *Psychology and Religion*; works not previously translated, such as *Aion*; and, in general, new translations of virtually all of Professor Jung's writings. Prior to his death, in 1961, the author supervised the textual revision, which in some cases is extensive. Sir Herbert Read (d. 1968), Dr. Michael Fordham, and Dr. Gerhard Adler compose the Editorial Committee; the translator is R. F. C. Hull (except for Volume 2) and William McGuire is executive editor.

The price of the volumes varies according to size; they are sold separately, and may also be obtained on standing order. Several of the volumes are extensively illustrated. Each volume contains an index and in most a bibliography; the final volumes will contain a complete bibliography of Professor Jung's writings and a general index to the entire edition.

In the following list, dates of original publication are given in parentheses (of original composition, in brackets). Multiple dates indicate revisions.

*1. PSYCHIATRIC STUDIES

On the Psychology and Pathology of So-Called Occult Phenomena (1902)

On Hysterical Misreading (1904)

Cryptomnesia (1905)

On Manic Mood Disorder (1903)

A Case of Hysterical Stupor in a Prisoner in Detention (1902)

On Simulated Insanity (1903)

A Medical Opinion on a Case of Simulated Insanity (1904)

A Third and Final Opinion on Two Contradictory Psychiatric Diagnoses (1906)

On the Psychological Diagnosis of Facts (1905)

†2. EXPERIMENTAL RESEARCHES

Translated by Leopold Stein in collaboration with Diana Riviere

STUDIES IN WORD ASSOCIATION (1904–7, 1910)

The Associations of Normal Subjects (by Jung and F. Riklin)

An Analysis of the Associations of an Epileptic

The Reaction-Time Ratio in the Association Experiment

Experimental Observations on the Faculty of Memory

Psychoanalysis and Association Experiments

The Psychological Diagnosis of Evidence

Association, Dream, and Hysterical Symptom

The Psychopathological Significance of the Association Experiment

Disturbances in Reproduction in the Association Experiment

The Association Method

The Family Constellation

PSYCHOPHYSICAL RESEARCHES (1907–8)

On the Psychophysical Relations of the Association Experiment

Psychophysical Investigations with the Galvanometer and Pneumograph in Normal and Insane Individuals (by F. Peterson and Jung)

Further Investigations on the Galvanic Phenomenon and Respiration in Normal and Insane Individuals (by C. Ricksher and Jung)

Appendix: Statistical Details of Enlistment (1906); New Aspects of Criminal Psychology (1908); The Psychological Methods of Investigation Used in the Psychiatric Clinic of the University of Zurich (1910); On the Doctrine of Complexes ([1911] 1913); On the Psychological Diagnosis of Evidence (1937)

*3. THE PSYCHOGENESIS OF MENTAL DISEASE
The Psychology of Dementia Praecox (1907)
The Content of the Psychoses (1908/1914)
On Psychological Understanding (1914)
A Criticism of Bleuler's Theory of Schizophrenic Negativism (1911)
On the Importance of the Unconscious in Psychopathology (1914)
On the Problem of Psychogenesis in Mental Disease (1919)
Mental Disease and the Psyche (1928)
On the Psychogenesis of Schizophrenia (1939)
Recent Thoughts on Schizophrenia (1957)
Schizophrenia (1958)

†4. FREUD AND PSYCHOANALYSIS
Freud's Theory of Hysteria: A Reply to Aschaffenburg (1906)
The Freudian Theory of Hysteria (1908)
The Analysis of Dreams (1909)
A Contribution to the Psychology of Rumour (1910–11)
On the Significance of Number Dreams (1910–11)
Morton Prince, "The Mechanism and Interpretation of Dreams": A
    Critical Review (1911)
On the Criticism of Psychoanalysis (1910)
Concerning Psychoanalysis (1912)
The Theory of Psychoanalysis (1913)
General Aspects of Psychoanalysis (1913)
Psychoanalysis and Neurosis (1916)
Some Crucial Points in Psychoanalysis: A Correspondence between
    Dr. Jung and Dr. Loÿ (1914)
Prefaces to "Collected Papers on Analytical Psychology" (1916, 1917)
The Significance of the Father in the Destiny of the Individual
    (1909/1949)
Introduction to Kranefeldt's "Secret Ways of the Mind" (1930)
Freud and Jung: Contrasts (1929)

‡5. SYMBOLS OF TRANSFORMATION (1911–12/1952)
    PART I
Introduction
Two Kinds of Thinking
The Miller Fantasies: Anamnesis
The Hymn of Creation
The Song of the Moth
                                                                (continued)

5. (*continued*)

PART II

Introduction
The Concept of Libido
The Transformation of Libido
The Origin of the Hero
Symbols of the Mother and of Rebirth
The Battle for Deliverance from the Mother
The Dual Mother
The Sacrifice
Epilogue
Appendix: The Miller Fantasies

*6. PSYCHOLOGICAL TYPES (1921)
Introduction
The Problem of Types in the History of Classical and Medieval
    Thought
Schiller's Ideas on the Type Problem
The Apollinian and the Dionysian
The Type Problem in Human Character
The Type Problem in Poetry
The Type Problem in Psychopathology
The Type Problem in Aesthetics
The Type Problem in Modern Philosophy
The Type Problem in Biography
General Description of the Types
Definitions
Epilogue
Four Papers on Psychological Typology (1913, 1925, 1931, 1936)

†7. TWO ESSAYS ON ANALYTICAL PSYCHOLOGY
On the Psychology of the Unconscious (1917/1926/1943)
The Relations between the Ego and the Unconscious (1928)
Appendix: New Paths in Psychology (1912); The Structure of the
    Unconscious (1916) (new versions, with variants, 1966)

‡8. THE STRUCTURE AND DYNAMICS OF THE PSYCHE
On Psychic Energy (1928)
The Transcendent Function ([1916]/1957)
A Review of the Complex Theory (1934)
The Significance of Constitution and Heredity in Psychology (1929)

* Published 1971.   † Published 1953; 2nd edn., 1966.
‡ Published 1960; 2nd edn., 1969.

Psychological Factors Determining Human Behavior (1937)

Instinct and the Unconscious (1919)

The Structure of the Psyche (1927/1931)

On the Nature of the Psyche (1947/1954)

General Aspects of Dream Psychology (1916/1948)

On the Nature of Dreams (1945/1948)

The Psychological Foundations of Belief in Spirits (1920/1948)

Spirit and Life (1926)

Basic Postulates of Analytical Psychology (1931)

Analytical Psychology and *Weltanschauung* (1928/1931)

The Real and the Surreal (1933)

The Stages of Life (1930–1931)

The Soul and Death (1934)

Synchronicity: An Acausal Connecting Principle (1952)

Appendix: On Synchronicity (1951)

*9. PART I. THE ARCHETYPES AND THE
COLLECTIVE UNCONSCIOUS

Archetypes of the Collective Unconscious (1934/1954)

The Concept of the Collective Unconscious (1936)

Concerning the Archetypes, with Special Reference to the Anima
Concept (1936/1954)

Psychological Aspects of the Mother Archetype (1938/1954)

Concerning Rebirth (1940/1950)

The Psychology of the Child Archetype (1940)

The Psychological Aspects of the Kore (1941)

The Phenomenology of the Spirit in Fairytales (1945/1948)

On the Psychology of the Trickster-Figure (1954)

Conscious, Unconscious, and Individuation (1939)

A Study in the Process of Individuation (1934/1950)

Concerning Mandala Symbolism (1950)

Appendix: Mandalas (1955)

*9. PART II. AION (1951)

RESEARCHES INTO THE PHENOMENOLOGY OF THE SELF

The Ego

The Shadow

The Syzygy: Anima and Animus

The Self

Christ, a Symbol of the Self

The Sign of the Fishes   *(continued)*

* Published 1959; 2nd edn., 1968. (Part I: 79 plates, with 29 in colour.)

9. (*continued*)
    The Prophecies of Nostradamus
    The Historical Significance of the Fish
    The Ambivalence of the Fish Symbol
    The Fish in Alchemy
    The Alchemical Interpretation of the Fish
    Background to the Psychology of Christian Alchemical Symbolism
    Gnostic Symbols of the Self
    The Structure and Dynamics of the Self
    Conclusion

*10. CIVILIZATION IN TRANSITION
    The Role of the Unconscious (1918)
    Mind and Earth (1927/1931)
    Archaic Man (1931)
    The Spiritual Problem of Modern Man (1928/1931)
    The Love Problem of a Student (1928)
    Woman in Europe (1927)
    The Meaning of Psychology for Modern Man (1933/1934)
    The State of Psychotherapy Today (1934)
    Preface and Epilogue to "Essays on Contemporary Events" (1946)
    Wotan (1936)
    After the Catastrophe (1945)
    The Fight with the Shadow (1946)
    The Undiscovered Self (Present and Future) (1957)
    Flying Saucers: A Modern Myth (1958)
    A Psychological View of Conscience (1958)
    Good and Evil in Analytical Psychology (1959)
    Introduction to Wolff's "Studies in Jungian Psychology" (1959)
    The Swiss Line in the European Spectrum (1928)
    Reviews of Keyserling's "America Set Free" (1930) and "La Révolution Mondiale" (1934)
    The Complications of American Psychology (1930)
    The Dreamlike World of India (1939)
    What India Can Teach Us (1939)
    Appendix: Documents (1933–1938)

†11. PSYCHOLOGY AND RELIGION: WEST AND EAST
    WESTERN RELIGION
    Psychology and Religion (The Terry Lectures) (1938/1940)

* Published 1964; 2nd edn., 1970. (8 plates.)
† Published 1958; 2nd edn., 1969.

A Psychological Approach to the Dogma of the Trinity (1942/1948)
Transformation Symbolism in the Mass (1942/1954)
Forewords to White's "God and the Unconscious" and Werblowsky's "Lucifer and Prometheus" (1952)
Brother Klaus (1933)
Psychotherapists or the Clergy (1932)
Psychoanalysis and the Cure of Souls (1928)
Answer to Job (1952)

EASTERN RELIGION

Psychological Commentaries on "The Tibetan Book of the Great Liberation" (1939/1954) and "The Tibetan Book of the Dead" (1935/1953)
Yoga and the West (1936)
Foreword to Suzuki's "Introduction to Zen Buddhism" (1939)
The Psychology of Eastern Meditation (1943)
The Holy Men of India: Introduction to Zimmer's "Der Weg zum Selbst" (1944)
Foreword to the "I Ching" (1950)

*12. PSYCHOLOGY AND ALCHEMY (1944)
Prefatory note to the English Edition ([1951?] added 1967)
Introduction to the Religious and Psychological Problems of Alchemy
Individual Dream Symbolism in Relation to Alchemy (1936)
Religious Ideas in Alchemy (1937)
Epilogue

†13. ALCHEMICAL STUDIES
Commentary on "The Secret of the Golden Flower" (1929)
The Visions of Zosimos (1938/1954)
Paracelsus as a Spiritual Phenomenon (1942)
The Spirit Mercurius (1943/1948)
The Philosophical Tree (1945/1954)

‡14. MYSTERIUM CONIUNCTIONIS (1955-56)
AN INQUIRY INTO THE SEPARATION AND
SYNTHESIS OF PSYCHIC OPPOSITES IN ALCHEMY
The Components of the Coniunctio
The Paradoxa
The Personification of the Opposites
Rex and Regina   (continued)

* Published 1953; 2nd edn., completely revised, 1968. (270 illustrations.)
† Published 1968. (50 plates, 4 text figures.)
‡ Published 1963; 2nd edn., 1970. (10 plates.)

14. (*continued*)
   Adam and Eve
   The Conjunction

*15. THE SPIRIT IN MAN, ART, AND LITERATURE
   Paracelsus (1929)
   Paracelsus the Physician (1941)
   Sigmund Freud in His Historical Setting (1932)
   In Memory of Sigmund Freud (1939)
   Richard Wilhelm: In Memoriam (1930)
   On the Relation of Analytical Psychology to Poetry (1922)
   Psychology and Literature (1930/1950)
   "Ulysses": A Monologue (1932)
   Picasso (1932)

†16. THE PRACTICE OF PSYCHOTHERAPY
   GENERAL PROBLEMS OF PSYCHOTHERAPY
   Principles of Practical Psychotherapy (1935)
   What Is Psychotherapy? (1935)
   Some Aspects of Modern Psychotherapy (1930)
   The Aims of Psychotherapy (1931)
   Problems of Modern Psychotherapy (1929)
   Psychotherapy and a Philosophy of Life (1943)
   Medicine and Psychotherapy (1945)
   Psychotherapy Today (1945)
   Fundamental Questions of Psychotherapy (1951)
   SPECIFIC PROBLEMS OF PSYCHOTHERAPY
   The Therapeutic Value of Abreaction (1921/1928)
   The Practical Use of Dream-Analysis (1934)
   The Psychology of the Transference (1946)
   Appendix: The Realities of Practical Psychotherapy ([1937] added,
      1966)

‡17. THE DEVELOPMENT OF PERSONALITY
   Psychic Conflicts in a Child (1910/1946)
   Introduction to Wickes's "Analyse der Kinderseele" (1927/1931)
   Child Development and Education (1928)
   Analytical Psychology and Education: Three Lectures (1926/1946)
   The Gifted Child (1943)
   The Significance of the Unconscious in Individual Education (1928)

* Published 1966.
† Published 1954; 2nd edn., revised and augmented, 1966. (13 illustrations.)
‡ Published 1954.

The Development of Personality (1934)
Marriage as a Psychological Relationship (1925)

*18. THE SYMBOLIC LIFE
Miscellaneous Writings

†19. GENERAL BIBLIOGRAPHY OF C. G. JUNG'S WRITINGS

†20. GENERAL INDEX TO THE COLLECTED WORKS

See also:

C. G. JUNG: LETTERS
Selected and edited by Gerhard Adler, in collaboration with Aniela Jaffé.
Translations from the German by R.F.C. Hull.

VOL. 1: 1906–1950
VOL. 2: 1951–1961

THE FREUD/JUNG LETTERS
Edited by William McGuire, translated by
Ralph Manheim and R.F.C. Hull

C. G. JUNG SPEAKING: Interviews and Encounters
Edited by William McGuire and R.F.C. Hull

* Published 1976.
† Published 1979.